Out of Sight,
Out of Mind

OUT OF SIGHT, OUT OF MIND

CLAUDIA KAERNER

Homeless Children and Families in Small-Town America

YVONNE M. VISSING

THE UNIVERSITY PRESS OF KENTUCKY

Scholarly publisher for the Commonwealth,
serving Bellarmine College, Berea College, Centre
College of Kentucky, Eastern Kentucky University,
The Filson Club, Georgetown College, Kentucky
Historical Society, Kentucky State University,
Morehead State University, Murray State University,
Northern Kentucky University, Transylvania University,
University of Kentucky, University of Louisville,
and Western Kentucky University.

Editorial and Sales Offices: The University Press of Kentucky
663 South Limestone Street, Lexington, Kentucky 40508-4008

Library of Congress Cataloging-in-Publication Data
Vissing, Yvonne Marie.
    Out of sight, out of Mind : homeless children and families in
small-town America / Yvonne M. Vissing.
        p. cm.
    Includes bibliographical references and index.
    ISBN 0-8131-1943-X (cloth : alk. paper). — ISBN 0-8131-0872-1
(pbk. : alk. paper)
    1. Homelessness—United States. 2. Homeless children—United
States. 3. Homeless persons—United States. 4. Housing, Rural—
United States. 5. United States.—Rural conditions. I. Title.
HV4505.V57   1996
362.5'0973—dc20   96-3749

For Edna and Richard Vissing

Contents

Preface

Out of Sight, Out of Mind is the product of six years of sociological investigation into the lives of people who are, or have been, homeless. About a dozen different studies, including both qualitative and quantitative research, helped me to develop an understanding of rural child and family homelessness.

The New Hampshire Department of Education financed my initial study of causes and consequences of homelessness among school-aged children and their families. This grant enabled me to interview forty homeless children and their families in five New Hampshire communities. Dover, Franklin, Manchester, Mascoma, and Monodnock were selected because they represented different types of communities within the states. Students were identified by school personnel and human service representatives. My research team traveled to each community and met the children and, when possible, their families. Sometimes we met at the school; other times we met at a homeless shelter, welfare office, health practitioner's office, or where the homeless person was staying. We recorded each interview, with the consent of the individual, and asked a series of questions from a semistructured interview schedule. We also interviewed school personnel and human service providers for each of the families. Each case was summarized and included in a report for the state (Vissing 1991; Luloff, Zaso and Vissing 1992).

The New Hampshire Department of Education also provided funding for me to speak with school and community groups about the findings of our report on the homeless and to engage in problem solving with communities across the state. I spoke to approximately three hundred people from a dozen organizations. The participants provided useful information about programs they had or needed to develop in order to help the homeless families. They also discussed problems, both personal and structural, they had encountered in serving the homeless. Some of the people attended the meetings were homeless, and I met with these individuals in follow-up meetings.

With the financial assistance of the Ella Anderson Trust of the New Hampshire Charitable Trust, I conducted a study to see what happens to homeless children during the summer. In the previous studies I had identified the school as the most helpful institution for homeless kids. Schools give them knowledge, support, food, clothes, and hope. But even when school is out for the summer, children's needs continue. I surveyed approximately fifty local community representatives and found that almost none of the communities had special summer programs for homeless children. I became convinced that "homelessness" was not a term that most agencies used when serving children.

University of New Hampshire photography students, under Professor Chris Enos's and my direction, worked with homeless children and families during a semester-long course in 1991. Fourteen students over six months met weekly with the homeless children and families, taking photographs and chronicling their lives. We surveyed and videotaped the students before they met their families, during their assignment, and again at the completion of the term. The result of this project was a traveling photography exhibit. Each student saw homelessness from a different angle; together, their work provides a broad view of what it is like to be a child who is homelessness in a small town.

The photographs were so beautiful that we wanted to enable more people to see them and learn about the photographer's experiences. The New Hampshire Humanities Council and the Durum Foundation of the New Hampshire Charitable Trust provided us with funding to put the experience on video. The result was a beautifully crafted twenty-minute videotape called "I Want to Go Home" (which can be purchased for $25 from the Baboosic Center for Child and Community Development, P.O. Box 547, Durham, N.H. 03824). It recently won two awards— as winner of the New Hampshire First and Finest in Film competition and as the artistic presentation of 1995 for the Ben and Jerry's One Heart–One World Festival.

Through a project supported by the Greater Piscataqua Community Foundation, Odyssey House Foundation director Joseph Diament and I conducted a count of homeless high school students in the seacoast of New Hampshire and Maine. Almost four thousand such students were enumerated in this study (see Vissing and Diament, 1994).

I also completed a resource and information guide for homeless students for the New Hampshire Department of Education. The first section of the handbook contains information about issues that most caregivers should know in order to help homeless children and their families. Questions included: What is homelessness? How can you tell if a student is homeless? What special problems do homeless students experience that makes it hard for them to succeed in school? Do home-less children have to be immunized in order to attend school? The second section provides strategies that educators and service providers can use to help children who are homeless. This section also contains a list of books for both children and adults, special curricular materials, videos, and theatrical plays that pertain to homelessness. The third section is a telephone directory of services homeless people can use. This handbook is being disseminated to schools and social service agencies in the state. (Copies can be purchased for $30 from the Baboosic Center.)

Additionally, I have garnered information on my subject from my service on the boards of directors for the New Hampshire Coalition for the Homeless and the New Hampshire Homeless and Runaway Youth Task Force, and as a consultant and public speaker for many organizations in New England. I have generated the material found in this book from my experiences with thousands of children, parents, and those who attempt to help them. Their stories supplement the findings published in hundreds of books, articles, and reports. Together these materials bring rural child and family homelessness into the American mind, so that these people and their problems will no longer be out of sight or out of mind.

Special thanks are provided to Dorothy Schroepfer and Richard Hodges at the New Hampshire Department of Education for providing the initial—and subsequent—opportunities to help homeless children. The insights of Tamara Chandler, Mary Connley, and Anne May were particularly valuable. Debra Cowan at the New Hampshire Charitable Trust has provided me, and the homeless of the state, with thoughtful assistance, as has Angela Matthews at the Greater Piscataqua Community Foundation. Chris Enos, Michael Bergeron, Fred Bloise and Claudia Kaerner have been willing to put their photography into action to help the homeless, and I am grateful to them. Homeless experts Beverly Toomey, Richard First, and Christopher Hudson have all provided me with valuable scholarly input to improve my work, and I thank them wholeheartedly. Michael Stoops at the National Coalition for the Homeless has also provided me with noteworthy assistence. State of New Hamp-shire leaders Nancy Rollins and Phyllis Powell have also afforded me opportunities to learn about, and help, homeless children. Mary Caldwell, Nancy Emerson, Beverly O'Brien, and Terry Warren also provided helpful information. The stories told by Yanali LaHaine and her family merit special thanks. Salem State College's Else Wiersma and Kenneth McNeil have also provided me with support for this project. Thanks are provided to Jean Corson Wolff and Anita Remengenti, who provided me with emotional support during difficult writing days.

One thing that I have learned painfully during the writing of this book is that we do not last forever. Thus, it is critically important to do all we can while we walk this earth to make it a sweeter place. My friend, Henrietta Charest, founder of the New Hampshire Coalition for the Homeless, died of cancer during the writing of this book. I learned much from her, and she is sorely missed. Bob Deane passed on shortly after he edited an early version of this book. He taught me to write without the purple pen and helped me to craft the document that you hold in your hands. Janet Fitchen, whom I knew only through her writings, provided me with insight about rural areas that was particularly valuable. The rurual communities will miss her contributions.

My greatest thanks goes to my family. I wish to express my gratitude to Jeffrey Salloway, whose faith, support, dedication, and critical thought made it possible for me to write this book. Kiki, Chris, Leah, and Jonah have exercised extreme patience with me during these days. This is a public recognition of my love for them and my appreciation for theirs.

Introduction

Like most people, I never knew that homeless children in rural areas existed. I never saw them, never read about them, and never heard about them from professionals working in health and human services. Homeless children in small town America were out of sight and out of mind.

But my lack of knowledge did not negate their existence. The numbers of homeless children and families have increased dramatically in rural areas over the past decade. This book describes my journey to identify and understand child and family homelessness in rural areas. It began as I completed two years as a National Institute of Mental Health post-doctoral research fellow in child and family sociology, working with the New Hampshire State Department of Education to describe the causes and consequences of child and family homelessness. This project led to half a dozen other projects about rural child and family homelessness, and within three years, I had contact with more than three hundred homeless children and families. I followed most of the homeless families for several months, until their situations changed and they moved. These are the people whose stories are told in this book.

It was impossible for me not to feel compassion for those I met in my fieldwork, when I ate with them and played with their children while they told their stories. As the photos contained in this book illustrate, children who are homeless are like every other child. They want to play, they need emotional and physical protection, and they dream of what they will be tomorrow. Their parents struggle with the same issues as do other parents: they worry about their children being safe, happy, and healthy. They fret about jobs and money, they stew over relationships with one another, and they reflect about what happened yesterday and wonder what will happen tomorrow. It was encouraging to identify their strengths and to share in their triumphs. It was distressing to learn how stable, employed, two-parent households were transformed into poor, emotionally devastated, single-parent homes

1

overnight. In so many ways, their homelessness could have been prevented. But it wasn't. Even the financially secure plummeted into the abyss of poverty and homelessness. In many ways, I found that those who were homeless were no different from me.

My scientific training would not allow what I saw and felt to go unanalyzed. My compassion wasn't useful unless dispassionately appraised. I evaluated and categorized the information I learned. To allow others to learn a bit of what I observed, I have concentrated my findings into four themes. The most basic theme is that rural homelessness exists, and it primarily consists not of single, "skid-row" men but of children and families (First, Rife, & Tooney, 1994).

The second theme is that the rural homeless experience is qualitatively different from that experienced in urban areas. Rural Poverty and homelessness are more problematic than urban poverty (Amato, Zuo, 1992). Rural culture and lifestyle result in different emotional, physical, and social functioning among those who lack housing. Also, there are unique strengths and weaknesses in rural areas that must be considered when developing prevention and intervention programs. What works in urban areas may not work in rural places. Rural communities may have a resource base that can be mobilized to develop effective, efficient, and humane programs for children and families who live in housing distress. But some rural communities have no resource base at all, which makes helping difficult.

Third, a different definition of the lack of housing in rural areas is needed. The stereotyped term *homelessness* does not convey the rural experience. As I indicate in the first chapter, a better way to view rural experience is to focus on the processes experienced by "displaced" children and families, or those who are in "housing distress."

The fourth theme is that while those who are homeless live in chaos, out of the chaos there results an orderly existence. If understood, this order can be used by rural communities to (1) develop programs to help those in need, and (2) unify the entire community in a model of caring and compassion that re-creates the spirit of rural communities. (Wagner 1993) This fourth theme requires that rural homelessness be viewed from a broad conceptual framework.

It is much more difficult to see the causes of rural homelessness than it is to see its consequences. Typically people only see the catastrophe of homelessness, of hungry, sick, dirty people living on the street. Most do not have the information and time to consider the complexity of the issue and, as a result, offer sophomoric explanations and simplistic solutions. To take the reader along the path that I walked, I would like to describe the conceptual journey that ultimately directed my investigation of homelessness in small town America.

I was initially intrigued by the topic of rural homelessness, in part, because while homelessness has become as a social problem, its presence was antithetical to what I believed should occur in rural areas. Small towns were the last bastions of beauty, safety, and community between neighbors, I thought. Yet even here, there was homelessness. The sociologist in me had to find out why. The social worker part of me wanted to do something about it. So I threw myself into the investigation of the topic. Where would this journey take me?

As my projects in the study of rural child and family homelessness evolved, I found myself evolving as well. At first, I felt overwhelmed by the catastrophe of the lives of those whom I met. But I did not feel helpless and hopeless, for the sociologist in me attempted to make sense of the chaotic, confusing, and tumultuous lives of those interviewed. I looked for patterns of similarity and difference between them. Over time, patterns became clear, and theories emerged to explain what I observed. Then, and only after I understood what was causing homelessness among children in small town America, could I make recommendations about "what should be done."

During this process, I read hundreds of books and articles that described homelessness and its solutions. Much of what was written simply didn't address what I observed about the homeless families and children I saw in small towns. This led me to look not just at the phenomenon of rural homelessness but also *how* it was studied. I concluded that the way scientists have studied social problems contributed to why homeless children and families in rural areas were not discussed (Snow, Anderson, and Koegel 1994). Instead of dissecting the whole into small parts for analysis—which left the rural homeless out of sight and out of mind—forming an inclusive model was more inviting.

I found such an alternate framework not in the social sciences but in post-chaos and complexity theory. This approach, initially described by Gleick (1987) and by Lewin (1992), and expanded by Cohen and Stewart (1994), focused on how to discover simplicity in a complex world. This new paradigm offers a way of seeing simplicity and order where formerly only the random, the unpredictable—or the chaotic— had been observed. I used this new paradigm to order rural homelessness. In doing so, I came to understand it as occurring in four distinct stages. In this first stage, homelessness is seen as the catastrophic result of personal chaos. It is "the most devastating condition that can happen to a child," according to homeless expert James Wright (1990). Homelessness is not a singular event or merely the lack of housing. With exceptions such as "immediate" homelessness caused by fires, tornados, or floods, homelessness is a *process* in which personal chaos occurs slowly, incrementally. Chaos, then, is the spiral of losing job, money, support networks, material possessions, and self esteem, which ultimately results in the catastrophe of homelessness, as Barbara's experience points out:

> I had all kinds of trouble. The kids' father started drinking and beating me up. He couldn't seem to hold a job. Things got so bad between us that he up and left. I started drinking, which messed things up worse. Social workers got involved, and they put me in detox and my kids in foster care. Once they were in foster homes, they cut my AFDC. Without AFDC, I had no money. So there I was in detox, with no kids and no money. My landlord threw me out of my apartment because I couldn't pay the rent. Then they wouldn't give me the kids back because I had no place to live. But they wouldn't give me back the AFDC before I got the kids back so I could get a place to stay with the kids. I've never really worked, so I can't find anyone who will hire me. So now I am homeless and I've lost my kids. And on top of it all—they blame me for it.

The impact of homelessness's chaos and catastrophe on the body, emotion, mind, and structure of the family is the focus of chapters 2 through 5 of this book.

The next four chapters analyze the complex patterns of factors, behavior, or situations that can describe why homeless children and families come to exist in small town America. What is the unifying set of factors that causes a child or family to become homeless in rural areas? There are several distinct patterns of social phenomena that contribute to the incidence of homelessness. Much of the literature about the causes of homelessness focuses on how personal pathology contributes to homelessness. Yet most children and families who are homeless in rural areas do not become homeless because of personal dysfunction. If the families do become dysfunctional, their problems are typically a consequence of social forces that are beyond their control. Rural homelessness is caused not by a single factor but by at least four interweaving sources: ideological frameworks, demographic trends, failures of the social infrastructure, and personal problems and dysfunctions. Both personal and social forces contribute to why one is in housing distress.

Complex as each single contributing factor is, it is possible to detect causes of rural homelessness and to identify large groups of people who are at risk of housing distress. For those who are homeless, their situation is chaotic. For those who analyze their housing distress, the topic is complex—but not impenetrable. The question that confronts us next is one of order. Is there, in this social phenomenon of rural child and family homelessness, a fundamental order that governs our society?

Do the rural homeless occupy a regular, ordered place in society? Is their status virtually ordained by the structure of their society? If so, what are the theoretical constructs that enable us to understand their situation?

We know that the lives of those who are homeless have orderable parts. Homeless people know where to get free food and clothes, where it is safe to stay, and on whom they can count for help. Some communities have few people who live in housing distress, while other communities have many. It is possible to understand why this occurs. Only by understanding the linkage between the causes and consequences of rural homelessness can one prevent it.

The last two chapters of this book provide tangible ways for rural communities to act in order to prevent and eradicate homelessness. The best way to solve the problem of rural homelessness is by creating a community in which "us" and "them" are regarded as the same, by recognizing that *all* children and families are in need of a community that cares—and that we *all* are responsible for building the tomorrow in which we must all live.

one

Identifying Homeless Children and Families in Rural Areas

"We don't have any homeless kids in our town." This was the common response among residents in small towns who were unwilling to think that homelessness might be in their own backyards. Homeless children and families in small towns are invisible. Because they are out of sight, they are also out of mind, thought not to exist. And if they do not exist, then nothing has to be done about, or for, them.

How does one know whether or not a child is homeless? Homeless children, according to the federeal Stewart B. McKinney Homeless Assistance Act (Public Law 100–77). are "those who lack a fixed, regular night-time residence." This definition was written with the urban homeless in mind. It is not particularly useful in defining homeless children in rural areas, as I learned when I began my investigation for the New Hampshire Department of Education.

School teachers, administrators, counselors, and nurses would scratch their heads as they pondered whether a particular child in the school fit that definition. It was easy for them to identify rural families who were in housing distress; it was harder to say for sure if they were actually homeless. As a principal of an elementary school pointed out, the official definition of homelessness got in the way of her serving displaced children. If attention was given *only* to children who were defined as homeless, children living a marginal existence in housing distress, and in poverty could be overlooked. And yet those on the margin may have been homeless before, and could easily be homeless again. These are children who do not fit tightly into the McKinney definition—but they do not fall entirely outside it either. Because of the nature of rural homelessness, those who lack housing are, in many ways, indistinguishable from rural people who are poor but not homeless (Snow and Bradford 1994; Snow, Anderson, and Koegel 1994; Patton 1987).

6

People in small towns are hesitant to label folks on hard times as homeless. It is easier to associate homelessness with urban images of skid-row bums and derelict bag ladies. Even people in small towns are familiar with an eccentric resident who may not have stable housing because he or she has personal problems that interfere with living a normal life. It is uncomfortable to think of the family down the road who had a "bad spell" and became evicted as homeless people. Rural folks on hard times are not seen as similar to the homeless of big cities.

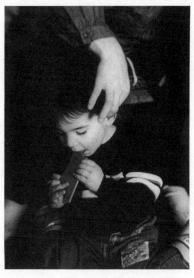

LISE RUSSELL

The typical definition of homelessness looks only at one dimension: lack of shelter. However, rural homelessness consists of more than lacking a regular, physical structure to sleep in. Rural homelessness consists of psychological, cultural, and social dimensions that must not be overlooked (Rossi 1994).

What do you envision when you are asked the question, "Tell me about your home?" Likely you are flooded with images about people, places, and things. You may see a physical structure—a place, a room, a yard, and material possessions. But "home" also consists of nonmaterial realities—interactions with family and friends, feelings that home is a certain place where you belong, where both you and your material possessions are safe. Home is a place of privacy, where you can choose who is allowed inside. It is a place where you have control over what you want to do and when you want to do it. A home is evidence of the continuity of your history, where memories of yesterday, realities of today, and hopes for tomorrow converge. It is from laying these internal and external bricks that the psychological construct of home is built for children in small town America.

Because there are different types of housing distress, there are different categories of people in rural areas who can be considered homeless. Many rural children and families have a roof over their heads and yet do not have a "home." They are, as homeless experts call them, "homeless with a roof" or those people who "rent a couch." The families described in this book are exclusively those who had lost housing for a minimum of several months. Yet almost all of them had physical shelter at the time of the interviews. Most of them had shelter of one form or another throughout the time they were homeless, since parents refused to allow their children to be subjected to rain, snow, and predators (both human and animal). While they may have had shelter, none of them were living in places they could call home.

The study of rural child and family homelessness requires that a different definition be used to describe their experience for four reasons: (1) The word *homelessness* carries too many urban stereotypes to be useful in understanding those who are homeless in small towns and their experience. (2) The term does not readily convey the *process* in which children and families come to lose housing in small towns. (3) While the rural homeless may have a roof over their head, shelter alone does not give one a sense of home. Psychological homelessness is as much of a threat to one's well being as physical homelessness. (4) The term *homelessness* has no positive attributes. Yet the rural displaced have integrity. They are generally not lazy, substance-abusing, mentally ill misfits. The rural homeless are folks who, largely, have fallen upon hard times that got the better of them. Therefore, rural homelessness is defined in this book as the lack of a consistent, safe, physical structure and the emotional deprivation that occurs as a result. The lack of housing denies children a secure sense of psychological belongingness within a community where other people have access to regular homes. The label of homelessness applies not just to families and children who are currently without a home, but also to those who are at imminent risk of losing the necessities of life.

In actuality, *homelessness* is an inappropriate term for explaining the rural experience. A better way to describe the rural experience is as "displaced" children and families or as those who are in "housing distress." In this book, the term *homelessness* will be used synonymously with the terms housing displacement and housing distress.

Today families and children—not single adults—are the fastest growing subgroups of the homeless in both urban and rural areas. Homeless children are not of one type. They include infants, preschoolers, and school-age children who are part of a homeless family, as well as older young people who are homeless but on their own, such as pregnant teens, teen parents, runaways, and older adolescents (Kryder-Coe, Salamon, and Molnar 1991; Robertson and Greenblatt 1992). A decade ago, homeless families and children were 10 percent of the national homeless population, but today they form about half or more of that population (Anderson 1987; U.S. Council of Mayors 1987; Coates 1990; Fagan 1990). The proportion of homeless families are higher in rural areas than in urban ones (Toomey and First 1991; Bassuk 1990). More than ever, this figure includes not only the destitute but also working-class and two-parent families. It appears from all sources that children who are very young—under age six—and in their formative years are the fastest growing group among America's homeless (Jennings 1988). Also, teens who live without a parent are ever increasing in all parts of the nation (Bucy and Nichols 1991; James 1992).

While some people may think that rural homelessness is a small problem affecting few people, the National Coalition for the Homeless (1989), the Coalition for the Homeless (1987), the Children's Defense Fund (Mihaly 1991), and the Housing Assistance Council (1990; 1992) all assert that it is a significant social problem. The growing income disparities between rural and urban areas has widened as income gaps among rich, poor, and middle classes have occurred. The result is that the rural poor are the most disadvantaged of all Americans (Barranick 1990). Data from the Bureau of the Census and the Department of Housing and Urban Development indicate that the problem of housing affordability in rural areas has worsened since the late 1970s. While improvements in housing quality have been made in some areas, substantial numbers of rural poor households continue to live in substandard housing (Lazere et al. 1989). Children, women, families, Native Americans, and migrant farm workers represent a larger portion of this population than the urban homeless population (Housing Assistance Council 1992).

The U.S. Conference of Mayors study (1987) found that homelessness is increasing by 20 percent each year. If these rates are unchanged, more than 18.7 million Americans will be unable to find affordable housing by the year 2003 (Jennings 1988). But homelessness may be increasing at a faster rate than the mayors expected. In a Columbia University study (Link 1993) that used a conservative method of sampling, researchers found that about 13.5 million Americans have been on the streets or stayed in homeless shelters at some point in their lives, and that almost 6 million of them had been homeless in the past five years. If one counted those who temporarily lived with others, that number doubled to 26 million Americans who have been homeless.

Conservative estimates indicate that about a third of the nation's homeless Americans live in small towns and that homeless children make up an increasing and significantly large number of homeless in both rural and urban areas (Mihaly 1991; Geisler 1988; LeBlanc 1988; Stark 1988; National Coalition for the Homeless 1989). A high number of homeless people is sure to be denied by those who want to believe that there just couldn't be many homeless people around. Typically, when one wants a definitive number of "how many" of a certain kind of people exist in an area, such information can be found in national census data. But until 1990, homeless people were not included in the census. By 1990 there were so many homeless people that the government could not ignore them and finally agreed that they should be counted. The U.S. Census Bureau's enumeration of homeless people nationwide used a flawed methodology that resulted in erroneously small estimates (Hudson 1992); the National Coalition for the Homeless (1991d) reports that they may have missed more than half of the homeless people. The counting errors appear most pronounced in rural areas. Therefore, how many people are homeless in small town America is still unknown.

Independent studies indicate that more people are homeless in rural American than traditionally thought. A rural Missouri count of homeless children yielded about eight hundred children in shelters. Half of these children were under the age of five. This represented a 29 percent increase over the previous year (Gray 1989). In Kansas, the majority of homeless people are single mothers and their children. In 1991 there were about fifty thousand families below the poverty level in Kansas, with more than six thousand homeless school-aged children and youth—an increase of 39 percent in one year alone (Buck and Dunlap 1991). In a count of homelessness in the heartland of America, the Illinois Coalition for the Homeless (1991) found that agencies reported increases ranging from 61 to 600 percent in the number of people requesting shelter. The Ohio Coalition for the Homeless has identified rural homelessness as "growing faster than we can keep track of it." The Housing Assistance Council reported that in a 1988 survey of 2,200 rural and urban counties in the United States, rural people accounted for at least a quarter of the people who used homeless shelters (Wilkenson 1988; Toomey and First 1994).

In New Hampshire alone, 20 percent of 3,635 New Hampshire teens stayed regularly in places other than their own homes, while 13 percent reported that there was at least one time during the past year when they felt they had no place they could stay. Five percent of the teens identified themselves as having been homeless during the past year, but the number of teens who identified themselves as homeless doubled to almost 10 percent when the number of teens who reported that they were unsure whether they had been homeless or not in the past year were included. Twenty-five percent, a quarter of all students, knew another teen who was homeless. Housing difficulties were significantly greater for boys than for girls. Twice as many boys reported that they experienced times when they had no place to stay in small towns in the seacoast region of New England (Vissing and Diament 1994, 1996).

In rural areas, accurate numbers of the homeless cannot be obtained by counting those who use shelters or social services. According to Henrietta Charest, former director of the New Hampshire Coalition for the Homeless, counting the rural homeless is a lot like counting people who are sick. "If you want to know how many people are sick and you only count those who are in the hospital, you are going to miss most of the sick people. If you want to count the homeless and only count those in the shelters, you are going to miss most of the homeless." This is especially true in rural areas where there are no shelters and few human services.

According to researchers who counted the homeless in rural Ohio, any national count which omits smaller jurisdictions is grossly misleading and fosters a common misconception that homeless people are only found in big cities (Toomey and First 1992).

Including people in rural areas and using a broader definition of homelessness would give a "truer" picture of the housing crisis in America, asserts sociologist Peter Rossi (Rossi et al. 1987:1337). What we see in the homelessness is just the tip of the iceberg. There are many millions of adults who have inadequate income. The pool of persons from which the homeless are "recruited" is a very large pool. But the numbers are secondary, because "whether it is 2,000 or 200,000, it is still a national disgrace." If one includes those people who are living on the margin—one paycheck away from becoming homeless—then the hidden part of the iceberg is enormous.

Thus, though it is unclear how many people are homeless in rural areas, we are left making the same conclusions as the Columbia University study (Link 1993)—that there are far more homeless people in small town America than we ever imagined.

Small towns are officially considered to be rural communities, not urban subsectors. Rural areas are typically defined as including areas with populations of under 50,000. The National Rural Health Association (Patton 1987) has identified at least four types of rural communities:

1. Adjacent rural areas, which are contiguous to or within metropolitan statistical areas (MSAs), and are very similar to their urban neighbors.
2. Urbanized rural areas that consist of a population of 25,000 or more, but are distinct from an MSA.
3. Frontier areas that have a population density of fewer than six persons per square mile.
4. Countryside rural areas that consist of the remainder of the country not covered by other designations.

All of the people interviewed for this book fell into one of these four categories, and more than three-quarters of them came from urbanized rural areas or adjacent rural areas.

Homeless people in small towns are much more like those in rural areas than those in cities (Zwickza, 1990). In a statewide study of urban and rural counties, the Coalition for the Homeless in Pennsylvania (Ryan, Goldstein, and Bartelt 1989) compared characteristics of homeless people according to county population size. They found more similarities between small and medium-size counties than between medium-size and large counties. In another Pennsylvania study, while families represented 20 percent of the homeless population in the state, they made up 30 percent of the homeless in small communities. Forty percent of the identified homeless were located in rural areas (Dawida, 1988).

Lifestyles, attitudes, values, and problems found in small towns are more similar to those experienced in rural areas than they are to those found in cities. Similarly, people who are homeless in small towns and rural areas are not necessarily like the homeless people found in urban areas.

As previously pointed out, families, single mothers, and children constitute the largest number of people who are homeless in rural areas. This is true in New England as well in other parts of the nation. The 1989 national conference on Health Care for Homeless Mothers, Children, and Youth reported that in general mothers of homeless children are young, with a median age of twenty-nine and a range from fourteen to fifty. Rural homeless mothers were found to be younger than the national average. More than half gave birth to their first child by age twenty, and one-fourth became mothers by age seventeen. The average size for homeless single-parent families was between two and three children. In the major National Institute of Mental Health studies of homeless rural families to date, Roth, Bean, and Hyde (1986) and Toomey and First (1992) found that homelessness is widespread in rural areas. Their work focused on the homeless of rural Ohio. Five subtypes of rural homeless were identified. These included:

1. Young families no longer able to close the gap between housing costs and total household income.
2. Individuals currently employed full-time or part-time but with too little income to afford housing.
3. Women unable to work because of child care responsibilities or limited skills to meet the demands of a changing labor market.
4. Men who are older, homeless longer, and more likely to be with few supports.
5. Disabled persons without social networks and supports.

The largest proportion of rural homeless were found to be children and families—particularly families with female heads of household. Single women with children constitute a much higher proportion of the rural homeless, with rates almost double that found in urban areas (32.3 percent vs. 15.8 percent). This is partially explained by the higher percentage of rural women who are married, and who thus have insulating effects of a spouse and two potential sources of income. When such marriages dissolve, lack of education and poor job skills, common among rural women, make homelessness a likely outcome for the newly single rural parent.

The National Institute of Mental Health studies found that most of the rural homeless were either permanent or long-term residents of the area. Families were found to be homeless for shorter periods of time (90 days) compared to single homeless people (268 days). Rural homeless were much less likely, compared to their urban counterparts, to be found in missions or shelters (11.1 percent vs. 37.1 percent) and were more likely to be sheltered by family or friends (40.7 percent vs. 10.7 percent). Employment and job history data indicated that the rural homeless were less likely to find work: 62 percent of the rural homeless compared to 44 percent of the urban homeless had looked for work and couldn't find it. The rural homeless were not found to be "lazy and shiftless." Ninety percent of the rural residents had worked for pay previously, and nearly one-third had worked in the month preceding their homelessness. Approximately two-thirds of the respondents received income, including earnings and Social Security.

Economic factors such as unemployment, problems paying rent, and eviction were experienced by almost half of the rural families in Ohio, while personal problems, including conflict and dissolution, were cited by a third as the cause of homelessness. Unexpected accidents caused homelessness among 10 percent of the families. Only 2 percent reported that drug or alcohol abuse was the major contributing factor to their homelessness.

Families were not likely to be identified as homeless: "mothers apparently are more willing to compromise on housing conditions to avoid exposing their young children to the risks entailed in literal homelessness" (Rossi 1994, 378). More than 60 percent of the homeless in the 1990 Ohio study lived with families or friends, while 10 percent lived in makeshift shelters like cars, and a third lived in cheap motels, or finally shelters or missions. Although many of the respondents stayed with relatives, income provided by family and friends was very limited (39 percent). Approximately half of the respondents stated, however, that relatives provided them with noneconomic support, which had been the source of their survival.

Health problems were reported more frequently by the rural Ohio homeless sample (32 percent to 1 percent), compared to urban homeless. A quarter of the population had health problems for which they should currently see a doctor. Most frequently cited health problems included heart and circulatory problems, respiratory problems, pregnancy problems, musculoskeletal diseases, injuries, and poisoning. Fewer rural homeless had serious drinking problems compared to urbanites. Only 10 percent reported drinking a lot, compared with 21 percent of the urban population. Although mental health statuses were similar for the two groups, access and utilization of mental health services was significantly lower for the rural group.

As I interviewed homeless families and children across rural New Hampshire, each had their own tale to tell—but the tales became increasingly similar. While not all of them were alike, certain categories of people emerged. As Frank and Streeter (1987) point out, the rural homeless are a diverse group which include the "traditionally homeless," the "new poor" who have suddenly lost their jobs, displaced farmers and regionalized workers, and "the new hermits," who include survivalists, veterans, and back-to-the-land advocates who have become isolated from mainstream American society. Also, some people are homeless for a long period of time, but most are homeless for only a short while.

It is important to describe the types of families and children who were interviewed for this book in order to put the material in context. There is not just one type of homeless family, nor is there a singular type of child who comes to live independently. The diversity of the rural homeless can best be exemplified through brief case studies of people I interviewed. Interviews with the rural homeless indicated that 60 percent of them were families—two-thirds of them single-parent families, while the remainder had both mother and father present. Forty percent of the respondents were children who lived "independently," without the day-to-day guidance, care, and protection of their parents.

When mom, dad, and three children bow their heads to say grace over their dinner, few people imagine that it is at a homeless shelter. Two-parent families who are homeless defy common stereotypes of the homeless. "With two parents, wouldn't you think that one of them could hold a job and earn a living?" is a common response to these families.

Most two-parent families, like Bruce and May Newton and their three children, have one parent working at least part-time. But given the economic depression, they do not make enough money to afford shelter for their families. The Newton family was typical of those two-parent families I met:

My husband was working as a car mechanic, and had been steadily employed there for two years. I worked in a bank as a teller. Times got rough, and there wasn't as much work for everyone at his job. So the boss decided he had to lay people off—and Bruce didn't have enough seniority and got laid off. His boss felt really bad about it, and said there may be a chance of a job for him with a branch of the business in Florida. We knew we couldn't make the bills on my bank job that paid just a little more than minimum wage. We decided the best thing was for me to quit and us to move to Florida to get that job. Bruce called ahead, and the boss down there said he could use a good mechanic like Bruce. We used all our savings getting there.

Once we got there, there was no job. It had been all talk. It was so disappointing. We figured that Bruce could get a job somewhere else down there, though. Anyway, we had no money to come home on. We stayed in a cheap apartment for a while. He got a job delivering pizzas, and we ended up eating pizza every night because we had little money for food. Then the car went kaput. Things kept going from bad to worse.

Finally, we wired my family for money so we could come home. On the return trip, we stayed in the car at rest parks, since we didn't have enough money even for a campground. When we got back, we didn't have a place to live, and we could only sponge off our relatives and friends for so long.

We have tried and tried to find jobs. There simply aren't any. We must apply for a dozen jobs every day. We read the want ads every night. We walk around looking for "help wanted" signs in windows. We are applying for jobs that we would never have considered before. And we can't even get them. We have to eat. We have to take care of our children. People look at us like, "what kind of losers are you?" It is so upsetting the way they look at us. We didn't do anything wrong. We just lost our jobs, and now everything is awful. How dare they look at us like that! It could happen to them—but I guess they don't know that.

In desperation, we ended up at the homeless shelter. We keep on looking for work and the length of time we can stay here is limited. We are terrified because we don't know what is going to happen to us. All these aid programs that supposedly exist make you wait forever to get help, or they don't give help for very long, or they have stupid rules that disqualify you for this or for that. People tell us that Bruce should leave me with the kids, because then I could get help easier. But we refuse to do that. We've lost everything else—I won't let my family be torn apart.

In all of the two-parent families who were homeless, the father had been laid off or lost his job because of economic problems. The mother, who often worked part-time, did not make enough money for the family to survive. "Most women still just don't make what men do, and it is harder to support a family on a mother's income," May pointed out. Given that women still make only sixty cents or so for every dollar a man earns, and female college graduates make about the same as male high school graduates (Faludi 1991), May's experience in small towns confirms the consequences of financial discrimination of women.

Two-parent households moved the most frequently of any group interviewed. Having some assets and job experience, they "up and moved to where the grass was supposed to be greener." "But the grass is always greener on the other side," parent after parent reported. There were no jobs, there were few social services for which they could qualify, and they found themselves in desperate straits.

Once located far from their hometown and friends, the families found no one there to help. The universal response from the two-parent families was that if they were going to be homeless, it was better to be homeless in the state they knew, where there would be family and friends who could give them emotional support, if nothing else.

Just as the Ohio studies found that homeless rural families were younger, few of the New Hampshire parents were older than thirty-five. Young families on whom we count to raise healthy children for America's future are in "extraordinary trouble," according to Peter Edleman and Joyce Ladner, authors of *Adolescence and Poverty: Challenge for the 1990s* (1991), and a study by the W.T. Grant Foundation (1988). Since the early 1970s, young families across the nation have suffered increasing economic distress that results in family disintegration. Young families have borne the weight of economic dislocation. Indeed, the greatest victims of poverty were young white families, young married couples with children, and young families headed by high school graduates—especially those in rural areas.

Evidence that the young family is losing ground is now incontrovertible. The real median income of families headed by a person up to twenty-four years old fell 27 percent from 1973 to 1986. Their ability to purchase homes also declined sharply, with home ownership among married household heads under age twenty-five falling from 39 percent to 29 percent between 1973 and 1986 (Grant Foundation 1988).

The problem is the greatest for the young breadwinners who live in rural areas. The Population Reference Bureau examined hourly wages and found that more than half of young workers in rural areas (57 percent in 1987 compared with 46 percent in 1979) earned hourly wages that were inadequate to support a family of four above the poverty line. Poverty still results even if the worker works at that wage full-time year-round, forty hours a week, fifty weeks a year. By comparison, 41 percent of urban young workers earned such low wages in 1987, up from 37 percent in 1979 (Sherman 1992).

Incomes of young families are low, in part, because young workers are often locked into low-paying jobs. The median hourly earnings of workers younger than age twenty-five have declined each year since 1973, with the women receiving consistently less than their male counterparts (Johnson et al. 1991). Almost twice as many young workers are paid below the poverty line today as ten years ago. Many young workers have the same financial demands and family responsibilities as older people.

It is estimated that these young families would have had to pay 81.1 percent of their total income to afford decent rental housing in 1987, up from 46 percent in 1974. Given these figures, it is understandable why young families are at special risk of being homeless.

Early struggles have always been a predictable part of any family's life cycle. However, today's young families have little prospect of a growing economy before them and start out far behind the generation that preceded them. Many will never know the economic opportunities that their parents enjoyed. Nor is their plight likely to improve with the passage of time or the benefit of experience. Once behind, they tend to stay behind.

In many ways, two-parent family homelessness is the worst of all. It "shouldn't" happen to intact families. Yet thousands of two-parent families are finding themselves in just that kind of situation. It is easier to understand how single parents end up homeless.

Single mothers are the largest group of homeless parents with children in both rural and urban areas. They accounted for two-thirds of the families interviewed in New Hampshire. Like other researchers (Coates 1990; Toomey, First, Greene, and Cummins 1992), I found that single parents are disproportionally represented among those experiencing housing problems, and numerically are the largest subgroup of the poorly sheltered population.

How many single parents are homeless? Because the counts of homeless people vary so much, it is hard to come up with exact numbers. But we do know that the real numbers of homeless women and children are likely much higher than those reported. Figures on homeless women and children are "the most questionable of the figures, since they are almost universally shy, uncommunicative, and fearful—that is, not very 'countable'" (Coates 1990, 27).

The rural experience of homelessness followed national demographic and economic trends. For instance, between 1980 and 1988, the number of children living only with their mother increased by 21 percent, from 11.4 million to 13.5 million nationally. From 1974 to 1986, the proportion of married 20- to 24-year-old males living with their spouses plummeted by half, from 39 percent to 21 percent. Not surprisingly, between 1960 and 1979 the divorce rate rose from 9.2 to 22.8 per 1,000 married women. Viewed differently, from 1970 to 1987, the proportion of children living with one parent more than doubled, while the proportion living with two parents declined by almost 15 percent. By 1987, more than 27 percent of all families with a child under age eighteen was headed by one parent. Only 3 percent of all family households are headed by men, and this does not vary by race. The number of unwed women who bear children has increased nationally from 4 percent in 1950 to more than 25 percent in 1988—a trend that extends to rural areas (Lamanna and Reidmann 1991; U.S. National Center for Health Statistics 1990; Rund Sociological Society, 1993; U.S. Bureau of Census 1989a). But the numbers of single parents have increased more rapidly in rural areas than in urban ones, which reverses the trend of the 1970s (Committee for Economic Development 1991; Sherman 1992). Most single women have difficulty juggling all the pressures placed upon them to hold a decent-paying job, find child care, and secure a home and household essentials. If women do not have good education, marketable job skills, and the self-esteem to get work, they are doomed to dead-end occupations or public assistance. Finding work in rural areas when one does not have a good education is especially difficult.

Between 1970 and 1987, the median income of children living in single-parent families declined by 19 percent. Among low-income families with children, average family income declined 14 percent between 1979 and 1987, compared with a 19 percent increase for the highest-income families. Approximately 43 percent of mother-only families are poor, compared to about 7 percent of two-parent families. As we will see in the forthcoming chapter 6 on the economic conditions of rural areas, small towns have been hardest hit by the economic downturn: earnings are lower and the plight of rural single mothers is even worse than that of their urban sisters. The average income of a mother-headed family is only 40 percent of the average income of two-parent families at the same age. Median earnings of young female householders were $3,005 in 1989, barely 36 percent of the official poverty level for a family of two and substantially below the poverty level for a family of three. Their economic hardship is compounded by the failure of many absent fathers to pay child support (National Commission on Children 1991).

Nearly 75 percent of all American children growing up in a single-parent family will experience poverty for some period during their first ten years, compared to 20 percent of children in two-parent families. Among children living only with their mothers, sustained poverty for seven or more years was found to be common; among two-parent households, such poverty is rare. Because so many children are expected to spend part of their childhood with only their mothers, the chances that an American child will be poor are far greater than in the past. Further, the chances that these children will live in poverty for longer periods of time are greater (U.S. House 1989). In this regard, the American dream is evaporating in small town America.

What is the result of economic deprivation and stress of single parenting? Coates (1990) found that homeless mothers frequently have backgrounds with complex psychosocial problems. Sometimes the problems are directly caused by poverty and homelessness, but sometimes the problems preceded their economic woes. Fully three-fourths reported a history of sexual or physical abuse, and 39 percent were abused before eighteen years of age. More than a quarter of them had lived with relatives other than their parents or were placed in foster care. Homeless mothers had experienced relationships with men who had drinking problems (42 percent), were physical abusive (32 percent), had poor work histories (31 percent), or had mental problems (15 percent). Approximately 40 percent of homeless women stated their relationship had none of these problems (Wood 1989). How do these findings compare with homeless women in my rural studies?

Homelessness in New Hampshire was often a consequence of separation or divorce, as shown in the case of single mother, Sarah.

Bill and I got married when I found out I was pregnant. He figured he could get work easier if he worked in his dad's construction business— but that was a long way from where my folks lived. I don't think either of us was really happy in the marriage. We always had money troubles and went from one crisis to another. He blamed me for all the troubles. He drank too much, said awful things to me, and sometimes knocked me around. Finally, he left me and the baby. I didn't want the divorce—I had no job skills and didn't know how I could support me and the baby. Bill left town and all his family turned against me. I applied for public assistance, but it took months to get the benefits. I had no one to talk to, no one to help me, and I was stuck in our house out in the country with no car. It was too long to walk with the baby, and I guess I just lost it for a while. I started drinking, and I didn't take too good care of my child. It wasn't long before I used up the few savings we had, and I got evicted. Having nowhere to live, I ended up at a shelter. Because of my personal problems, my daughter was put into foster care "for a while." I lost my husband, child, home, my sense of respectability, and my ability to live a normal life—all within two years.

While single parents are usually thought to be female, dads are single parents too. There are an increasing number of homeless fathers raising their children: approximately 8 percent of our respondents fell into this category. The homeless fathers interviewed were loving dads who were trying very hard to make the most of life for their children. All of them had lost their jobs while attempting to be the primary care-givers to their small children. They found that day care was not available or affordable and that their children were often frightened or sick and needed them at home. "There was nothing else to do. I had to choose between my kids and my job." They didn't always know how to cook or how to braid little girls' hair, but they loved their children. In each case, the mother had been present but suddenly decided to leave the family. When the mother left, the father was not able to manage both home and job responsibilities, as in the case of Carl.

> We had been getting by, and we'd had our share of troubles. Then, one day, their mother just left. No warning, nothing. She ran off with this guy who did drugs and promised everything. She left town, and left me to take care of our kids. For a while I had friends watch the kids while I worked, but one of them got sick, and I had to stay home with her. My boss understood that I had to take care of the kids, but he had pressures on him too. So I had no choice except to quit my third-shift job. The boss promised he would get me on first shift as soon as a spot opened. Mean-while, I couldn't pay the rent, and we ended up here at the shelter. I never knew how tough single mothers had it until now. We've been here six weeks. I do the best I can, but I know it ain't enough. But I just got word that a spot has opened up on first shift and that I will be going back to work. I have already started looking for a place for us to live, where we can get normal. We haven't heard from their mom, so I guess she isn't planning to come home.

The most distressing group of homeless single parents I met was those young women who were under age eighteen. Though legally the guardians of their children, they themselves had no guardians who could give authorization for them to receive services. This resulted in their falling through the cracks of the system all the time. As an ex-ample of this, consider the story told by a shelter provider:

> A sixteen-year-old girl with her baby came to us, wanting shelter be-cause she had no place to live. Family shelters have rules that we cannot accept anyone under eighteen without parental consent. This girl had no parental consent for her to be housed, even though she could authorize for her child to be sheltered. Foster homes and host homes are not equipped to deal with children who have children. The best offer we

could give her was to put her in one place, and her baby in another facility. The young mother refused this option, and left with her baby. God only knows where they went.

A member of the New Hampshire Homeless and Runaway Youth Task Force's commented, "We do not know how many people like her are out there, because they know the system is ill-equipped to help [them]. If the best options that we can provide are separating families, or having the police involved to help, then we surely will not get many of these kids who need so much help coming to us."

Parents with children were not the only ones to find themselves homeless. Sometimes the children were homeless all by themselves. Forty percent of the people I interviewed were teenagers who did not live with parents or guardians. Caught betwixt and between, the homeless children who live "independently" are teenagers who do not live as children, yet do not have the resources or legal status of adults. They are expected to act responsibly and independently but do not have the skills or resources with which to do so. This makes them extremely vulnerable. When they seek help, they frequently find that they do not qualify for assistance.

The following types of "independent children" were identified in the rural areas by my studies:

1. Those who become homeless in order to be safe (20 percent)
2. Those who are kicked out of their homes (20 percent)
3. Those who are pushed out of their homes (35 percent)
4. Those who can't go home (10 percent)
5. Those for whom homelessness is normal (5 percent)
6. Those who had previously lived in foster care (10 percent)

Almost a quarter of all the teens interviewed became homeless because they realized that it was safer for them to live on the street alone, facing uncertainties, than to stay at home with the certainty of abuse. Some of them were considered runaways, while most of them lived quietly so that no authorities would know they were homeless. The problems they experienced that led to their homelessness took on distinctive patterns—conflict with parents that could not seem to be resolved; physical, sexual, and emotional abuse; overt and covert threats of danger and exploitation; and substance abuse by their parents.

Children are routinely the target of abuse by the parents who are supposed to be loving and protecting them (Vissing et al. 1991). Coates (1990) found that up to 90 percent of the kids on the street were sexually or physically abused before they became homeless; all will likely endure further abuses once on the street. The teens I interviewed who fell into this category of homelessness were desperate to live else-where, anywhere. Their home life problems were seldom a secret to those who knew these kids—but adults who could have intervened either didn't or couldn't come up with enough "proof" to be of much assistance to the teens. As a result, many rural teens who fled for safety found solace by living with other disenfranchised kids.

The National Network of Runaway and Youth Services estimated that in 1987 more than 3 million teenagers were wandering across the nation looking for a safe place to stay. In 1988 there were 450,700 run-aways and 438,200 "lost, injured, or otherwise missing" children na-tionally, not to mention the 12,800 who run away from juvenile facilities (Finkelhor, Hotaling, and Sedlack 1990). The Children's Defense Fund (1995) found that 1.5 million children run away from home each year—about half of them to escape abusive homes. The official totals of run-away children likely underrepresent the actual number of children who run away (Office of Human Development Services 1983).[2] While home-less, runaway, and high-risk youth come from all kinds of backgrounds, they are more likely to come from families with few resources (National Network of Runaway and Youth Services 1991).

Consider the case of Randi, a rural teenager I met in a New Hampshire shelter:

> My father began molesting me when I turned twelve. I believe he was devastated because he lost a good job for some scam his friend talked him into. He was never the same after that. Our family was happy and good. Then this happened. He got more unhappy, and he started hitting on me. My mom never believed me. But the school counselor did, and I was put into a group home where I didn't want to be at all. So I started acting up to get what I wanted. I wasn't gonna get anything any other way. Finally, they kicked my ass out, said they'd had enough of me. So I was free! But I had nowhere to go, so after I got pregnant by this dude I had to move back home. My dad made it very clear that I could stay if I would be "available" for him. 'Cause I wouldn't, he threw me down the stairs, and my mom pulled his hands off my neck in time. Yeah, I could go back there, but who in the hell would want to?

Teens who run for their lives find it hard to explain to others how being homeless was better than living at home, as Teddy explained: "People tell kids how they are supposed to live when they don't know anything about what goes on at home for them. They don't know how it is better to be treated badly by strangers than be treated badly by your own family."

While some teens run for their lives, others are told by parents that "it's my way—or the highway." Homeless children in this category are usually teenagers who experienced poor communication and extreme conflict with one or both parents. In almost all of the cases found in this study, the father or father surrogate was the person with whom the conflict was greatest. The teens reported that the mothers appeared helpless, choosing to stand by their men rather than prevent their children being kicked out of their own home.

Although a majority of teens who have blowouts with their parents return home, many do not. The common misconception is that these children could go home if they wanted to. But many children have been kicked out and are not allowed to come back home (Finkelhor, Hotaling, and Sedlack 1990; Rothman 1991; Kryder-Coe et al. 1991).

Parent-child conflict causes this kind of homelessness. Interaction between parent and child becomes so tense, so riddled with disagreement, that even routine conversations become volatile. Typically, the parents cannot accept their children's desire for independence or view their behavior as unacceptable. Children, on the other hand, feel that their parents have unrealistic expectations and will not work with them to find a compromise. What are the behaviors that pose the greatest conflict? They are typical parent-adolescent problems, which include disagreements about the child's friend selection, sexual behavior, drug and alcohol experimentation, money, chores, and hours for coming and going. Elizabeth reflected upon her conflict with her father:

> I became homeless because my father disapproved of my friends and the way I was living my life. I don't think that I was doing anything that other kids my age weren't doing. In fact, I think I did a lot less, only he wouldn't listen to that. Nobody I hung with was any good, nothing I did was right. He wouldn't listen to me—he ordered me around all the time. One day I came home from school, and he had thrown all my clothes, my books, my records,—everything I owned—in a pile on the front lawn, and set them on fire. I screamed and asked him what he was doing, and I was told to "get the hell out of here, and don't you ever come back." I couldn't believe he just kicked me out. I didn't do anything that was all that bad. I was just being a normal teenager, doing the stuff that kids do. I was hysterical at first, then determined I could do it alone. But it is hard out on your own. In the past six months I have lived in eight different places. I'm very embarrassed about my situation and I always try to hide it from the other kids. It's really not my fault, but I feel guilty. One day I called to see if they would let me come back. Mom stuttered around, and he grabbed the phone and told me to never call again. So I haven't.

While the teens admitted that their behavior contributed to their being kicked out of the house, it must be remembered that they are still children—children who make mistakes, children who need to be protected, children who learn, as sixteen-year-old Jonathan told me: "I've had enough. I want to go home. But they don't want me back, and I don't know how to make them want me. I've picked up the phone a hundred times to call them; sometimes I do, and then I hear their voice. I can't talk. My throat clamps shut, and I hang up the receiver."

Once kids are kicked out of their homes, they often find themselves thrown out of the places where they seek refuge. This was a common experience among teenagers I interviewed, who had been kicked out of their homes and later kicked out of their alternative housing. The most common pattern experienced by teens in housing distress in small towns is first to seek short-term shelter at the home of a close friend. However, the family of the friend is likely not able, or willing, to support the displaced teen on a long-term basis. Looking for some place to stay, teens most likely stay with other displaced teens. But with each teen having many family problems and few financial resources, the "homes" that they create are likely to be short-lived.

Boys appear to have a somewhat easier time making it in these collective living arrangements than do girls (Vissing and Diament 1993). Parents more often seem to feel that if the boys want to act like men and violate home rules, they can leave and take care of themselves. Boys find others in similar situations with whom they can live. Small town girls, on the other hand, typically leave in such emotional distress that they look not just for shelter but for emotional support as well. Girls who feel helpless frequently see boyfriends as potential Prince Charmings who can whisk them away from their troubles. But their care and protection is not without cost, and more often than not, the sexual nature of the relationship is the appeal for the boys, as Alexis pointed out: "Right now I am living with a new boyfriend and his parents, and been there for about a month. They know we have sex, and they figure it is normal. Everybody does. I feel like every time I stay with a guy, I got to put out in order for him to let me stay. If I say 'no way,' then I am afraid he will kick me out, and I don't know where I will go."

But not all teens who experience housing distress in rural areas are kicked out. Some are made to feel so uncomfortable that they just leave. This type of homeless child typically enjoyed the social atmosphere of being a teenager, exploring friendships, staying out late, being sloppy around the house, exploring sexuality, and experimenting with drugs or alcohol. These behaviors become problematic for parents who do not know how to handle them. The teens are sometimes intoxicated with their sense of freedom and see parental authority as something to rebel against. When parental authority is challenged, the parents may increase threats and penalties in the attempts to gain control, inevitably resulting in greater conflict with their teenagers. Typically the interaction between the parents and the teen has become so conflict-ridden that the parents have resorted to the ultimatum: "You can't live under my roof and disobey me; if you're going to do that, you can move out."

Both parents and teens think that their perspective is the correct one, and if only the other would see things their way the problems would disappear. Both sides unyielding, many teens feel as if they are not listened to or respected and feel pushed out of the home. Typically the parents do not want their children to leave but cannot accept their behavior, resulting in situations in which neither parents nor teens are happy, as Frankie reported:

> I was born on [a South Seas Island]; my father was an American GI and my mother an island girl. I never met him because he left when the GIs were pulled off the island. My mother ended up marrying another GI and moved to the United States, leaving me in the care of my grandmother. A few years ago, Grandmother felt I should get to know my mom, so she sent me here. It has been awful. I don't feel like I belong here, and I can't go back there. My mother and stepfather watched every move. They didn't want me, and I didn't want them. If they had wanted me maybe it would all have been different. They said if only I would do just what they wanted, then I could stay. But who could please them? I wasn't in any trouble, I didn't do drugs or get wild like they seemed to think. Since they won't change, and I won't change, it is easier for us all for me to be on my own. But damn, it is hard.

Most rural teens pushed out didn't have to deal with these cross-cultural issues. Usually, the conflict revolved around communication and boundary issues. For both Frankie and Kristen, the issues were more intense because they were in stepfamilies:

> My parents were divorced when I was eleven. I lived with my mom okay, until she got remarried. I fought all the time with my mother and stepfather, and nothing I did was okay. They seemed to think I was so bad, but I really didn't do much of anything. The conflict between us got worse and worse. I refused the offer of my real dad to live with him, because I don't like his new wife, who is just a couple years older than me. I did my best to stay away from home by holding down two part-time

jobs and attending high school. Eventually, I couldn't stand it any more
and moved in with a boyfriend. That situation didn't work too well, and
I have been on the move ever since. I figure after I graduate from high
school I can get my own place, and then things will be better.

These students do have homes that they could go back to, if they
were willing to pay the emotional consequences. Some teens, however,
I found had no home to go back to.

Many displaced teens found that once out of the house, they were
out for good. Their parents had gone on with their lives without making
room for them. The teens no longer had a room to go to or a place set at
the table. This category of homeless children no longer belong to the
family, to the household, no matter how much they wished they were.

It doesn't really matter why these children became homeless.
Maybe they were thrown out, pushed out, or maybe they just left. The
point is, they want to go home. But that is now impossible for them.

In some cases the parent has moved away: "I got a letter from my
mom, and she and her boyfriend moved to Colorado. They've only got
a one-bedroom apartment. I called her and asked if I could move there
too—I've always wanted to see the Rocky Mountains. But she said
there was no room. But she said maybe I could come visit her there one
day."

Other times, the parent has transformed the child's room for another purpose, and no longer has room for the child: "They rented my
room out to a friend of theirs. They said they needed the money. There
is no place for me to sleep there anymore. They said if I could pay my
share of the rent, then maybe they would throw him out."

Sometimes, parents—even affluent ones—set up opportunities to
be rid of children, as Missy learned:

> My parents thought I would do better if I went to school in another state
> where I could live with some friends there. But the situation didn't work
> out, and I wanted to come home. But my dad and his girlfriend had sold
> our house and moved into an apartment—and there was no spare room.
> I had not lived with my mother in over a dozen years and did not feel
> comfortable with her or her roommate. Neither one really wanted me to
> live with them, so both parents offered money so I could find a place of
> my own. So I have enough money to get by on, but I don't have a home.

Once the kids are out of the house, some parents just don't want
them to return, as Billy found out: "I had been gone a couple of
months. They made it real clear that they didn't want me around. But I
got homesick, and decided to stop by one night around supper time.

When I got there, other people were living in my house. They told me my family had moved [to another town]. The message was 'Good luck—you are on your own for good now.'"

Most of the teens who experienced housing displacement did so because of family problems. But there was a small subsection of respondents for whom leaving home and living independently was a normal rite of passage into adulthood.

Debbie chose to leave home because it was normal for adolescents in her family to "try it on their own" during high school. Her mother had left home as a teenager, each of her older brothers had moved out to be on their own, and it was a rite of passage into adulthood for her to try her wings of independence:

> When I was sixteen, I decided to move out and live with my boyfriend. My older brothers had both left home during their high school years to live independently. While my mother did not approve of my moving out to live with my boyfriend, it also seemed normal to her for teenagers to want to do that. When I moved out, my mother gave her legal guardianship to [Debbie's boyfriend, who was "older"]. When we broke up, no one else was willing to serve as my legal guardian. That has been a problem, because I can't get no aid without a guardian's signature, and my mom won't sign. I've been staying with a boyfriend and his parents. While they aren't willing to be my guardians, they are willing to let me stay with them until I graduate in June.

While a few teens thought their housing distress was a normal part of existence, there were those who did not think that moving from place to place was normal. These were the kids who were in foster care. Now in rural areas—just like cities—foster children are not considered homeless. But professionals who work with displaced teens in rural areas know there is a relationship between foster care and homelessness (Institute for Children and Poverty, 1993). When I met with a homeless youth task force in a rural New Hampshire community, the representative from the state organization that oversees foster care was constantly under attack by other task force members. He was confronted with stories of displaced kids who needed help and were not getting it. The worker defended his organization and pointed out that children under his jurisdiction were *not* homeless. Children placed into foster care by state divisions of child protection are not officially considered to be homeless.

The other community members had seen his foster kids grow to be too old for successful foster care and end up on the streets or doubled up with others. These kids demonstrated the most obvious link between physical and psychological homelessness. Feeling that they were not cherished in their biological homes, they found themselves unwanted in the homes of strangers.

The data on the relationship between foster care and homelessness is a recent topic of inquiry. A report by the Institute for Children and Poverty (1993) found that homeless families whose heads of households grew up in foster care are at the greatest risk of dissolution. Individuals who grew up in foster care are 30 percent more likely to be substance abusers and 50 percent more likely to have a history of domestic violence than the overall homeless population; twice as many of these heads of households lose at least one child to foster care. Why do people become homeless from a system that was designed to provide them with homes?

Nearly 500,000 children are currently in foster home placement. If current trends continue, by 1996 that population is projected to increase by an estimated 73.4 percent to 840,000. The number of children placed in foster care doubled from 16 percent to 30 percent between 1983 and 1985, and there has been no significant progress in reducing the average length of stay of children in foster care. A 1988 U.S. House report found that a greater proportion (42 percent) of children who entered foster care were under six years old. While the majority of children in foster care are white, minority children increased 46 percent, more than twice the percentage of minority children in the nation's child population. The length of stay for black children in foster care is one-third longer than the national median. Foster family homes are too few and far between to meet the demand, even in rural areas.

Because a state coordinates and pays for the placements, officials deny that a foster child should be considered "homeless." Yet one can argue convincingly that "a house alone is not a home." Placing a child in a "house" with people the child does not know does not mean that this child then has a "home." The mobility and emotional scars carried by countless foster children often qualify them in their own minds as "homeless." In the words of one social worker: "The state says that foster kids and group home kids are not homeless. But they get moved so often and some placements are so bad that the kids are better off taking care of themselves. These kids do not think of these placements as their 'home.' Home is something they once had, that they long for again, and that they don't have now. When will the state wise up and admit that just because they pay for a kid to go somewhere, that money and force doesn't make a home?"

Foster children are supposed to have access to food, shelter, and emotional support. While ideally foster homes result in supportive, nurturing environments for children, many children are shuttled from one home to another, experiencing a variety of abuses along the way. This is particularly true for older adolescents.

As an indictment of the failures of our foster care program, in the Children's Defense Fund (1990) report we read:

> Children are put in inappropriate placements, not designed to offer family counseling, psychiatric treatment or drug treatment . . . Children are usually placed at great distance or even in other states . . . Little or no work is done to return children to their families. Most programs consider home visits to be a privilege, and visits are used as rewards for good behavior rather than as reunification tools . . . Too many foster children are . . . separated from their brothers and sisters because of the lack of a sufficient number of appropriate foster homes. . . . too few visits between birth parents and/or siblings, and far too little attention given to foster parents and foster children. [42]

Many of the rural homeless children I interviewed had once been in foster care. Sixteen-year-old Roxanne barely remembered her biological family. She had been in "maybe 45 different foster homes" that she could remember. Most of the time, she and the family didn't "fit." Sometimes the family did not like her. Roxanne had behavior and learning problems from having been moved around so much. Sometimes the family abused her—sexually and physically—and she was routinely the butt of verbal and emotional abuse. "Most of the time, nobody cared," Roxy reported. When she thought of "home," she recalled one foster home in which she felt the family was kind to her. The mother "would bring me soup when I got sick, and she made a dress for me that matched a dress she made for her real daughter. I still got a square of that material that I keep." She was at that home less than a year.

Foster homes do not give a child a sense of long-term security, especially when all a child knows is foster care. Several children whom I interviewed had been in foster care almost all of their lives, as in the case of Susan. Her shelter worker explained her situation:

> We understand that Susan was born to alcoholic parents of meager means who didn't understand about developmental disabilities. They didn't want a "slow" child. She was borderline mentally retarded and had a range of behavioral problems. Moreover, she didn't look like what the parents had dreamed about when they had their first baby. She was too fat, too clumsy, too goofy-looking to be considered pretty. Susan was two when first placed in foster care, and now she is eighteen and been moved around to over thirty different homes. When she became older

she ran away five times from one foster home. There was nobody left in her town or nearby communities who would take her—her reputation, you know. So she ended up in our shelter. She keeps in contact with her parents, and once they asked her to move home. We were suspicious about this, but Suzy needs to know that they want her, so she went. It was less than a month and she was back. It seems that her biological parents only wanted her there because they were out of work and figured they could cop her Social Security payments. Susan's not too quick, but even she figured out that her parents really did not want her. She has now moved in with substance-abusing "friends," who her caseworker reported were the only group who will accept her. Her caseworker is looking for yet another placement for Susan, but to date has not found one that will accept her.

Teens commonly tested their foster families, to determine how much they really cared. Learning disabled, Tim was placed in a boy's group home since the mother did not feel she could manage him. When fiscal problems closed the group home, he was put in foster care placements. Tim reported that "Basically, I wanted to see if they really wanted me or if they were just keeping me to get the money. So I did what I wanted to do. I smoked marijuana, stayed out all night, and got drunk at parties." As a result, none of the placements have worked out for very long. "I really want my mom to take me back. When I hear kids say they hate their moms and they can't wait to get rid of them and stuff like that, I'm like, wait till you don't have one anymore, then you realize what you're missing."

Child and family housing displacement is the most common form of homelessness in small town America. As the National Academy of Sciences points out (Jennings 1988) the growing phenomenon of homeless children is nothing short of a national disaster that must be treated with the urgency such a situation demands. With homelessness come health risks, concomitant health problems, alcohol abuse, family violence, educational problems. These are exacerbated for children in areas where there are fewer services, not as many professionals, and a paucity of resources with which to address problems. While homelessness is hidden in rural America, it is an example of how rural areas are no longer removed from the problems that confront urban areas.

The displaced rural poor live more invisible lives and try to manage their problems on their own. But when they cannot manage their personal chaos, catastrophe results.

t w o

The Catastrophic Assault on the Family

> It's hard to be homeless . . . We can't afford to do the things we used to, and we are so busy that we are exhausted, showing nothing better for us at the end of the day than at dawn, no matter how hard we try. My kids get sick like they never used to only now we don't have money to take them to the doctor. My husband and I fight when we never used to. Before, we were a loving family with a house and friends and respect. We were able to help others, and now we can't even help ourselves.
>
> Judy, homeless mother of three

When a rural family is at imminent risk of homelessness, chaos tears away at the fabric that holds it together. When the family fabric finally rips apart, the catastrophe of family disintegration results. This is true not just for rural families but for families in every community of every size across the nation. According to Sylvia Hewlett, author of *When the Bough Breaks: The Cost of Neglecting Our Children* (1991, 11), "Across the face of America, children are failing to flourish. Rich kids, middle-class kids, poor kids—all deal with risk and neglect on a scale unimagined in previous generations. Problems of poverty, divorce, out of wedlock births, absentee parents, latchkey kids, violence, and drugs are no longer confined to the ghetto. They reach deep into the mainstream; they belong to 'us' as well as to 'them.'"

Never before has one generation of American children been less healthy, less cared for, or less prepared for life than their parents were at the same age (Fordham Institute 1989). According to an index that measures the social health of children and youth, the well-being of children has declined dramatically over the last twenty years. In 1970 the index stood at 68; by 1987 it had plummeted to 37. Because of social conditions, homelessness in rural America has become commonplace, even if it is not readily apparent (Conger and Elder, 1994). The rural homeless

FRED BLOISE

families I interviewed experienced a number of chaotic family-life problems, including financial distress, employment obstacles, strained family interaction, domestic violence, and fear of losing their children.

People who have good jobs in growing economies generally do not become homeless. But economic problems in rural areas (which will be discussed in more detail in chapter 6) have resulted in people losing jobs or resorting to part-time employment when once full-time jobs were available. In depressed rural areas, homelessness becomes a likely outcome.

Once homeless, rural families run into bureaucracy, social stigma, and economic stone walls. Many adults I interviewed worked full-time, yet they and their families were homeless. How could this be? People worked temporary jobs, at menial pay—because such jobs were the only ones available. These jobs grossly underutilized the abilities of the worker. Mostly they were dead-end jobs, such as dishwashers, newspaper carriers, restaurant workers, janitorial workers, pizza deliverers, or retail clerks. These jobs pay low hourly wages and do not include insurance or other benefits. Such jobs require that the person work nights and weekends—hours that are long and difficult for parents with children, as Rod pointed out: "I work at least forty hours each week—more, if I can get it. Yet I cannot make enough to get us out of the shelter. We'd lost everything, and we were so happy when I got this job. But we can't come up with a month's damage deposit and a month's rent all at once, plus everything else. Besides, there are no places available that we could afford."

Most of the parents I interviewed worked part-time. They would like to work full-time but could not find the jobs. Just as the people working full-time ended up in dead-end jobs, so did those who worked part-time. If people cannot make it on one parent's full-time salary, they obviously can't make it on a part-time wage! All of the people did not start working less than full-time but ended up doing so because "any work is better than no work at all." Savings were depleted as economic distress increased. Betsy described the part-time worker's dilemma: "My husband has been working this week for a construction company. Last week he couldn't work but a couple of hours at this other business. Before that, he couldn't find work at all. He used to be a manager, and now he can't get anything more than scraps of work here and there. We surely can't live this way." The situation for people who work part-time is only marginally better than for those who have no work at all.

While 15 percent of the rural homeless parents had completed some college, and almost all of them had graduated from high school or obtained their GED, education could not assure employment. Although most had worked in the past year, almost all were currently unemployed. Parents reported the same nightly activity—reading the want ads in order to look for work the next day. Seldom did they see themselves as overqualified for a position; they would take any job they could get. But there were few jobs for the unskilled. Employers for low- to middle-range-skill jobs had so many applicants that they could pick the best of the large applicant pool. Looking for work only made the homelessness worse, because not being able to get even the most menial jobs crushed already low self-esteem, as Billy pointed out: "What kind of man do you think I feel like, when my kids see me looking for jobs in the paper every night? If you think it hurts your pride to have your kid say, 'Hey Daddy, here's an ad you could get,' just think about what it is like when you go apply for it and get rejected? How can they respect their old man? God, I hate it all!"

"If you can't get work, volunteer!" This directive has long motivated the unemployed, who believe that volunteer work will give them both skills and references that will make getting a "real" job better. Sometimes it works, as it did for Dwayne: "I had a really rough time. I couldn't hold a job. My self-confidence was gone. So I began doing some volunteer work at the shelter. They said I did really well, and they asked me to work more hours. It's been a year now, and I got a promotion. Now I get to drive people to the store to use their food stamps or I take them to appointments. I am doing really good now."

While Dwayne is steadily working his way up toward paid employment, most rural homeless volunteers are kept working for no pay. Volunteerism is a single mother's dilemma, according to several women interviewed. For instance, Paula realized that she had no job skills. The elementary school had been so supportive of her that she decided to do some volunteer work there. Three years later, she was still doing volunteer work. While her self-confidence had increased, her bank account had not. "I wonder when they will finally pay me for what I do? I have learned so much there and know I do as well as some of the paid people."

Margaret, a single mother of three children, found that volunteer work could be hazardous to keeping her welfare benefits, and a disincentive to work:

> I decided to volunteer at the shelter because they had been so good to us when we were homeless. I told [the welfare worker] that I was doing this volunteer work, and hoped it would be useful when I finish my GED and look for a job. Some woman from [the welfare office] saw me working there, and since I guess I looked like I was doing a good job, she went back and said I was working and they cut my benefits off. They didn't even tell me. One day, there was no check. When I found out, I explained that I was volunteering, but I had to call seven offices, including the state capitol, to get reinstated.

When parents cannot find paid employment, children may end up being the only ones in the family who can find work. "Kids can get paper routes easier, or places will hire them quicker because they get to pay them less than they would have to pay adults," according to one father who counted on his children's part-time jobs to subsidize the family. "We get welfare, but it doesn't pay near enough for all the things a family has to have to get by on."

When the small town kids worked to support their households, it was a tremendous emotional burden for them. "I don't feel I can quit, the way that other kids can when they don't like their jobs," said Mikey. Tracy agreed, stating "I knew my mom could not pay the rent if I didn't work. It was so hard to keep up my school work and work, but there was no choice. Mom worked two jobs, and I knew she was doing all she could, and I must too." But the emotional toil of embarrassment that the parents feel is just as great, according to Mrs. Beyers: "We could not make our rent if Sherry didn't work. I know she has high school and has to do good there, but if she doesn't work, we will be on the street. I feel awful about it all and how I can't make enough to take care of the girls." Almost all of the rural teens—those living with parents and those living independently—worked even though they still attended high school.

Families quickly learned that when you have no job, it is hard to get another. It is even harder when one is homeless. Transportation is a significant problem for the rural homeless. Their cars, when they have them, often are in need of repair. As a result, driving long distances for work may be prohibitive. If jobs are not on a public transportation route—and few rural areas have buses or cabs, much less trains or subways—it is hard for the person to keep the job once it is obtained. Paying for routine car insurance, registration, and gasoline may be impossible for homeless people—and yet in rural areas, how can they manage without an automobile? Consider the transportation woes of this two-parent family who were trying "to hold on to each other, because we are all we've got."

The Wexler family had been out looking for work throughout the town. Because they had been homeless for four months, they were totally dependent upon financial assistance programs to help them. The registration for their car came due, and they could not afford to pay it. Feeling they had to use the car to apply for jobs, and once they had a job they could pay the registration, they continued to drive the car. The mother was stopped by the police and given a ticket for the violation. Having no money to pay the ticket, the family continued to drive the car. After they received another ticket and were unable to pay it, a bench warrant was placed on the parents.

When one has no stable address or phone number, it is difficult to get telephone calls or letters about possible employment. When one applies for a job, seldom is the person hired on the spot. Employers may want time to think about their selection, call references, and gain approval from superiors. Employers may want to call the applicant on the telephone to offer the position. However, homeless people do not have telephones. Even when they live at the shelter, they are reluctant to give the shelter address or phone number on a job application. Job hunters believe that no employer will hire them if the employer learns that they are homeless. Since homeless people move frequently, the phone number they have at one location may be different from where they currently reside. More often, there is no telephone at all where the homeless person can be contacted. An employer is unlikely to go to great trouble to track down the person; there are countless other qualified applicants who are easier to find. It is not likely that an out-of-town or out-of-state applicant will get a job, my respondents told me. "They aren't going to spend the money for a long distance call when they got hundreds to choose from locally."

When people are homeless, their schedules are not their own, I learned. Homeless families live in crisis, and a housing, financial, or family problem may arise unexpectedly, causing the displaced worker to be late for work—or to miss work altogether for a time. Employers may not be sensitive to such personal problems and may not tolerate violation of work rules. Additionally, on-the-job performance may be influenced by lack of sleep, poor diets, and high stress. So even when the homeless work, they bring along a variety of problems that make it difficult for them to be highly productive.

Employment problems inevitably lead to economic woes, which directly cause housing problems—especially when housing costs half or more of one's income!

Interviewed rural families were homeless from a week to eight years. No one was chronically homeless, but several families had experienced intermittent homelessness over the years. Most of the families and children had not been homeless before. The number of dwellings in the past two years for the surveyed families ranged from two to twenty-five, with most people living in six different residences during that time. Most of the rural homeless were not transient; respondents said that the longest time they had lived in one home as adults was ten years, with the majority having lived in one location for three or more years.

When the displaced people talked about the process of their homelessness in rural areas, they went through a clear progression of housing arrangements, as shown below:

Stage 1: The rural family found themselves in economic distress. They could no longer afford to keep up their house and felt they could make ends meet better if they sold the house and moved to an apartment. Almost all of those interviewed had lived in their own house at some point in their lives. But they usually found that apartments cost less to rent than houses: "I didn't want to sell the house. But we simply couldn't make all the payments associated with it. It broke my heart then, and I still well up thinking about it."

Stage 2: Almost all of the homeless people had lived in an apartment or mobile home shortly before becoming homeless. Apartment or trailer life was desirable because the cost was cheaper than owning a house. Also, once the down payment and first month's rent were paid, it would take at least two months to be evicted if subsequent rents could not be paid. This would "buy" desperate families an extra two months of shelter at no additional cost. Families would learn to use this strategy and hop from apartment to apartment—often in different towns—in order to avoid being evicted.

Although the apartment cost less than the house, financial problems were not sufficiently alleviated. Willie reported: "A family can cut back on recreation, or on what you eat, or how you dress. But you can only cut back the necessities so far, and then there is nothing left to cut back on except how much you spend for rent. So we moved from the house to a condo. It was beside the local dump, and our groundwater was contaminated. So we looked around, and found a little apartment. No matter how bad things got, there was usually a cheaper place to stay somewhere—if you could stand it."

Once in crisis and homeless, rural folks frequently moved to other areas in hopes of securing cheaper housing and better jobs. This made the maintenance of normal interactions with significant others more difficult. Moving frequently also disrupted the building of new social relationships. As a result, isolation was great in new communities, and distressed families found themselves wanting to "go home" to the community from which they had come. As Bassuk (1990) points out, social isolation is both a cause and a consequence of being homeless.

When no place was inexpensive enough to house the distressed family, they looked to their relatives and friends for help. Most frequently, this help was given by allowing them to double up—for a while.

Stage 3: It is common among poor people in rural areas to depend on family and relatives to help them during times of distress. At some point during their homeless time, most of them doubled up with family or friends for a period. In the New Hampshire studies, like other studies of homelessness in rural areas (Fitchen 1991), friends and family did help the family who experienced housing distress. Those doubled-up, who are often referred to as the hidden homeless, have no security in such tenuous living arrangements and may find themselves vulnerable to literal homelessness. Children and teens were frequently found living with relatives but without their parents (McCallum et al. 1991).

But over time, the friends and family members become overwhelmed by ongoing requests for help. A growing cause of homelessness includes families' growing reluctance to shelter their own relatives

(Jencks 1994). Supportive loved ones, who may also be struggling to get by, find themselves unable or unwilling to sacrifice scarce time, space, food, and resources. The family members in crisis soon "wear out their welcome" and find themselves alienated from the people on whom they have counted for help.

Because friends and family members conveyed to the distressed family that they were too great a physical and an economic burden, the family would leave and fend for themselves as best they could. Only a handful of the rural homeless had gone without asking people in their informal network for help. Even then, help may not be provided very long, as Emily found out: "My sister knew that my husband was drinking again and beating me and the kids up, so she said we could come stay with her. I don't think any of us expected how crowded her apartment would be with us all of us living there. Her husband said it was okay that we come, but it was clear from early on that he saw us as intruders. We traveled all the way across the country to be with them. Then, in just two days, we all agreed that it was better if the kids and I move to the shelter." I learned from my subjects what Bassuk and Gallagher (1990) found from theirs—that most homeless women lack extensive kin networks, which makes them vulnerable to chronic homelessness.

Stage 4: After being kicked out of the homes of friends and relatives, the rural families found themselves confronted with even fewer housing options. Some people went to shelters, while others tried to make it on their own for as long as they could. Campgrounds were the most frequently used shelter, since the daily camping rates were inexpensive and the family could keep their possessions in the tent and their car. Others stayed in cars, on the streets, in hotels, or in trailers.

For those who came to the shelters, this was "the last resort." Wanda's sentiment was common: "We had owned our own home; we had flowers in the yard, and had tried hard to fix it up. But when he lost work, we lost the house. For a while we imposed upon our friends; for a while they put up with us, but after a while they let us know we were no longer welcome. So we hung out best we could until things got so hard that we had no choice but to come to the shelter."

In a shelter, a parent loses control over the establishment of rules and regulations for the child. If a family is forced to live with family members, friends, or in a shelter, they are then subject to living under other people's rules. This makes it virtually impossible for a parent to discipline, nurture, or set up the guidelines that once structured their family life (Boxill and Beaty 1990; Molnar et al. 1990). "I just want to be able to hang pictures on the wall if I want to. I want to sit on the couch with my feet on the coffee table, eating ice cream with my kid while we watch TV. I want to decide who comes into my house, and if I want to answer the door or not. It's these little things that you never think about when you have a home. It's these kinds of things that really make a home, you know."

Shelter providers create the basic daily structure for the child, not the parents. Shelters decide what time people should get up, what time breakfast should be fixed, and when lights are to be turned off. Only in unusual circumstances are shelter residents allowed to stay there during the day; residents are supposed to be out looking for work, meeting with resource providers, and getting a place to live. Rules exist for when residents can come back to the shelter, how neat they must be, and how they are to behave when they are there. Shelter providers, not necessarily the parents, decide what is appropriate discipline. Though the providers are well-intended, the result is the usurping of parental control (Boxill and Beaty 1990). Shelters have been found to undermine parental ability by their staffs' becoming involved in regular aspects of the families' lives. Boxill and Beaty (1990) report that families, instead of being empowered, are often disempowered by shelter staff. Parents and children are told what, when, and how to do tasks. If parents don't do them "right," the staff has the power to assume an authoritarian role over parents and children alike. A white, middle-class value structure in shelters all too frequently reigns.

In short, the role of the family as the central unit for the child's well-being is drastically influenced by the homeless state. It is not destined that homeless parents will be ineffectual in carrying out roles as parents, employees, and competent human beings. But homelessness makes it more difficult for them.

Stage 5: "Solution" housing for those who live in temporary accommodations must be found. People who are in shelters are supposed to be provided with social service assistance to help them find housing on their own. Sometimes this is through applying for Section 8 housing, finding inexpensive apartments, or being subsidized by welfare. If one lives in a makeshift shelter in the woods or in a car, cold weather will make living there uncomfortable and unsafe. Long-term housing is the aim.

While the goal was to get housing that could last, frequently rural families found that they were put in places that one would never call home. A welfare director in one rural area noted they had no apartments in her community, so the homeless were placed in motels for extended periods. Yet they could not live a normal life in the motels, because it was illegal for them to cook there. "It was the best we could provide for them," she explained.

Some small towns have their own "ghettos." While they look little like urban ghettos, such places are where the marginal people congregate. A single mother with three children told me about the accommodations provided by the welfare department in the town where they were living: "We are good and decent people, and they put us in with that trash. We don't want to be put there anymore than you would. Just because we are poor don't mean that we approve of any of that behavior. There are drugs everywhere. There are prostitutes and my kids see things they shouldn't. And at night you can sometimes hear guns or fights. It is a terrible influence on my kids, and we will get out of there just as soon as we can."

Where can children and parents get information on where to go and how to work the system? While the homeless in urban areas have places to congregate and talk, the rural homeless do not. There is no rural street subculture from which they can obtain sympathy, support and information. People do not gather in areas where they see one another. The result is that rural homeless families become invisible, rely upon themselves, and become increasingly isolated from mainstream society. Once homeless, it is difficult to get rid of that stigma and be seen as "normal people"—even after one gets a home. The stress of not having a home is often enough to break a family apart.

Divorce and separation are the major causes of single parenthood in the United States, where we have the highest divorce rate in the world (National Commission on Children 1991). At the present rates, approximately half of all marriages in small town America are expected to end in divorce. Over a million children are affected each year by their parents' decision to separate.

In the New Hampshire studies, the biggest reason children became homeless was the separation of their parents. Seldom was life rosy for the homeless families before their worlds turned upside down (McChesney 1988). They had endured a variety of problems for a long time before they actually became homeless, as observed in the story of Mollie: "Life hasn't been stable for us in a long time. We've moved a lot. When me and my husband lived together he was always getting into trouble. Finally, we split up, and I ended up living on the street with the kids. I ended up living up with this guy to share expenses. But he ended up going to jail and I couldn't afford the rent, so me and my sister moved in together. But she had trouble, and that's how I ended up homeless."

Alcohol use and domestic violence associated with economic problems that led up to homelessness were common reasons for divorce in rural areas, I learned: "I couldn't take his drinking any more. He would always drink, and then he would be mean to me and the kids. Sometimes I drank with him, but it never helped. One day I picked up quietly and left. I took the kids to the shelter where he could not find us. It is better for me to start my life over, even if it is rough and I have to do things by myself."

Frequently the men who left had a pattern of family dysfunction, were involved with new partners, or did not have the personal resources to make it through difficult times. Tim left his wife, who became homeless as a result. His wife talked about the experience:

> Their father got laid off and didn't bother to tell me. The bills didn't get paid, and when he didn't come home for two weeks, I didn't have any money for anything and I had to do something. We were evicted from the apartment, even though I had a three-week-old baby, two other children under age five, and a ten-year-old boy. My oldest daughter (from a previous marriage) is in foster care because Tim tried to suffocate her with a pillow. Tim beat me, drank all the time, and then wanted to come home. Now I think this is a good time to start anew, so I refuse to move back with him. But I don't know how I am going to manage all this. I got a new baby, four kids, no husband, no money, no schooling, no job, and nowhere to live.

Sometimes women decided to leave because they had enough of a problematic relationship and being alone seemed better than staying with the "wrong" partner: "This marriage was going nowhere. I'm almost forty years old, and my life was going nowhere. My kids had absolutely nothing in their lives. There was no consistency, things just weren't working out, so I said, well, forget this, and I left. I haven't seen or heard from him since."

In a few cases, fathers became homeless single parents because their wives left them. Women, longing for adventure or feeling trapped in situations from which they felt they could not escape except by leaving everything behind, left their homes, husbands, and children to pursue another way of life. All too often, substance abuse and extramarital affairs played a role in these separations. Five-year-old Mandy's parents had been divorced most of her life. She had been living with her mother until the mother brought the child (who was ill with undiagnosed pneumonia) to her sister-in-law's house and left town. Allegedly the mother had run into trouble with the police regarding a drug-related problem and had to leave town quickly. Mandy's father came to care for the child but had to resign his second-shift job to get her the emergency medical care she needed. He resigned with the understanding that when a first-shift position became available, he would get it.

Unfortunately, one did not open for many months, and his savings ran out, forcing the father and daughter into the homeless shelter.

Before parents separated, many of them experienced domestic violence. Indeed, many rural mothers fled for their lives into homelessness. Domestic violence has become so common in our society that it, sadly, could be considered normative. Despite its frequent occurrence, it can produce devastating emotional consequences for the family. Women often stay in abusive relationships for longer than they want because of the financial, emotional, and social dependencies that result (Browne 1987). Homeless women who are victims of domestic violence are not much different from their sisters who are abused and who do not become homeless. But clearly, domestic violence, family disintegration, and divorce contribute directly to thousands of women becoming homeless.

Many homeless single women were found to have experienced domestic violence at the hands of their male partners. They endured the abuse for years but at some point decided that they could no longer live this way. By choosing a safer, independent route, they also chose poverty, isolation, and homelessness, as is illustrated in the case of Sophie and her family. The family was living out west when the father became increasingly abusive toward the mother. She had no support system there. His work became increasingly irregular, and the abuse increasingly regular. The mother decided she could no longer tolerate this type of living situation, packed up her four children, and made a 3,000-mile trip back home. "I didn't realize what I was taking on. I thought I was going to slide right into a job and housing, and it didn't work out that way."

Similarly, a small town counselor recalled how in Andrea's family "there was substance abuse, neglect . . . the husband had threatened the stepmother with a rifle and the kids were scared. They ran away. They figured it was safer to live anywhere else than in that household."

The impact of these family problems is most severe for women who have little money, poor education, and few personal and social resources (Bean, Stefl, and Howe 1987). Leaving an abusive spouse may be most difficult for a woman who has little possibility of supporting herself and her children, as shown in one social worker's report: "When the father and mother would drink heavily, the dad would be physically and verbally abusive toward the mother. She 'hated it—but what could I do? I didn't have no education, never worked outside the home, and I got a bunch of kids.' She drank to be his buddy and keep him happy, but it only caused things to get worse."

Homeless women sometimes found that even though they left their home and security, they were unable to stop the pattern of abuse: "He heard where I was, though I tried everything to keep us underground. I even changed our names so he wouldn't know. That man wouldn't give money for our kids' shoes or put food on our table. He only used his money for himself and the things he wanted. When he found us, he paid money to have two huge bags of garbage sent two thousand miles, with a note that this is what we were—garbage. He still calls us and harasses us. I have had to move often to try to keep him from coming and hurting us again."

The women who became homeless because they refused to live in abusive relationships found great pain and suffering, both in and out of the relationships. The sacrifices they made to stay in the relationships were significant, but their sacrifices in leaving were perhaps even greater:

> My Prince Charming turned out to be a violent and vicious man. After having two children and I was pregnant with my third, he left. If I were as horrible a person and mother as I was being told, and if I wanted to destroy my life, I felt that was my business—but I had no right doing that to my children. So three months after my third baby was born, I decided it was time for me to give the children up. I believed that if I truly loved my children then I would want the very best for them, no matter what the cost to me . . . Sometimes, I think it takes more of a woman to walk out a door than it does to stay.

Nationally, there has been an increase of 225 percent in child abuse reporting over the last twenty years (Children's Defense Fund 1990). Much of the early child abuse literature (Gil 1971) associated child abuse with poverty. If this relationship was accurate, one would expect to find homeless parents abusing their children. But the families in this study were generally not physically abusive to their children. There are no official statistics that suggest that homeless parents abuse their children more or less than the nonhomeless population. However, crowded, chaotic environments create ripe conditions for conflict and violence. The accumulation of stress and frustration may push homeless parents beyond their limits. One could regard any homeless child as a neglected child because of the lack of housing, lack of secure food source and preparation unit, and austere poverty. In the past this allegation has been used to take children away from their parents. Alperstein, Rappaport, and Flanigan (1988) reviewed hospital emergency room records for rates of child abuse and neglect of homeless children and found a rate of 8.8 per 1,000 for the homeless group and 2.3 per 1,000 for the housed group.

While child abuse was more the exception than the rule, three categories of abuse were observed in the New Hampshire families: (1) Some children experienced physical abuse at the hands of their parents. (2) Older children appeared to experience more emotional and verbal abuse. (3) It was not uncommon to learn that teenage girls were victims of sexual abuse. All forms of abuse were more likely to occur during the downward spiral into homelessness, rather than after one became homeless.

Given the stress and strain of homelessness and the fact that national levels of child abuse were high, it was surprising how little physical abuse appeared to be occurring within rural homeless families. There are a number of possible explanations for this. Since homeless families are at risk of disintegrating, many come to care for one another more intensely. Children give parents reasons for living, reasons to keep on trying—even in the darkest moments. Also, there has been a historical pattern of children being taken away from their parents merely because they are homeless, so many parents go to extremes to prove that they are good parents. Having lost everything else, the children are the one thing that parents like Mrs. Madison refuse to lose: "I would never hit my children before, and I am less likely to hit them now that I am homeless. I doubt that hitting solves anything or makes a kid behave. Besides, if I did hit my kid, people would point and maybe try to take him away from me. I couldn't stand to lose my kid. He is the most important thing in the world to me."

Ms. Jackson affirmed this line of reasoning as she cuddled baby Michelle in her arms: "The only thing I have in the world is my kids. Nothing means more to me than them. I am a good mom, and would do anything to make sure they are okay. When everything else in our world is crummy, they need to know that I love them, that I will take care of them, and that I will always be there for them."

Sometimes the stress of homelessness made it difficult for parents to do a good job taking care of their children. Sometimes parents made poor decisions or had too few resources to parent adequately. Such abuses were not intentional but the result of having too many things to manage with too few resources. An example is Mikey. Mikey's mother abandoned him soon after he was born. His father was ill equipped to deal with raising a child. He drank, couldn't hold a job, and had few real friends. He and Mickey lived on the street in his truck for a while. After the truck was demolished, they lived in a park and slept in alleys. After a while, the boy became too much of an imposition. So the father put the eleven-year-old boy on a bus in California and sent him to live with relatives in New Hampshire. As Mikey recalls, "I was scared of those creepy people on the bus. I was all by myself. Not even the driver was the same, they changed every so many miles. I didn't have much money to get anything to eat, and I didn't have anything to do except look out the window that whole trip. When I finally got to the bus station, no one even came to get me. I figured no one wanted me. So I just sat down and waited, figuring out what to do. I had no place to go. The bus station people ended up calling the police, who helped me find a place to stay."

Time after time, parents talked about how homelessness put them under tremendous stress and how they knew that stress could make them more prone to abuse their kids. Since one mother was afraid that she could not control her anger, she chose no longer to spank or hit her children to assure that she will not hurt them. "I love my kids more than life itself. I will not hurt them, I will not lose them. They're everything I've got, and I'm everything they have."

Therefore, while child abuse occurs among homeless families, it is a symptom of the stress that the family is under. When homeless parents of small children know their behavior is being monitored by social service agencies, they appear to be less likely to abuse their children. Oddly, the threat of abuse seems to help parents monitor their behavior more closely. Parents of older children do not operate under the same constraints, and adolescents may be the ones most at risk of severe physical and emotional abuse. Older girls also appear particularly prone to sexual assault.

It was not uncommon to find that teenage girls who were homeless in small towns decided to flee their homes to escape sexual abuse. This is consistent with work by Bassuk (1990), which suggests that many homeless urban girls and women were sexually abused by both their caregivers and their partners before their becoming homeless. In New Hampshire, there were few cases of biological fathers molesting their daughters; the abuse was more prevalent among stepfathers or friends of the family. Fifteen-year-old Lynn's story was similar to those of other girls: "I was raped by my mom's boyfriend, who kept doing it, and no one would listen to me to make him stop. So I moved out with people where things didn't go very well. The guy there started to hit on me. I moved out from there, to where I really didn't know the people. Finally, it got too much for me and I moved in with my boyfriend [whom she had known for two weeks]."

This type of sexual exploitation was routine among homeless girls in small towns. It seemed even more predominant among girls who had the least going for them. Terry, who was developmentally disabled, reported: "Some friend of my dad's tried to have sex with me, so I told my mom. They all said it was my fault, and they put me into foster care. One day when I was visiting them, they were drinking and doing stuff I didn't like. My uncle tried to have sex with me. I screamed, and he said he would kill me with a knife. My dad came out and told him to put the knife away. No one there cared about me; they just wanted to fuck me and get ahold of my Social Security checks."

Therefore, while the small town girls lacked the sophistication of girls in urban areas, they were subject to the same pressures for sexual activity. They tolerated it for as long as they could and then resorted to fleeing to their informal network of friends. Uniformly, they did not report the sexual abuse, nor did they seek help from social service agencies.

Clearly, parents who are homeless have greater problems in carrying out normal parental roles and responsibilities. They may fail to provide the essential physical, material, and emotional resources that a child needs in order to thrive. Parents vary from being authoritarian to having no control; either situation results in problems for the child. However, inappropriate parenting behavior should not be regarded as an indication that one is not trying to be a "good" parent, as one social worker reported:

> The bus terminal was busy that time of day, and many feet pounded around where the boy was playing. As the child began to wander off and misbehave, the mother snatched the child by the neck and began to verbally and physically accost him. While one could say that she was physically, verbally, and emotionally abusive to the child, she was attempting—in the only way she knew—to instill a sense of safety, responsibility, and proper behavior into the boy. She was trying to be a good parent, although her behavior violated the rural town's norms of what constituted acceptable discipline.

Parents may try to do the right thing for their children but find that their situation makes them unable to do so. Imagine how much better and more appropriate poor, distressed parents would be if they had the same resources as other parents!

Intergenerational disempowerment, especially in families who are chronically dysfunctional, is not uncommon. Children learn what they observe. If children do not learn how to take care of themselves while they are young, they may grow up with an inability to care for themselves and others.

Children have more positive views of themselves when they understand the world as a supportive place. As Rowe (1982) notes, it is a curious paradox of life that while we can actually live in the present, we give meaning to the present in terms of our past and our future. The causes of our actions lie in our past and the intentions of our actions lie in the future. "And so we construct our world, a world which turns on the aegis of our beliefs and which we must always strive to see as being firm and solid, since it is the only world which we construct that keeps at bay the formless chaos of reality"(6).

It is unrealistic to expect that a homeless parent can do the same job of parenting as middle-class, employed, housed parents. The struggles that the homeless parent must confront are tremendously different from—and more difficult than—the experiences of financially secure, housed parents. The problems in parenting that many homeless parents experience may be situationally acquired or they may be learned. As children grow up not having their needs met, clearly they themselves will have difficulty parenting as they mature to adulthood. This makes the homeless parent as much the victim as the child he or she is parenting, since those whose needs are unmet today may likely have insufficient personal resources to take care of others tomorrow.

Not having a place to live was not necessarily an indication of poor parenting, I learned through my interviews with homeless parents in small towns. They loved their children, just as housed parents love theirs. No parent is perfect, and the stresses of economic and housing distress take their toll. But the housing displacement often seemed to bond parents and children together in unexpected ways.

The premier fear of every parent interviewed in this study was losing their children because they were homeless. Their fear is not unsubstantiated. In many areas it is common practice for homeless people to have their children placed in foster homes. Once the child is in a foster home, the parent becomes ineligible for assistance. Without any assistance, it becomes virtually impossible to improve sufficiently to regain custody of their children. In urban areas, like New York, the Supreme Court ruled that the city cannot withdraw a mother's welfare payments, even if her children are in foster care, if doing so causes her to lose her home and makes it impossible to reunite the family (Sullivan 1989). However, not all states have developed such a position. Rural areas that have never had to address homelessness before are not necessarily so progressive in their treatment of homeless parents.

Several single mothers reported having family members or friends who had a child removed from the home before, and they felt that the system could take a child away just because the parents were homeless.

Always, the parents believed that they were doing the best they could for their child, given their situation. Yet they realized that social workers might not think that their best was good enough. In other cases, parents knew of other people whose children had been removed, and they were terrified that this could happen to them. This terror was greatest among the single mothers. "I am so scared, more scared than you can ever know, that one of those people will come up and take my kids away from me because we are homeless. They probably wouldn't ever look to see how hard I have tried to keep us together, to make sure my kids are okay. Not having a house doesn't mean that I am a bad mom, or that they aren't okay."

Love of the children was clearly stated and conveyed in their behavior. Children became a motivating force for the mothers to do all they could to get their lives in order, to make sure that their children were set up with the best future possible. "I am a good mom, and I love them more than anything. I try really hard to let them know that they are not responsible for this mess we are in and that things will be better. I make sure they do good in school so that things like this won't happen to them when they get big. I build them up wherever I can, to help them keep their self-esteem up during these hard times."

When parents cannot provide their homeless children with the love and nurturance so essential to the development of a positive sense of self, children will look for some other way to achieve acceptance. Sometimes they cling to adult role models in shelters, schools, or social service agencies because there is no other strong role model with whom they can identify. This is especially the case for homeless girls like Judy, according to her shelter director: "Judy sees me as her mother, the mother she never had. She follows me everywhere I go. There is no way that I can begin to fill her empty cup; nobody could do that now that she is a teenager."

When asked if she could choose one thing to change in her life, Judy wanted to "stay in one spot. I just would like to stay in one spot." As one caretaker said of the teen, "She is one more who will always be caught between the cracks." Judy needs a supervised home setting, workers who can nurture her and diffuse her anger, yet her social worker is unsure how that will come about. The long-term problems of an erratic childhood are now carved in stone for her.

The importance of role modeling and identification cannot be overestimated (Danzinger 1970; Maccoby 1970; Bandura 1965). Identification with role models is critical for the child's social well-being. Through conscious and unconscious identification with role models, children are able to see themselves as significant adults in their world. If children see parents as competent, successful, engaging, and resource-ful, they will learn both the attitudes and the behaviors that make it pos-sible to develop these attributes within themselves. Similarly, when children see their parents as victims, helpless, hopeless, frustrated, and failing to "be all that they can be," children integrate these experiences and may see such behaviors as the only ones they can realistically incor-porate into themselves (Danzinger 1970).

Strong role models and a positive sense of self may be more im-portant at some points during the child's life than at other times. Devel-opmental theorists note how there are certain times in a child's life when he or she needs to establish forms of security. This is seen through Erik Erikson's stages of development (1951) and through the work of T. Berry Brazelton (1994). If a child is in a crucial stage of physical or psychosocial development when he or she is homeless, the long-term consequences may become more devastating than if the child had become homeless at another developmental stage.

One of the best gifts that parents can give to their children is being positive role models. A child's ego and sense of self-competency are of course better served by seeing parents steadily employed than by seeing them unable to find work, by seeing them with enough income to provide the necessities and a few "extras" than by seeing them unable to make ends meet, by going on a family outing to a restaurant and a movie than by waiting outside an office in hopes that this time there may be a job for the parent.

Eleven-year-old Tilly stated:

> My dad and my mom both had good jobs before my dad lost his and we moved to Florida for him to get another. We spent all our savings going there, and then he found out no job really existed. Neither of them could find work. Every night we would sit with the papers and look for places where they could find jobs. Day after day us kids would go with them while they went into the buildings to apply for the jobs. We would just sit on the steps until they finished—it was boring, but we all gotta stick together. So far, they haven't found work yet. It's hard to look at them psych themselves up for the interview, and to come out looking so sad and mad. We know it's for us kids that they want the work, so they can take care of us like they used to. School is coming up, and we can't get new clothes, or shoes, or even paper and pencils. It just doesn't seem fair. They try so hard and get nowhere. Sometimes I wonder—what is going to happen to me?

Compare Tilly's defeating experience with the case of nine-year-old Ricky:

My dad left my mom and me. She took me to live with my grandparents for a while. But they kept telling her what to do and how to raise me. She didn't think they were right, and she moved us out. Dad told us to move back to town and he'd help us. We didn't know he'd moved in with his girlfriend. Since we didn't have any place to go or any money, we had to stay with my dad and his girlfriend for a while. That was really hard on my mom. But she knew we needed a place to stay and put up with it to take care of us. She then found a shelter for us to live at for a while, even though she didn't like the idea of us living there because she was afraid people would talk badly about us. But she held her head high, and we moved in there. She signed me up in my new school, told people that we were on hard times, and that she would be getting things together and needed their help. Over the next couple months, she got us an apartment, went to some vocational training, and she is now working at her first job. She is doing really well. She makes sure I get my homework done. I am on the honor roll this term. We are doing good. I am proud of my mom—she didn't let anything beat her. It has been hard, but I want to grow up to be like her.

Tilly felt hopeless and helpless, while Ricky was empowered because of the way his mother managed the situation. Both are homeless; both have parents who are trying to take care of them and establish a good home for them. Situational factors appear to account for the parents' differential opportunity to get out of homelessness. It is important to realize how much the situational context influences parental ability and the child's perception about what is and is not possible.

Role reversal also occurs in homeless families when the child nurtures and supports the depressed and distraught parent. Parents may have no one to talk to who understands the situation like the immediate family. Thus, a child may become the primary person with whom the parent talks about his or her problems. The parent may need support, but a child's loving gesture can be met with parental reactions that range from anger, humiliation, or gratitude. A mother explained: "My son knew I was doing the best I could. I would sit and cry, and he would hold my hand, saying, 'Don't worry, Mommy, everything will be okay. I'll help you.' And he did. He did the cleaning and sometimes fixed dinner or breakfast for me. He sold his guitar to another kid so that he could get me a Christmas gift. That year, I could barely hold things together. He helped hold me together. I could not have managed without him. He is exceptional, wonderful. Now that I am back in charge, he can go back to being a kid."

Being good parents is hard for the homeless. The cards are stacked against them. The will of these parents to take care of their children and not give them up conveys strength, love, and concern that merits acknowledgement.

So are homeless parents good role models? Perhaps they cannot "do" the same things as housed parents. But the parents conveyed dedication and strength when they were put to the test, weary and worn out. In this context, the parents could be considered good models for their children.

The future of rural areas—indeed, the entire nation—will be dominated by changing demographic and social forces that influence the family. Homelessness is but one of a series of adverse situations that loom for the future of the family, if current trends continue. The implications of these trends are made clear in the National Commission on Children's report:

> America's future is forecast in the lives of its children and the ability of their families to raise them. Most American children are healthy, happy, and secure. They belong to warm, loving families. For them, today is filled with the joys of childhood—growing, exploring, learning and dreaming—and tomorrow is full of hope and promise. These children will become the competent and caring parents, employees, and community leaders upon whom America's future depends. But at every age, among all races and income groups, and in communities nationwide, many children are in jeopardy. They grow up in families whose lives are in turmoil. Their parents are too stressed and too drained to provide the nurturing, structure, and security that protect children and prepare them for adulthood. Some of these children are unloved and ill tended. Others are unsafe at home and in their neighborhoods. Many are poor, and some are homeless and hungry. Often, they lack hope and dreams, a vision of what their lives can become, and the support and guidance to make it a reality. The harshness of these children's lives and their tenuous hold on tomorrow cannot be countenanced by a wealthy nation, a caring people, or a prudent society. America's future depends on these children too. [1991, 2]

The problems that have beset rural families have occurred as the national waves of change have encroached upon rural America's shores. Rural families are no longer able to escape the chaos once confined primarily to urban areas. The problems that homeless children and families experience are not accidental but systematic.

three

Homelessness:
It's Enough to Make You Sick

Homelessness and illness go hand in hand in both rural and urban America, because poverty and its accompanying consequences know no geographic, age, gender, or racial boundaries. Therefore, health consequences of homelessness are great for children everywhere. However, because of the higher proportion of people who live in rural poverty and the lack of medical facilities and health care practitioners in rural areas, children and families who are displaced there are at even greater risk for health problems than are those from urban areas.

There is scarcely any aspect of a homeless existence that does not compromise physical health, or at least greatly complicate the delivery of adequate health services (Boxill and Beatty 1990). Life without shelter is extremely corrosive to physical well-being. Minor health problems that most people would solve with a palliative from their home medicine cabinet become much more serious for people with no access to the medicine chest. Ailments that are routinely cured with a day or two at home in bed can become major health problems if one has no bed. One of the healthiest things Americans do every day is take a shower, a simple act of hygiene that is largely denied to the homeless population.

For the homeless, there is no bed to crawl into when one has the fever and chills. There is no stove on which to make chicken soup, and there is no medicine cabinet from which to get aspirin or cough syrup. There is no bathtub in which to soak and no refrigerator from which to get ice (Hillenbrand 1994). As Jonathan Kozol wrote of homeless urban children, whose health situations are not drastically different from their rural counterparts, homeless children

> grow up surrounded by illnesses no longer seen in most developed nations. Whooping cough and tuberculosis, once regarded as archaic ill-

SCOTT CHARETTE

nesses, are now familiar in shelters. Shocking numbers of these children
have not been inoculated and for this reason cannot go to school. Those
who do are likely to be two grades behind grade level. Many get to class
so tired and hungry that they cannot concentrate. Others are ashamed to
go to school because of the shunning by their peers . . . [who] don't want
to sit beside them. Even their teachers sometimes keep their distance.
The children look diseased and dirty. Many times they are. Often unable
to bathe, they bring the smell of destitution with them into school . . . in a
terrifying sense, these children have become American untouchables.
[1989, 52]

Information gathered by the National Health Care for the Homeless project (Institute of Medicine 1988; Wright 1987) indicates that
homeless children up to twelve years old are twice as likely to be
treated for minor upper respiratory infections and ear infections as to
other children. They are at least three times as likely to be treated for
gastrointestinal problems, four times as likely to be treated for skin

ailments, and ten times as likely to be treated for poor dentition. For children between the ages thirteen and nineteen, the National Health Care for Homeless Project documented similar patterns. Rates of nearly all acute disorders and traumas were higher in the homeless youth. Nearly twice as many homeless youth suffered from one or more chronic disorders, including hypertension. Pregnancy rates were extremely high, as were rates of alcohol and drug abuse (Molnar et al. 1990).

Homeless children are twice as likely to have one or more chronic health problems, such as cardiac disease, peripheral vascular disorders, endocrine dysfunction, and neurological disorders (Molnar et al. 1990). When compared to housed children, homeless kids are twice as likely to have elevated blood lead levels, a condition associated with developmental and psychological delays (Alperstein, Rappaport, and Flanigan 1988). Homeless children suffer from asthma at a rate two to three times higher than other poor children, according to David Wood of the RAND/UCLA Center for Health Policy Studies (Mihaly 1991). Although no national count for child mortality among the rural homeless is available, information from about twenty communities indicated that about a thousand homeless people died in 1991, and half of these deaths occurred on the street. Causes of death included exposure, accidents, alcoholism, and homicide, as well as diseases such as AIDS (Williams 1991). Problems created indirectly from poverty and homelessness were not included in these figures—and these are the problems the rural homeless are more likely to experience.

Most of the health problems experienced by the small town children and families I interviewed were preventable. Poverty, stress, irregular schedules, exposure to unhealthy environments, and a lack of basic necessities created health problems. Two of the most basic health necessities lacked by homeless children in rural areas were nutritious food and regular sleep.

Those who experienced housing distress in rural areas reported two nutritional problems—not having enough to eat and eating an imbalanced diet. Nutrition needed for good health and development is compromised for homeless children. Their families may be so financially strapped that they have to choose between paying for adequate food and paying for transportation to a job interview or for a down payment for an apartment. Cheap food frequently cheats the children of necessary nutrients. Studies indicate that homeless children are iron-deficient, resulting in anemia; lack of vitamin C, causing poor wound healing; and lack vitamin B, affecting the central nervous system (Winick 1985; Molnar et al. 1990).

Homelessness restricts what can be eaten, which results in poor nutrition and health. Lacking refrigeration, many homeless mothers in small towns keep their children's milk and medications cold by putting them in a cooler or in the tank of the toilet. Without stoves, they are forced to cook outdoors over a fire or to eat foods that do not have to be cooked. The New Hampshire homeless ended up eating foods that require no heating or preparation—foods that are seldom as high in nutrients as "home cooking." As one counselor pointed out:

> When I was counseling a homeless teenage boy about the importance of eating breakfast, he agreed he may feel better if he did. He never ate breakfast. The next day, he proudly greeted me with his breakfast in hand—a bag of pretzels and a cream soda! I didn't know whether to laugh or cry—he did eat breakfast, but oh, his selection was terrible. Really, his choices were limited to the food in the convenience store across the street from my office. I could educate him on better foods to eat, but he had no way of preparing them anyway. He didn't even have a can opener, much less a place to heat up even canned soup.

As a result of dietary limitations, poor people may be too skinny, or obese. Because of the carbohydrate-loading and high-fat/sugar/salt content of convenience foods available to the homeless in small towns, I saw many more overweight people then thin ones. Within some families, all of the members were overweight. Their weight was clearly the result of the types of diets they could afford on limited incomes. A few teenage girls I met were bulimic; they reported not being able to hold food comfortably in their stomachs after having been without food for long periods of time. "I sit down, so hungry, and wolf down food. Then I feel so miserable that I throw it up. But I am still so hungry."

Lack of good nutrition resulted in children being hungry. Homeless parents are five times as likely as housed poor parents to report that their children go hungry (Molnar et al. 1990; Children's Defense Fund 1990). Where can one get free food if one is hungry in rural areas? If families qualify, they can receive food stamps. Families may also use food pantries and soup kitchens. Children sometimes can get free meals if they are in school but in many rural communities, I found school breakfast and lunch programs being eliminated as school funds were cut. Current food stamps and school food programs are still not be enough to keep children from being hungry and malnourished, and one can predict that poor children will suffer even more under the proposal block grant re-allocation formula proposed by the contract with America advocates.

Homeless children may rely on school breakfasts and lunches as the only meal they get. As Molnar et al. (90) observed, it is not uncommon for homeless children participating in free breakfast programs to eat three and four bowls of cereal, as that may be all they have had since the previous day's school lunch.

Free lunch programs are available in many rural schools, giving many homeless children their only hot meals each day. Some schools have free breakfast programs, but many rural schools do not. Why are free breakfast programs not implemented, if they do so much good? As one principal pointed out, political realities of the school sometimes override the needs of the students:

> We knew many children were coming to school hungry, so we started a free breakfast program. It worked okay at first, because enthusiastic parent volunteers put it together. But as the novelty wore off and time went by, the volunteers dwindled off. So teachers started coming in early to serve up the breakfast. But this made it hard on them. Finally, when winter came and the kids came in before school with snowy boots, the mess under the tables became so great that the custodians had to clean up before lunch could be served. They put up such a fuss, and there was no one else with the time to clean it up. So our free breakfast program went down the drain.

While all homeless children are hungry, it is easy to focus on small children and forget about the plight of teenagers. My interviews yielded that teenagers were frequently hungry and malnourished. Most of them received no economic support and relied entirely upon free lunches from the school or friends who gave them handouts. Even though hungry, many students could not eat when food was available, finding themselves too stressed to eat, as Amanda pointed out: "I want to eat, I am so hungry, but when it comes to the chance to eat, I look at the food, and I just can't swallow it. Later I wish I had, but the same thing happens over and over. I think it is my nerves."

The manner in which free food is given has much to do with how well it is received in rural areas. I met dozens of hungry kids who refused to eat the free lunches at school because they would be ridiculed: "Everyone else either brings their lunch or eats at the snack bar. Everyone knows that the people who eat the regular school lunch are losers and poor. I don't want anyone to think that of me. I would rather go hungry. And I do."

Soup kitchens were once used only by adults, but today they have become a center for young and old alike. However, soup kitchens and food pantries are often nonexistent in rural areas. Typically only larger communities have them, and most have very limited hours of operation. When food pantries exist, they serve a large geographic area and only a two- or three-day food supply is given. Many rural food pantries have rules that one can come for food only once a month. This leaves a family with twenty-five or more other days per month to fend for themselves.

Most soup kitchens in rural areas are sponsored by religious organizations or groups like the Salvation Army. Typically the soup kitchens are located in the county seat, since that is the largest community within the area. In larger communities there is often a system of regular meal provision in which different churches or community groups are responsible for a meal each night of the week. But in most small towns with soup kitchens, a meal is not provided each night. Some soup kitchens are open only one night a week. This leaves people who are dependent upon soup kitchens hungry on the nights in which no meal is provided.

Since different people usually work at soup kitchens each night, it is often impossible to identify people who are in chronic distress. Also, some soup kitchens refuse to serve people under age eighteen who are unaccompanied by a parent. Knowing that even the soup kitchens will turn them away, adolescents who are homeless in rural areas become even more invisible.

One night as we prepared dinner at a well-organized soup kitchen in a small town in New Hampshire, we looked at the log kept by volunteers in the days before us. The log noted how many people were served, by which civic group. It appeared that about thirty-five people were in usual attendance. This particular soup kitchen developed a menu around bulk foods that were donated. On chili night, we prepared food for thirty-five. People came . . . and came . . . and kept coming. Who were they? Parents with infants and little children came, and so did teenage boys who averted their eyes as my same-aged daughter put out food for them. And single men and women came as well. The long tables were filled to capacity with this unlikely collage of "family" members. Hungry fathers and sons set up more tables, as women smoothed out tablecloths after them. And people waited patiently as we cooked all the food we could find and still ran out. They silently left after clearing away their own dishes, simultaneously expressing gratitude and trying to save face.

There is frequently little coordination of menus when different groups are in charge of the soup kitchen each night. Because the kitchens operate on donations, they have no long-term planning for balanced nutrition. Almost no menu had fresh fruit; fresh vegetables were also rare except during the summer. The menus were almost exclusively carbohydrate. Spaghetti, chili, macaroni and cheese, and baked beans were very common. While chicken was fixed once or twice, meat dishes were rare. Meals were high in carbohydrates. One menu included pasta, corn, and bread. Cake or cookies were always provided for dessert. Coffee was always available, although milk and juice ran out quickly. Once in a while, one of the guests at the soup kitchen would inquire why a certain food was—or was not—available. When one woman complained about the menu, her complaint was met with a short, "beggars can't be choosers" rebuff from a volunteer. Upon talking to her later, I learned that she was a diabetic who was trying to control her health problems by dietary intake. She did not have health insurance or money for doctor visits. She did not mean to be ungrateful; she was trying to survive as best she could with the resources that were available to her. If one had cholesterol or other dietary restrictions, one was simply out of luck when eating at the soup kitchens. One could eat what was served, or not eat at all. (See Eliot Liebow's *Tell Them Who We Are* for more information about shelter and soup kitchen life.)

Rural food pantries were never designed to be the main source of food for those in need. Food stamps are the main source of food for the poor in both rural and urban areas. While some welfare providers reported that food stamps should be available for a family within a week after application, I met no homeless family who received them in any less than three weeks. In some cases, it took over four months to actually get food stamps. How is a family to survive during that time?

While food selection becomes easier when one is on food stamps, it is best at the first of the month. All of the parents I interviewed made it clear that the amount of food stamps they received was insufficient to feed a family all month. As Ralph pointed out: "At the beginning of the month I shop very carefully and plan meals for the whole month. But it is hard to stretch the stamps, even when we have pasta four times a week. If we run out of food stamps before the end of the month—and we always do—then my kids have to do without vegetables, fruit, meat, and sometimes even milk and bread."

To make food stamps last, people often buy the cheapest food available. More expensive food items such as meat, milk products, and fresh fruits and vegetables were the hardest for the New Hampshire families to obtain. "They give us food stamps, but they don't go near far enough to feed seven kids and two adults. I shop real wise, and use coupons, but mostly we get macaroni and cheese dinners and peanut butter and stuff like that which will fill them up but don't cost so much. It's the only way."

Poor budgeting of food stamps was the explanation one a social worker gave for why the homeless often don't have enough to eat at the end of the month. But this allegation is simply untrue, according to Barbara:

> We don't get many food stamps to feed us. They say we get what we are entitled to, but when it comes time to feed us all, it cannot be done. The social worker told me that I had to divide up the food better. She told me to give kids 3/4 a hard boiled egg, or a half a peanut butter sandwich for lunch, because that officially meets their nutritional requirements. What do they think I am going to do—feed hungry kids just a dab to please government recommendations? They are crazy. I end up giving them my share, because I will not stand for my kids to go so hungry.

Low-income pregnant women and small children can qualify for the federally funded Special Supplemental Food Program for Women, Infants, and Children (WIC). This program provides milk and food so that children in their most formative period can grow up healthy. But in a related study (Knickman and Weitzman 1989), it was found that among sheltered pregnant or new mothers, only 60 percent were receiving benefits from WIC. Only one of the mothers I met reported receiving WIC supplements.

If a homeless family can get into a shelter, the chances for the family to have access to food and a regular meal schedule increase. While the quality of life may be better once a family is in a shelter, how much a family will be helped will depend upon the type and quality of the shelter.

The rigid content and schedule of meals in most shelters and soup kitchens where homeless families eat can actually cause problems in getting children fed. Many school-age children miss breakfast so they can get to school on time. This only compounds their academic problems. Families complained of the loss of family cohesion and parental authority when meals were no longer prepared and eaten together by the immediate family members. Because most public shelters are not equipped with cooking facilities, families are forced to cook on illegal hot plates, eat at fast-food restaurants, or subsist on junk food.

In some shelters, the family has absolutely no control over what they will eat. Being hungry and in need of charity, they are expected to eat and be grateful for anything that is served. When there are collective kitchens, the families may cook at different time periods to avoid confusion. This means eating when it is your time, whether you are ready to eat or not. At other facilities, everyone may cook all at the same time. This destroys the interpersonal interactions that occur in kitchens when members of a single family cook together. In the attempts to feed large numbers of people, normal interpersonal relations within the family are sacrificed.

Shelter directors found that sometimes children would hoard food because they were not convinced that tomorrow they would get enough to eat. As one woman who worked with homeless children pointed out:

> New shelter children were given stuffed animals to give them a sense of comfort. But we found that many of them were stealing food out of the common food supply, hoarding it. At first we got upset—how dare they steal food! There will be plenty for them while they are here. But one night I tiptoed into a room and saw a blond-haired boy around five years old asleep, clutching a jar of peanut butter and a box of crackers. The stuffed animal was on the floor. He had gone hungry for so long that the food gave him more comfort than the toy. This scene really rocked me to my senses. I will always see this sleeping child clutching food to his heart. Now I am more understanding about why people steal food.

Another factor that creates preventable health problems for homeless children is the lack of sleep. It is hard to get a good night's sleep when you are homeless. Sleep problems were experienced by almost of the children I interviewed, especially teenagers. Homeless teenagers who worked after school at late-night jobs found themselves exhausted when they had to be at school early the next day. Linda's story was repeated time after time by homeless teens across the state: "I have to work or I have no money to pay my share of the rent. But when I work so late, I can't get my homework done. So when I get home, I sit down to do my homework. But then I stay up so late that I wake up too late to get to school on time. It is a crummy, vicious circle."

Children who live doubled up with other people cannot control where they will sleep, what time they will get to bed, if they will be awakened during the night, or what time they will get up. This makes it hard for them to get adequate rest. "My children's behavior gets rough when they aren't on a normal eating and sleeping schedule—but when you are homeless, you don't have a schedule at all that you can keep, even when you try," reports Jesse. But as Darryl points out: "I can't complain because I haven't got anywhere else to live, and I really am glad to have a place. But they sit up and listen to music really late, and they talk loud. Sometimes they laugh and laugh, or they get into fights. But no matter what, it means that I can't get to sleep. I sleep on the couch in the living room and there is no way to escape the noise. So I grin and bear it, because I don't have a choice."

Darryl was thrown out of his home by his father and found refuge in the homes of friends. He knew that if he complained, the only option he had was to scrounge around for another place to stay—and he had already stayed nearly everywhere he could. As Kelli reported:

"I worry all day about where I will sleep the next night. Some of the places I end up sleeping aren't too great. Sometimes it is so noisy, or I get scared because I don't feel safe. So even though it is night, I can't sleep. Sometimes even the worry wears me out. You never realize how much having a place to crash means until you don't have one."

Homelessness disrupts the sleep of those children whose parents have found work. Mrs. Baxter explained:

> My husband finally got a job washing dishes at a resort forty miles from here. We only have one car, and I take him and pick him up because I need the car to get to nurses' training. He gets off work at midnight. By that time, the kids have been asleep for hours. What am I supposed to do—leave them asleep at home while I am gone for an hour picking up their dad? What if something happened? I could never forgive myself. So I have to wake them up and have them sleep in the car while we go pick up Dad. I don't like doing that, but it is better than leaving them at home alone.

When a person is sleep-deprived, it is difficult to think clearly, to act rationally, and to fight off preventable illnesses. Warding off disease is even more difficult for homeless children, who frequently do not have all necessary immunizations.

While underimmunization and nonimmunization are national problems for children, they are disproportionately high among homeless children. When parents are concentrating on moment-to-moment survival, they tend not to focus on remembering that it is time to have their children immunized or what shots the kids had in the past. This is complicated for parents who find that there is a shortage of doctors in rural areas. "We haven't taken new patients in years," one receptionist in a rural medical practice informed me. Because many people who live on the margin of homelessness do not have health insurance or the money to pay for health services, immunizations and preventive care are easily put lower on their list of priorities.

In national studies of homeless children, delays in obtaining infant immunizations ranged from 27 to 51 percent of the homeless families (Alperstein, Rappaport, and Flanigan 1988; Molnar et al. 1990; Acker et al. 1987; Miller and Lin 1988). Percentages of immunization delays among the homeless were four times as high as among comparison groups. Even when children are immunized, it may be difficult for highly mobile parents to find the children's immunization records. Few of the mothers of preschool children interviewed knew if their children's immunizations were up-to-date. It is difficult to keep up with small pieces of paper like those that record immunizations when one moves frequently. Many different providers will have seen the children in different towns, so it is difficult to reconstruct a record of each child's immunizations. As Edie told me:

> I know that all of my three kids got some shots, but I also know that they missed some. Which ones? Gosh, I don't even know. I used to have it written in their baby books, but somewhere along the way they got lost. We have moved so much that I don't remember which doctor in what town gave which kid which shots. There has been just too much under the dam for me to remember things like that. So I guess they will have to get all the shots all over to be able to prove that they are healthy. But will you tell me how I am supposed to afford it?

The Clinton administration has acknowledged that a significant proportion of all American children are poorly immunized. President Clinton alleged that his national health reform package would have allowed for all children to get immunizations free of cost. But even if clinics had made the shots available for free, it would still have been difficult for transient children in rural areas to receive the immunizations they need when they are supposed to get them. One thing is for certain: new babies who need immunizations will come, whether or not their parents have housing.

One of the most overwhelming health problems experienced by rural homeless girls and women was unprotected sexual involvement. A high number of those interviewed were sexually active—even at young ages—and used no protection against pregnancy or sexually transmitted diseases.

For a teenager, to be pregnant or a parent is a crisis. To be homeless is a crisis. When these problems occur together, each exacerbates the other. Both conditions increase the risk of a poor birth outcome. While pregnancy and parenthood heighten a teen's need for health care and other services, homelessness reduces the ability to gain access to these services. For teens who have not completed high school, have poor employment skills, and are not socially, psychologically, or financially "mature," parenthood provides yet another obstacle to achievement. The young rural women interviewed for this book were similar to those found in the Shelter Committee of Illinois's Caucus on Teenage Pregnancy. Many were runaways and throwaways who became pregnant after leaving home, while others ran from foster home placements.

The National Health Care for the Homeless Project (Wright 1987) found that pregnancy rates sharply distinguished homeless girls from other girls. Young girls became pregnant ten times more frequently when they were homeless; girls age 16–19 got pregnant 3 times more often than did housed girls that age.

I found that the rural girls who became homeless and pregnant were looking for somebody—anybody—who might give them love and protection. Many girls who were estranged from their families hoped for a white knight to charge up and whisk them away from their misery. Girls like Brenda had became sexually active as a way to maintain relationships that they hoped would keep them from being out on the streets alone. As her counselor reported:

> Brenda became homeless when her father disapproved of her friends and her lifestyle. He told her to get out and never come back. In six months, she lived in eight different places. She has lived in houses, apartments, and trailers, with friends and alone. She lives with some friends for a couple of weeks, then has to find a new place. Mostly, the friends she lives with are male. The longest she lived with one boyfriend was a month. Brenda currently lives with another boyfriend, his parents, and his two brothers. She has lived there for two weeks. She is sexually active with him and thinks he treats her 'bad' sometimes, but she tolerates him because she has nowhere else to go. She uses no contraception and depends on her boyfriend to use condoms—which he frequently refuses to do. While she admits staying with him is not good, she has no other place to go and she dreads the inevitable day when they will break up.

Brenda is not pregnant—yet. But the chances are good that before long she will be. Heidi and Joe, sexually active teens, found themselves pregnant and homeless. They lived in a homeless shelter from March through high school graduation in June after being kicked out of their homes. Thanks to a caring shelter director, they were able to access Medicaid and provide Heidi and baby with prenatal care. She was "luckier than most" because of the support she was able to engender from human service professionals who met these "hard-working, good kids" (Vissing 1992; Vissing, Schroepfer and Bloise 1994).

Homelessness markedly reduces the chances of having healthy babies. Chavkin et al. (1987) reviewed birth certificates and found that of four hundred women known to be homeless, only 60 percent received even minimal prenatal care, compared to about 90 percent of other women. One out of six homeless mothers (16 percent) delivered low-birth-weight babies, compared to about 10 percent of other women. Low birth weight is associated with a variety of handicapping conditions, including mental retardation, hearing and visual impairment, behavior problems, and learning disorders (Molnar et al. 1990). Chavkin also found an infant mortality rate of 25 per 1,000, double the rate of babies born to nonhomeless women.

The work of Chavkin became real when I met Lora at a shelter— who had just delivered her fourth baby a few days earlier. The mother was painfully thin and admitted smoking and drinking during her pregnancy. She described high stress levels and poor nutrition throughout the pregnancy. As she talked, her new son's head bobbled unsupported over her arm. The baby made no eye contact and demonstrated a weak startle reflex. He had little ability to grip fingers or objects. The mother remarked how he wouldn't nurse and didn't much like bottles. He didn't coo, he didn't cry—he just lay quiet, staring out at the world during the several hours I was with him.

There are few riskier behaviors today than being sexually active with nonmonogamous partners that one does not know well. Such behavior drastically increases the risk of sexually transmitted diseases—including AIDS. Vulnerable kids, whether they are in the cities or the country, become easy prey for all kinds of victimization once they are homeless. Most homeless youth have multiple voluntary and involuntary sexual experiences, most of which are unsafe and put them at risk of HIV infection. Although IV drug use among homeless youth is low, sexual intercourse with people who are infected with HIV is not uncommon (Athey 1991).

While none of the small town teens interviewed reported using intravenous drugs, most put themselves at risk of contracting the disease by having multiple sexual partners. Many of these teenagers have been, or will be, exposed to AIDS (Schutt and Garrett 1992). None of the New Hampshire teens had been tested to see if they were HIV positive, nor did they really believe that they would contract the deadly disease.

Teenage girls exchanged sexual intimacy for a place to stay and for someone to love them. Consider Tammy's story: "I am staying with Bobby because he is nice to me. He is giving me a place to stay, he feeds me, and he is nice to me most of the time. If he didn't take care of me, I would have no place to go. Sure, I have sex with him. How could I tell him no, after all he's done for me?"

Tammy had learned that being sexually receptive would enable her to meet her basic necessities. Typically, her relationships were short-lived, maybe after a day, or a few months. But always, she would be cast out and forced to look for someone else who would take care of her.

One could apply a broad definition of prostitution to these small-town girls who exchange sex for homes and relationships instead for money as many homeless urban girls do. Adolescent prostitution has increased dramatically during the 1980s and 1990s, with estimates ranging from 90,000 to 900,000 young "prostitutes." I found that teens did not like this type of sexual exchange or want this lifestyle. Homeless urban and rural adolescents all find themselves struggling with typical problems of survival, along with the added risks of being raped, assaulted, incarcerated, and degraded. Homeless teens who prostituted themselves were likely to become depressed, alienated, lonely, frightened, and suicidal (Greenblatt and Robertson 1993). While most of the sexual exchange to escape homelessness was found among girls, boys were not immune to these pressures. In a few cases, when boys found themselves cast out into the streets with no place to call home, they resorted to exchanging intimacy for survival, as one social workers reported:

> Donnie's father had committed suicide some years ago, and his mother subsequently became incapacitated from severe mental illness. She was unable to work and unable to care for her son. As he became a teenager, he found himself floating from friends' homes to makeshift shelters. One day, as he was hanging around in a local restaurant, he was approached by a man who was passing through town. He offered the boy anything he wanted on the menu, if he would go back to his room with him for the night. The weather was cold and stormy, and Donnie had been wondering about where he could crash for the night. Given his options, he took the man up on his offer. After that, Donnie found that there was always another way to get a "bed with clean sheets and orange juice in the morning" if he was willing to pay the price. Unfortunately, Donnie has been put in contact with a network of sexually active homosexual men who engage in casual sex with strangers. This fact alone puts him at grave risk of contracting AIDS.

In sum, homeless children are at risk of unplanned pregnancy and AIDS. Given that many young women do not use contraception, the chance of there being a generation of homeless AIDS babies being born is not small—even in small town America.

When people are under stress, accidents become more likely (Seyle 1956). Also, poor and homeless people become exposed to situations that are more hazardous, making accidents more likely for them than for upper-middle-class people. Take for example, Patrick's story of a work disability:

> I was working construction and was always lifting heavy things here and there. My back had been pretty tender, and I was trying to leave it alone as best I could. But my foreman told me to carry a load of heavy boxes. When I told him I was worried about my back, he told me to do it or I could look for another job. So I did, and my back went out. They had to take me to the hospital and found I had three herniated disks.

Evidently the years of that kind of work took its toll. A couple of surgeons looked at me, and said "no way" about operating, for fear I'd end up paralyzed. I had only another week to go before I was off probation and would have had health insurance. So I got just a little bit of workman's comp and can't work. I went to a vocational counselor to see if she could get me work, but my back is such a mess now that I can't stay in any position too long, sitting, standing, lifting—I just can't be employable any more.

Thus, Patrick's work disability led to his being unable to work and support his family—and their becoming homeless. I met people of all ages who were suffering from broken arms, broken legs, twisted ankles, and necks in spasm. There were also people who had experienced accidents a long time ago but who were still afflicted with problems from them. Consider the story of Laurie, as told by her mother:

Laurie was five when she was smacked in the head by a baseball that her brother hit. She just stepped in the path of that flying ball, and it hit her so hard that it knocked her off her feet, breaking several of her front teeth. Now she's eight, and somebody who don't know her can barely understand her when she talks . . . Getting hit with the baseball in the side of her head also seemed to mess up her hearing; she don't hear so good on that side. At the time of the accident, we took her to the emergency room. But we never was able to get much more treatment because we had no money to pay for doctor care. Her problems are just something that we all learned to live with.

Only upon her arrival at the shelter did Laurie get the type of medical attention that she needed three years earlier. The audiologist did not believe that the baseball incident had anything to do with her loss of hearing. Her speech pathologist reported that, through therapy, Laurie may be able to speak normally enough to function.

Most health problems that the New Hampshire children experienced were the results of the lifestyle that accompanied being homeless. Stress, irregular schedules, exposure to unhealthy environments, poor diets, and lack of sleep were universal. Emotional problems for homeless children (discussed in the next chapter) abounded, making the children more susceptible to communicable diseases. Pneumonia, colds, and respiratory infections were common, as were broken limbs. More than eight million children in America are not covered by any public or private health insurance (National Commission on Children 1993); hence, even minor ailments go untreated because families cannot afford health care.

In providing health care to the homeless, physician David Hill-fiker (1994) found that he provided medical care that one would expect to see delivered in third world nations. Even the simplest treatment—bed rest—was impossible for people who were homeless. One New Hampshire mother summarized the experiences of her three children: "My girls just keep getting sick, with one cold after another. They just can't get well anymore; either we don't have the money to get them the right foods or medicine, or we are moving around so much that there is no time or lace for them to get the rest they need. My son is just now healing up from a broken arm, and now twisted his ankle real bad. It is just one thing after another."

Homeless children in small town America are sicker than those who are just poor, according to those who work with both populations. "Being poor is bad enough, but being homeless exacerbates every problem of being poor! These kids are at grave risk in every sense of the word," according to one nurse. Therefore, the chaos that comes with homelessness destroys a child's physical foundation.

Homeless children are at greater risk for developmental and language delays than the general population. As many as half of homeless children, in both urban and rural areas, exhibit developmental delays that are related to living in substandard, overcrowded living conditions (Bassuk and Gallagher 1990). When young children spend a significant amount of time in transient situations, it is likely that their cognitive, emotional, and physical growth may be impaired. Homelessness influences both physical and psychological development. Developmental delays have been found to be common among shelter children (Bassuk 1990; Bassuk and Rubin 1987). Bassuk found that the pressures of shelter living exacerbated children's difficulties and create new problems. Moreover, homeless children were found to be in the mentally retarded range at three times the expected level (Whitman, Accardo, Boyert, and Kendagor 1988).

More than one-third of the homeless New Hampshire children interviewed had a readily identifiable developmental problem. Undoubtedly, many others had problems that were not observable to the eye during the interview process. I learned that many children had preexisting health conditions that were exacerbated by their homelessness. Some of these preexisting conditions included visual impairment, mental retardation, speech and hearing problems, and learning disabilities.

Blonde-haired Diane, whose chubby belly showed the effect of eating too many white bread and peanut butter sandwiches, had trouble seeing the board at school. However, no one had ever tested her vision.

When the school nurse at her fifth school identified the problem, the family had no insurance or money to pay for her glasses. The local Lion's Club donated money for her to get the needed spectacles.

Sean, age seven, was called "slow" by his mother. While living at the shelter, the director found he had never received any formal cognitive or emotional assessments. He kept to himself most of the time, playing with few of the other children there.

Mattie "looked and acted retarded." She was a "throwaway" child who had been diagnosed and received state assistance. She was bounced from one foster home to another. Her homelessness made it harder for her social worker to secure services.

Few children received assistance for their developmental problems before they became homeless. The problems only got worse through the lack of care.

Regressive behavior was commonly observed in homeless preschool children. Many previously potty-trained children had regressed to wetting their pants after they became homeless. Speech and language use was found to deteriorate. This is similar to what Bassuk et al. (1984) and Molnar et al. (1991) observed. Over half of the preschoolers Bassuk et al. (1984) studied suffered severe developmental impairments. These children had difficulties with language, motor, social, and personal development skills. Generally, their skills lagged far behind other children their age. Homeless toddlers were found to experience attention deficits, speech delays, withdrawal, dependency, poor coordination, and toilet training problems. Bassuk and Gallagher (1990) found problems in language delays, problems in conceptualizing cause and effect relationships, problems with time sequencing, difficulty organizing behavior, a lack of empathy, and difficulty sharing (Molnar et al. 1990). While these behaviors were identified in urban-based studies, they were also observed among my subjects.

Whether one is living doubled up with others or in one of the few small town shelters, living with others creates health risks. Shelters are naturally unhealthy places because congregate living situations make communicable disease more likely. Communal living breed germs, whether it is through the sharing of bathroom facilities, cooking and drinking utensils, or confined sleeping space. There are airborne, fecal, oral, and direct contact modes of transmission of disease. Common disorders spread in shelters include diarrhea, pinworm, ringworm, strep throat, chicken pox, conjunctivitis, meningitis, influenza, lice, tuberculosis, measles, and AIDS and other sexually transmitted diseases (O'Connell and Groth 1991).

The communicable disease problem is greatest when there are more nonrelated people living together, such as at the homeless shelter. Shelters provide food, a dry place to stay, and varying degrees of social assistance. However, they vary widely in their acceptance policies and health restrictions. Some shelters may be unsanitary, overcrowded, and inadequately heated or cooled. These factors can cause serious health problems. Diarrhea is common among shelter children in these areas of congregate cooking, eating, and bathing. Though diarrhea is easily cured, after a few days it weakens children, leaving them vulnerable to other illnesses. It is easily cured, but it can be fatal if untreated.

Communicable diseases, including tuberculosis, are common—even in rural areas. As one shelter provider in the larger town of a rural area pointed out, "We don't want to talk about the presence of TB at the center. It would scare people and make the homeless look even more undesirable than the people in town already think they are." As another shelter worker noted, "By the time people get to the shelter, they are already sick. Everything is gone for them, including their health."

There is another way in which shelters are not healthy places. Sometimes people have hidden weapons, are under the influence of drugs or alcohol, or have violent outbursts. This puts the other residents at risk (Kozol 1988b).

Illness can be both a cause and a consequence of rural homelessness. Left untreated, people who live on the margin of housing distress are assured of having minds and bodies that will be ill-equipped for healthy, productive citizenship.

four

Homelessness:
It's Enough to Drive You Crazy

Homelessness causes not just physical and social problems but psychological distress as well. In rural communities where there is a great emphasis placed on the home, the psychological impact of having no place to call home can be more devastating than the physical impact of having no place to stay. If one has a stable sense of where he or she belongs, short-term homelessness, as in the case of a flood, fire, or hurricane, will probably not result in long-term psychological trauma. But for a child who consistently has no place to call home, permanent emotional scars are likely. The long-term social, emotional, and developmental toll that homelessness takes on a child who lives in a small community where everyone else seems to have a home cannot be overestimated. "The physical impacts are bad enough, but the emotional problems for these children both now and in the future are substantially worse . . . The scariest part of this crisis is that most of the homeless family members are children, and more than half of those children are under six years old" (Fagan 1990).

Just as Vietnam veterans or sexual abuse victims have difficulty adjusting after the trauma (Russell 1986), homeless children also experience forms of post-traumatic stress disorder. All childhood trauma originates from the outside, and none is generated solely within the child's own mind (Terr 1991; Garbarino and Gilliam 1980). Once the events take place, a number of internal changes occur in the child that can last a lifetime.

Psychological trauma is likely among homeless rural children and families for four reasons (Goodman, Saxe, and Harvey 1991). (1) The loss of one's home—whether sudden or gradual—can be a stressor of sufficient severity to produce symptoms of psychological trauma. (2) The conditions of shelter life or moving from place to place may produce trauma symptoms. (3) Many homeless children and their mothers

FRED BLOISE

are homeless as a result of experiencing physical, sexual, or emotional abuse that led to their being homeless. (4) Being without housing in a tightly knit community where everyone else seems to know one another's private business can psychologically isolate a person. This psychological isolation makes the rural child subject to more psychological trauma than urban children who have a larger peer group who also live in identifiable housing distress.

Two types of childhood trauma have been identified; Type I trauma, which includes full detailed memories, omens, and misperceptions, and Type II trauma, which includes denial and numbing, self-hypnosis and dissociation, and rage. I observed Type II trauma in many of the rural children.

Many homeless children, for example, denied the importance of the homelessness or events surrounding it. They had a preoccupation with the homelessness, worrying about where they were going to sleep, what they were going to eat, and so forth. They experienced confusion when they tried to think, learn, or figure out what was going to happen next. Frequently children had an orientation toward the past, which was a more pleasant time for them than the present.

The homeless children also showed emotional signs of trauma. Anxiety, frustration, anger, fear of recurrence, oversensitivity, depression, grief, guilt, resentment, self-destructive behavior, psychic numbing, and detachment were readily observed among most of the homeless children. Physical signs of trauma included fatigue, increased illnesses, and pounding hearts owing to emotional upsets. Behavioral signs of trauma, identified by Terr (1990), included sleep problems, social withdrawal, out-of-control behavior, the need to talk compulsively, relationship or family problems, substance abuse, memory problems, aimlessness, and dejection. Terr notes that for preschool and younger children, withdrawal, denial, anxious attachments, fears, and regressions are common ways of managing the trauma.

Given that the children interviewed for this book were followed typically less than six months, it is unclear whether they will suffer long-term effects from the trauma of being homeless. Clearly, the signs of psychological trauma were present among most of the children at this time. This is an important area of inquiry for future research.

Psychological problems among the rural homeless seem to be the result of housing displacement and living on the margin rather than the cause of the homelessness. This is different from urban typologies of homeless people, who are alleged to be homeless because of personal dysfunction (Schutt and Garrett 1992; Limbaugh 1993). The psychological problems I observed in small town children and parents are examined in this chapter in alphabetical order.

Acting out. Embarrassed about their homelessness, most homeless children are not open about their housing distress. Indeed, some go to great pains to deny it. Acting out is a cry for help among children who cannot otherwise ask for assistance. Homeless children I observed relied upon adults to pick up on the cues and inquire about what was going on that made them act out rather than punishing them. However, many children found that it took several incidents of acting out before adults asked the "right" questions and detected the housing distress.

Younger children were more likely to deal with their homelessness by withdrawing rather than acting out. Among elementary-age children, school performance declined and behavior fluctuated wildly. Sometimes younger children would get angry at the drop of a hat, over seemingly inconsequential problems. Punching another child quickly got the teacher's attention! Compensatory behavior, obsessive talking, and behavior changes occurring among previously trouble-free youth were signs of problems (Bassuk and Gallagher 1990).

The older school-age children were more likely to act out their problems rather than withdrawing from them. What kinds of acting out were common among older children? Drug use, sexual promiscuity, truancy, low self-esteem, self-criticism, preoccupation with themselves, displacing anger, and being "too old too fast" were characteristic (Terr 1991). Sometimes the homeless kids violated minor rules in the rural areas, but they were rules that would get the attention of adults who could help them. Seldom did they violate major rules or cause major disruptions. Most of the time, homeless teens were "pretty slick, pretty sophisticated" in their attention-getting, as in the case of Jonas, according to one assistant principal:

> I had this boy who had never been a problem in school, and then, all at once, he was constantly in trouble. He was smart-mouthing the teachers, not doing his homework, walking out of class without getting a pass—it was all so unlike him. It was almost as if he was thumbing his nose at us. We couldn't figure it out—and frankly, we didn't spend too much time trying to. Teacher after teacher would give this kid detention. He had so much detention that he had to come into school early to do it, or he would have to stay after school. But when he was on detention, he was as sweet a kid as before. One teacher wondered why this stark behavior shift. She began asking questions. Then we found out that he had no place to live. He was staying wherever he could—which meant a car, most nights. This kid was cold. If he could get into school early, it cut the night a little bit shorter. If he could stay after school a while, then it kept him safe and gave him something to do. He could not have said, "Help me, I don't have anyplace to live." He managed the only way he could and [retain] any dignity. He got into trouble. Not big trouble, just lots of little trouble. He could manage the trouble, and didn't care what others thought. He just didn't want others to know how awful his life had become.

Jonas went to great pains to preserve his dignity and tried to belong to the community he claimed as his.

Belongingness. Belonging is of utmost importance in the construction of healthy children. "To be rooted is perhaps the most important and least recognized need of the human soul. It is the one need that is the hardest to define" (Weil 1952, 41).

Children who move frequently do not have the opportunities to be rooted into a community the way stably housed kids are. After being uprooted from one community, just as they meet people and are start to build relationships, they have to move again. If this happens a number of times, the impact on the child is devastating for several reasons. First, children come to believe that there is no place where they belong. Second, they may lose their willingness to invest time or emotional energy in building new relationships, because their experience has shown them that nothing is stable. Third, even when they attempt to integrate, personal and structural barriers are constructed to assure that they cannot.

The comfort and security of a home is an essential foundation of childhood. It can be devastating for children when their family has nowhere to live—and they have lost their friends, school, neighborhood, and most of their possessions. Because poverty, family breakup, financial emergencies, and loss of a job often lead to homelessness, children lived in stressful conditions for some time before they found themselves without homes.

While one's informal network may be very helpful in managing problems that lead to homelessness, one's problems can be too much for friends and family to address. I found that the informal network—people who often were barely hanging on themselves—was incapable of providing all the financial, social, personal, and survival support that the families in crisis needed. Leslie noted:

> My brother said he could help me and the kids until I got back on my feet. We felt bad about moving in on him and his family, but we had no choice. At first, it was awkward, but everyone was good about it. Then, his wife started resenting us living there. I couldn't get work quick and had no money, so they paid for our food and stuff. They had no privacy anymore, and they made it real clear that we were a burden. They kept leaving out job ads and were snottier until we knew we couldn't stand it anymore. If you don't belong with your own family, then where can you go for help?

When one is homeless, one has a marginal position in the extended family, friendship network, community, and nation. When people lose their homes, they are frequently thrown into housing situations with people with whom they have absolutely nothing in common—except momentary poverty. "They threw us in with drug dealers, violent people, troublemakers, and people who are unstable—I guess they figure we must be just like them," said fourteen-year-old Adrianna.

Homelessness occurs as a process of disaffiliation—a process of increasing detachment from intimate support networks, traditional institutions, and social roles (Bahr 1970). In this context, homeless people ultimately do not belong anywhere. Disaffiliation has physical as well as psychosocial determinants. By shrinking the size of social networks, disaffiliation reduces the array and magnitude of material assistance, advice, and information that the individual can call on to meet basic needs. With no home and weakened ties to the community, the homeless people may feel less obliged to behave in conventional ways (Duncan 1978). This path of continuing loss of support leads to social isola-tion and entrenchment in homelessness.

The situations that predispose people to become homeless are often those that also increase disaffiliation by dislodging individuals from both housing and their sense of belonging. Normal social ties and affiliations become weakened and disrupted. Eviction from a house separates the individuals from neighbors. Loss of a job severs normal relations with coworkers. Divorce strains relationships with one's family. The intensity of these kinds of disaffiliation is exacerbated if the homeless person moves to a new community in an attempt to regain self-sufficiency.

Affiliation and social bonds have long been considered essential to psychological well-being. Social isolation is, conversely, associated with stress-related illness, alcoholism, and psychopathology (Cohen 1984). The need for affiliation prompts people to make friends, join groups, and develop a sense of community. Without it, both mental and social health suffers.

Children who do not have a sense of belonging to a family, neigh-borhood, or community likely feel no attachment to it. If a symbiotic relationship with the community is not created, the child grows to feel he or she is getting nothing from it and has no reason to give anything back in return.

Increase of crime, substance abuse, violence, suicide, vandalism, and alienation surely are related to this lack of belonging. Work by Edwin Sutherland and Harvey Locke (1936) indicates that when people become involved in any sort of deviant behavior, they do so because they are marginal to the mainstream society and have come to belong to more fringe groups. If the dominant social order has no place for them, children will fulfill the basic human need of belonging by finding some-body, some group, to which they can affiliate. These are consequences of the failure to belong, which one could see as an extension of the cul-ture of homelessness.

Homeless people, because they don't "belong" to a community (or at least they are not claimed by them), even lose the "right" to vote (National Coalition for the Homeless 1992). Homeless people have diffi-culty belonging—and the fact is, many of us don't want "those people" to belong to the same social circles as the rest of "us." For this simple—and embarrassing—reason, inaccurate stereotypes of the homeless abound.

Denial. Those who experience housing distress in small towns know all too well the urban stereotypes of homeless people, and they deny that the stereotypes fit. The reasons for this seem to be twofold.

First, the stereotypes really don't fit! Second, the only way to preserve any self-dignity is to deny the label of homelessness, and all that label signifies. Allie made it clear that she was not like "those homeless people you find in New York City, who are crazy, dirty, and scary people. Those people, well, maybe they were partially responsible for their problems. But us, we were just living our lives like people are supposed to, and then somebody changed the rules while we weren't looking and we found ourselves out of our home, out of money, and out of luck."

Time after time, young and old alike in small towns made it clear that they did not fit the stereotypes of homeless people. Some, in fact, denied that they were homeless, despite the fact that they were living in a homeless shelter. "We are just having a hard time right now. After we get things together, we will be fine," said Louis.

The negative stereotypes are wrong as they pertain to homeless families in small towns, according to every person surveyed. As one mother mused:

> I thought I knew what it was to be homeless, but actually, I never really knew. To me, it was those people with the shopping carts, maybe an old man with a bottle. Homelessness was nothing that could ever happen to me. I had too much going. I was too popular, too well off, too many people would help me . . . there was no way I could possibly lose everything. But I did. Now when people hear that I am homeless, they don't see who I am. First, they see in their heads that old bag lady, then they think of me, and somehow try to figure out how we are alike. Damn them!

If there is any possibility of them maintaining social dignity, it is by keeping the homelessness a secret. Rural people will seek help from others who they identify to be supportive before they will ask for help from strangers. "They are homeless but they will do every thing they can to keep you from finding that out," according to former New Hampshire Coalition for the Homeless Director Henrietta Charest. "They try to manage on their own."

Most of the rural children had learned the rural ethic of taking care of themselves and keeping their problems private. It was unclear whether or not the children denied the problems to themselves, but it was clear that they downplayed their problems to others. As one young man who had no place to live beyond next week reported, "I live independently. I take care of myself. Sure, I have problems that other kids don't have, but I don't go around talking about them all the time." While he may not have talked about his problems, he certainly was not a happy, carefree person. He carried the weight of the world upon his shoulders and seemed unhappy about not being carefree like his peers.

Depression. Depression was common among homeless children, especially among homeless teenagers. Almost every person I interviewed in the course of my research admitted to being depressed. I did not conduct psychological tests to determine to what degree they were "clinically" depressed. Rather, I took their word for their own interpretation of the situation. Besides, it seemed logical that depression would be a normal and appropriate response to the catastrophe of not having a home. Additionally, previous studies of homeless children and parents have found that even among young children, depression related to homelessness is typical (Bassuk 1990; Bassuk and Rubin 1987; Parker et al. 1991).

Homeless rural children and parents did, on occasion, experience serious cases of depression, chronic fear of abandonment, and an inability to form relationships because they lacked basic security, orderliness, and belonging (Parker et al. 1991). Depression in homeless families in small towns is associated with the general economic decline found in rural areas (Fitchen 1991). Patton (1987) has suggested that the continued economic stress on families in rural areas is responsible for tearing the community fabric. Friends and families are less able and willing to assist those in need. When people have less money, they are under more stress.

Depression was characterized as more than just sadness. Those I interviewed transformed their depression into other reactions, such as losing hope.

Loss of faith, hope, and trust. Homelessness can destroy children's self-esteem. It is difficult for children to watch their parents go out day after day to find work, only to come back empty-handed. Seeing optimistic, competent role models suddenly turned into beggars as parents go to agency after agency pleading for jobs, food, clothes, and housing causes children to devalue their parents—and themselves. Ultimately, questions about social justice enter the minds of the children. "How can things be better for me when my parents can't make it?" asked Roberta. "Why doesn't anyone in those agencies or in the government care about people like me? All they say they do they don't do, and they set people up. The places that are supposed to help you only rip you off," said Fred.

Children are taught to go to adults for help. When they do, and the adults can't do anything for them, "that's real sad. It violates everything they have been taught," said one social worker. "After the child is denied services, or falls between the cracks of different delivery systems, they learn that no one *really* cares about them."

All homeless children, regardless of age, have been found to see life as beyond their control (Coles 1967; Gewirtzman and Fodor 1987). Mary Connley, a visiting nurse in Manchester, New Hampshire, pointed out that children who do not see their parents able to manage their world and secure the needed services will lose hope, not just for today, but for the rest of their lives. These children have no role models who can teach them how to use the system effectively, so they are unable to learn empowerment. Helpless, hopeless children can grow into adults who are unable to grapple with the future demands. This may be the greatest of all the negative impacts of homelessness on small town children.

Loss of people, places, and things. Homeless children move so frequently that they lose contact with people who are near and dear to them. They lose familiarity of a house, neighborhood, or community. And they also lose material objects that mean a great deal to them.

We know that when people become transient, they lose important people in their lives. It is difficult for them to build, and rebuild, attachments with friends and acquaintances. Even relationships with relatives dissipate because of homelessness. If our relationships are the looking glass of who we are (Cooley 1932), how many times can children reconstruct their entire social networks and still maintain healthy, consistent pictures of who they are?

The conditions that precede homelessness are naturally isolating. People can sympathize with you, but they cannot share your problems. Your problems are your own. This is the lesson learned by the homeless families in New Hampshire.

As the not-yet-homeless person's life starts to unravel, and as problems increase and resources decrease, the homeless families in New Hampshire all called upon family and friends to help them when they could no longer manage alone. For a while, they did receive help. But, as Jennifer stated, "They said if I ran into trouble they would help me. Maybe I expected too much. Maybe I needed too much. Whatever, the longer I stayed, the worse it got. Finally, they told me to leave. I felt betrayed and abandoned. Once your family lets you down, where else can you go?"

Over time, the marginal and homeless rural people become increasingly isolated from their support network (Bassuk 1990). Even having family members in the area does not mean that one can count on them for assistance. Sometimes the hardest ones to ask for help are one's family. And sometimes family members just aren't there emotionally for one another, as a newly single mother pointed out: "I was left pregnant with three children after he up and left. Although I am from the area, half my family don't know where we are. Guess you could say that we're not close-knit. When I called my mother and told her we were at the shelter, all Mom could say was 'sorry.' None of my family never even came to see the new baby, or offered to help at all."

Homes embody the history, memories, and experiences that shape who we are. Battling back tears unsuccessfully, a homeless boy grieved, "I miss my house and yard. There we had a dog, but we had to get rid of him when we moved. I had this special tree I played under. I had my own room, and a window that overlooked the street. I miss my neighbors and friends too. I want to go home."

When people move frequently they may experience what Durkheim (1897) called anomie, feeling they don't fit in anywhere. "I can't live with my mother, I can't live with my dad, I can't stay too long at any of my friends', I've got no where I belong," reported one teenage girl.

Moving from place to place across town can be problem enough for a child, who must adjust to new surroundings. But moving to different communities, states, or countries can be increasingly problematic. "The rules for everything change when you move, especially if you are receiving assistance," said one mother. Another single mother pointed out the difficulties of moving to a different culture: "I am from Puerto Rico. I fell in love with this American who was visiting the island, and I ran off to marry him. I did not know him well, and soon I realized that I had made a mistake. He drank alcohol all the time, and then he would beat me bad. I was afraid all the time. I had a baby and decided this was no way to live. I left the man, and had no money and nowhere to go. So I went back and asked my family if I could live with them. And they said no, that my place was with my husband. This was true no matter what, and they would not let me stay."

When one is homeless, it is impossible to move or protect valued objects. Material objects provide emotional security, and link one with the past's memories and dreams. For young children, loss of toys can be upsetting: "I had a Barbie doll and lots of clothes. But when the fire came, they all got burned up. Mama says we can get new ones, but they just won't be the same as my dolly," said five-year-old Amanda.

For older children, clothes, books, pictures, and music were the major keepsakes. These items were linked directly with their sense of identity. When Jan's father kicked her out of the house, she had only the clothes of her back. He would not let her back into the house to claim any of her possessions. While losing keepsakes was difficult for her, her immediate problem was that she now had nothing to wear. "I don't have hardly any clothes and stuff, so I don't feel I look good like the other girls at school. If some of my friends hadn't given me clothes, I wouldn't have anything."

But for other teenagers, losing things is better than losing personal integrity: "I gave up my room with the lace curtains. I gave up my pink satin comforter. I gave up my wardrobe and my stuffed animals and my records and books. I gave it all up, because I couldn't stand my old man coming in, locking the door, and wanting me to have sex with him. Whenever I refused, he'd hurt me. So I gave it all up because it was safer on the street than living at home."

Parents too suffered from the loss of things. While clothes, kitchen supplies, and knickknacks were missed, the thing most longed for was the nice home they once had. Parents mourned the loss of "my flower garden and my kitchen sink with the window that overlooked the meadow. We had worked so hard on that house, and now we have nothing."

Mental illness. One of the most commonly held stereotypes about homeless people in general is that they are mentally ill (Lamb 1984; Roth, Bean, and Hyde 1986; Stimpson 1984; Wright 1988). But this stereotype is generally inaccurate, and it does not reflect those I met in rural areas.

Some argue (DiIulio 1991) that mental illness's role in the creation of homelessness has been greatly exaggerated. Two-thirds of homeless people nationally do not suffer from mental illness, according to the National Coalition of the Homeless (1989). The Institute of Medicine (1988) found that most homeless parents and children do not suffer from major mental illnesses. Reliance on the mental illness explanation for homelessness—especially for child and family homelessness in rural areas—is simplistic and misleading (Shinn and Weitzman 1990).

Rural homeless families are not afflicted with the same intensity of mental disorder as single or urban homeless adults (Toomey 1992). Children prove to be a stabilizing influence for parents, giving them someone to care for and live for. In a study examining the psychosocial difficulties facing homeless mothers with small children, Dail (1990) expected to find that homeless mothers were not in good psychosocial health, yet she found differently. Despite the difficulties of being homeless and having children, the mothers appeared to be coping relatively well. She attributes this, in large part, to the presence of the children.

Homelessness does increase the presence of psychiatric problems over the effects of poverty alone. Bassuk (1986) found that a larger number of homeless mothers, compared with welfare mothers who were not homeless, had minor psychiatric problems. While mental illness hospitalization rates for adults range from 10 to 35 percent in the homeless population, the rates are 4 to 9 percent for nonhomeless adults. But I only found two homeless individuals in rural areas who had been hospitalized for mental disorders, leading me to wonder if mental illness is a greater problem for the single, urban homeless person.

Mental illness and emotional problems experienced by the children and parents in rural areas appeared to be more a reaction to the homelessness than the cause of it. Few of the people I interviewed sought professional intervention for emotional problems—partly because they couldn't afford it and mostly because they regarded their problems as situational, external—not caused by psychological pathology. In fact, while many of them had social workers to help them locate jobs, food stamps, and housing, the professionals were more likely to report that "they have a good grip on reality, and they are managing the multitude of problems as well as could be expected." *If* the families had jobs, adequate housing, and some stability, the majority of their emotional problems would likely go away on their own.

Overcompensation. It was not uncommon to find homeless rural children nurturing others whom they perceived as being at risk. When parents were emotionally distraught or busy taking care of survival arrangements, younger children found ways to help and gain positive attention by taking on adult responsibilities. This is seen best in their care of younger children. Take, for example, this story:

> Gina at age six was the woman of the household. Her mother had abandoned her and her two younger brothers. Gina's father was forced to quit his job to take care of them, which resulted in their becoming homeless. The little girl decided to help her father as much as she could. She fed and diapered the baby, scolded her other brother, and entertained them while her father was busy. She prepared simple meals for her father and siblings and would clean the kitchen and encourage others to be "neat." Proud of her little mother status, she had no playtime or childhood of her own and was, for all functional purposes, the mother.

Older children took on this nurturing role by "helping other kids at school who are having a hard time. I know what it is like, and I have been able to make it, so I enjoy taking others under my wing and showing them the ropes," said Robin. Boys and girls alike were found to feel competent and wise when they were able to help distraught peers. While it gave them momentary credibility, it also aligned them with peers who were even worse off then they were—giving them little support for upward mobility.

Even parents overcompensated in order to deal with feelings of their own inadequacy. Madeline, mother of an adolescent boy, wanted to open a home for abused children because "I know what it is like to be abused, and I won't stand for anyone to hurt kids. I would kill anyone who tried to hurt kids. They need a safe place to go, and I would take good care of them."

Rage. Instead of fleeing, some of the homeless children interviewed kept their feelings pent up inside. They could not talk freely about their feelings, and they were not empowered enough to take action. Instead, they walked around with subdued anger that would eventually blow up in a rage. These children wore anger across their faces. While smiles might creep across from time to time, the frustration and rage were undaunted:

> Steve had been through so much, trusted so few people, and was so upset that he walked around angry all the time. At school he kept to himself and would only get caught once in a while pushing other kids in line. Generally he would function fine—until those moments when he pounded in the face of another boy on the playground. He would do okay at home 90 percent of the time—until something hit him wrong and he would kick his foot through the wall. His social worker was helping him to get control of his anger, fearing that if he did not, he could become an explosive and dangerous adult.

Kids like Steve don't want to be angry. They want the same things in life that everyone else seems to have. Too many burdens for people too small have toughened these kids so that they can survive. As one social worker put it, "You can take care of these kids now, or pay the price later. Now he is little and can be managed. But when he is big, when he is on is own, his empty holes will get bigger and one day his anger will flood out. He will spill his problems out onto the rest of us, even those who are innocent and unsuspecting. We will wonder 'why?' and blame him."

Some children were more overt than Steve with their anger. They used their aggression as a means of coping with their homelessness. These kids were angry at their homelessness, at their parents, at their brothers and sisters, at their friends, at their teachers, at other adults, at strangers—and at themselves. Being young, they did not know how to direct their anger. Breaking toys, running away, yelling, scowling, and being a general problem were ways that rage seeped out.

Self-esteem and reference groups. As one father asked me, "How would you feel if you had worked hard all your life and suddenly found yourself homeless?" He felt angry, cheated, frustrated, and blamed for a condition that was out of his control: "We had always worked hard and had a good home and life for our kids. Now we are homeless. We know it is the economy's fault, but when we can't buy our kids birthday presents, when we can't get a job, when we exist on handouts from others—how do you think we feel? We feel really awful about ourselves, and everything."

Again and again, the issue of self-esteem, stigma, and the invisibility of rural homelessness became apparent: "I tried to keep the fact we had no place to live a secret. As long as no one knew, I figured no one would treat my kids differently," said one mother. When people knew her child was homeless, sometimes they did treat her differently. The child felt that peers would make fun of her if they knew she was homeless: "The popular kids won't have anything to do with us because we are poor and homeless. We are left to associate with the losers, or we have nobody at all to talk with at school."

In small towns, people can maintain integrity by taking care of themselves and not burdening others with personal troubles. One boy hid his living at the shelter from his classmates: "When I visit friends and they drove me 'home,' I will ask his mom to let me off two blocks from the shelter. I act like I am going into this fancy house, and wave them on. As soon as they are out of sight, then I will run on back to the shelter."

While virtually all of the families in the small towns tried to manage their situations without the help of shelters, schools, social services, or mental health agencies, sometimes there was no other choice. As one mother pointed out, "My kids needed help. I needed help. The only place I knew to go for help was the school. So I swallowed my pride and marched in one day and told their teachers and principals. To my amazement, they have become our best friends. They do special things to help my kids and have gotten them into special programs. The counselor has brought us clothes. The nurse helped us get some medical care we had been needing. I now have people I can talk to and someplace I can go for help."

Younger children seem to care less where children live and more about how well they play, as Danny reported: "Nobody at my school cares that I live at the shelter. I am just another kid to them." The way children felt about their homelessness—and themselves—was dependent upon the way they are treated by others. Children look to primary group members to help them understand who they are and to provide meaning to the world. A person's notion of self grows out of interaction with others and is thus a reflection of the ways others view the self

(Cooley 1932). Opinions of others are indeed an important influence on the self-concept. People judge us by our behavior, and, in turn, we tend to see ourselves in terms of other's judgments. This process explains in part how relationships with others are stored and how they affect later behavior, even when these others are absent (Manis 1955; Sherif 1936; Kohlberg and Kramer 1969).

Reiss (1981) asserts that children experience a constant bombardment of stimuli that they must organize in some way to know who they are and how they are to function in society. Parents, teachers, and peers, as major socialization units, play the central role in this process, providing the child with a knowable, structural coherence that underlies who they come to believe they are and that explains the experienced world (Reiss 1981; Boyce 1985; Kobosa 1982).

Reference groups provide the context within which the normative patterns and techniques for behavior and personality are acquired (Parsons and Bales 1955; Parsons 1964, Brim 1958; Longfellow 1979). If a parent, teacher, or friend, for instance, responds to the child in a particular way, the child will come to view himself or herself in a similar manner (Rosenthal and Jacobson, 1968; Lightfoot 1978; Rist 1973).

Stress and anxiety. Stress levels were high in all of the displaced rural children and their parents. Regardless of age, homeless people were concerned about where they were going to stay and what they were going to eat. They were worried about not having the same material objects as others and were afraid of being ridiculed. Four general types of stress were experienced by the rural homeless: financial, physical, psychological, and social. The impact of stress and the coping mechanisms used were partially determined by the age of the child.

The younger children interviewed exhibited a wide range of stress-related behaviors. These included regressive behavior, as with Sally, who was once potty-trained but had so many accidents that her parents resorted to diapering her again. Feeling insecure, little children wanted to climb up in laps and be held as if they were infants. They resorted to the speech and behavior of much younger children, and they demonstrated increased tantrums and crying.

Homeless children generally dealt with anxiety in one of two ways. They would either become angry, boisterous, and overtly problematic or become withdrawn, calling no attention to themselves at all. The former children were more visible, hence their homelessness was identified more quickly than those children who were quiet. "The squeaky wheel gets the oil, so we give kids that cry out for help attention. Unfortunately, we forget to look at the children who don't call out, to those who ask for nothing but need so much," said one social worker.

It was unclear why one child would become withdrawn while another child would become aggressive. But it was clear that even siblings who experienced the same events were likely to deal with their problems differently. For instance, in one family, each of the children exhibited dramatically different ways of dealing with the stress of homelessness. The youngest withdrew and hid in a world in which only he could go. The middle boy was angry, burning inside with rage. He would yell, hit, bite, and regularly call attention to himself when he was upset. Their sister dealt with the situation by being busy all the time, doing for others.

Older homeless children were too busy surviving to engage in normative childhood behaviors. Many became old beyond their years, and they learned how to get food, housing, clothes, and assistance without calling attention to themselves. The chances were good that they would take part-time jobs. While working was one way to obtain money and reduce financial stress, it added another stressful dimension to their lives. Monica's caseworker described the stressful life that many homeless teenagers in small towns experienced: "Monica's stress levels are very high. She attends school all day and works until midnight most nights at a fast-food restaurant. She doesn't have a lot of time to do her homework and feels frustrated because she does not do well in school. She reports always being tired and hungry. She depends heavily upon her boyfriend, even though they fight a lot. She has no one else she can turn to and is upset that 'nobody at school understands what life is like for me, and nobody really wants anything to do with me.'"

There were some factors that produced stress for virtually every small town teen surveyed: lack of money, not knowing where they were going to be living, lack of transportation, tension with people they were staying with, time pressures, and feelings of inferiority.

Children who attend public schools need money in order to fulfill many of their assignments—especially in rural areas where the state expenditures are low. It may be difficult for homeless children to find money to make class projects. For instance, in a biology class, a student had to buy special bug mounting pins in order to fulfill an assignment. Although the pins only cost three dollars, that is a lot of money if a child has none. There are also monies needed for class trips, yearbooks, school dances, and the like. While these costs may be regarded as incidental by most people, they pose real dilemmas for impoverished children. It is embarrassing for a child to ask for financial assistance every time the school creates situations that demand the use of money. As Lucy complained, "I would have to be begging every day for something, if I decided to do that. It is easier to scrape up the money somehow and keep my personal business to myself."

A single father told a story about not being able to afford to provide his son with the same opportunity as his classmates:

> All the fifth graders go off to environmental camp for a week. While the school pays part of it, you still have to come up with forty-five dollars. This is hard enough, but then you gotta buy a sleeping bag, canteen, spending money, and this and that . . . We just couldn't afford it. So my boy sat in study hall all week with one other boy while the rest of the kids went off for the adventure of the year. Then, the next week, he got to hear from the other kids about how camp week was "the best week of my life." On top of it, all the teachers' class examples related to the camp experiences. I guess that would be okay—but not if you can't go. It just keeps rubbing salt in the wound.

Substance abuse. One of the most commonly associated stereotypes of homeless people is that they are alcoholics or drug abusers. Substance abuse has been found to contribute to the development of homelessness, as well as being an outcome of it (Parker et al. 1991; Institute of Medicine 1988; Cooper 1991). But in the Ohio study of rural families, only 13 percent were high consumers of alcohol, and 54 percent reported not using alcohol at all! Systematic epidemiologic research has not determined the prevalence of addictions among homeless families, and estimates of the rates of drinking problems in the homeless population range wildly from 2 to 86 percent (Struening and Padgett 1991; Fisher 1991; Bassuk 1990; Toomey 1992).

Substance abuse was not found to be a major cause for homelessness among the New Hampshire families. While some people did use—and abuse—substances, the majority of displaced rural parents and teens did not. Why? One mother summed it up: "If I get blitzed, I cannot take care of my kids or manage all the things I have to deal with. We have to survive, and we won't if I don't keep it together."

Homeless people who used substances consistently said their use was the result of the housing displacement—not the cause of it. As one mother reported: "I never abused alcohol before all the trouble started. I would drink now and then, but I never had a problem with it. As things got worse and worse, I couldn't see any way out. The drinking stopped the pain for just a little while."

Time after time, the rural ethic of hard work and sobriety appeared to keep in check the use of substances, so that, as in the rural Ohio study, catastrophic substance abuse was not great among those I interviewed.

While alcohol is still the drug of preference in rural areas, homeless children, like urban children, get exposed to a variety of drugs. Substance abuse not only brings psychic relief and momentary escape from problems, it also brings with it opportunities for economic gain: "I'll be honest with you. One of the only ways I could find to make money for my family was to sell drugs. A couple of times I really thought about it. That's a hell of an alternative if you've got children. But what is a man supposed to do if he can't get a job?"

Drug dealing may provide income for a while—if one doesn't get caught or hooked on that which is sold. A former model twisted the end of her hair as she recalled: "For years I had been managing. I was making it financially. When I was working and dealing drugs, sometimes I would make $500 or even $2,000. I had gotten involved with cocaine and other drugs, had become addicted to alcohol, started dealing, and things just kept going downhill."

When parents get hooked, they have trouble working and taking care of their children. A nurse discussed one girl's situation: "her mother and mom's boyfriend were misusing a lot of drugs. There was never enough money to pay the rent, so they got evicted. They were both working, but they were using their money for drugs, not rent."

Clearly, children live what they observe. As one mother reported, "I was drinking everyday, and my kids would see me. A couple weeks ago my son ran up, and he wanted to take a drink. I said, 'Little boy, you are nine years old; you're not drinking.' But he sees me drinking, he sees his father drinking, he sees our friends drinking, so he thinks its all right to drink too."

But most rural homeless people did not abuse drugs. A single mother put her experience into perspective: "I don't use drugs or alcohol. I don't enjoy them, and they do not help me cope with all I have to handle. But given everything you have to manage when you are homeless, well, I don't believe anyone should pass any judgment on people who try to get a little relief for a while, or on those who make a little money when there is no legitimate way for them to earn a living. If they—we—had better options, don't you think everybody would take them?"

Suicide. Rural children and parents felt they were at fault for their housing distress. While adults often became angry and blamed the system, children were more helpless and hopeless. Depression, behavior problems, and suicidal tendencies are not uncommon among homeless children (Shaffer and Caton 1984). Homelessness is isolating, stigmatizing, and frustrating, as fourteen-year-old Rolanda pointed out: "I couldn't stand it anymore. One night I took a kitchen knife and I carved up my wrists. My family found me bleeding. That hurt too much, so the next time I took pills and tried to overdose. But when they pumped my stomach, I guess I didn't take the right kind of pills that could really kill me. So they put me away for a while to get 'help' . . . I don't really want to die—but I sure don't want to live like this."

Suicide attempts, for the rural teens, were typically cries for help. When distressed teens felt there was no one to share their burden, they felt there was no way out except death. Sam had tried to manage on his own, but:

> This one night, I hit bottom. It was the fourth night in a row that I had no place to stay, after several months of staying here and there. It was snowing out and there I was sitting on a bench downtown trying to do my homework. Life didn't seem worth living. I had enough money for a cup of coffee, and went inside Dunkin Donuts to figure out how I could end it all. I stayed there as long as I could without getting hassled and was getting ready to go and do it when some guys I knew came in. Turns out I was able to say with one of them for awhile. Then things got better . . . and I'm still here.

But even having friends and family around doesn't always prevent suicide. Homelessness creates a sense of isolation and puts children yet again on the margin of their social world. Being without housing makes adolescents helpless and hopeless. One teen asked, "If my parents can't make it, how can I?" Another teen asked, "Is life like this really worth living?"

Withdrawal. The squeaky wheel gets the oil, so kids get more attention when they cry out for help. Unfortunately, many at-risk children bring no attention to themselves and ask for nothing. Some rural children adjusted to being homeless by trying to run away from it or hide from it. Sometimes the withdrawal was physical. Whenever two-year-old Daniel became afraid, he would run to the cupboard and shut himself inside where he felt safe. Because he had moved so many places in his short life, the only stable place he knew was this cupboard. He would pull out everything in the bottom and crawl into it, the only place where he felt comforted.

Most children would go away not physically but emotionally. Rather than dealing actively with the world in which they were forced to live, they created a fantasy world that was nicer. In Marsilla's dream world, she could be with princes, in castles, and wear exquisite clothes and dine on china plates. She could live in her "real world," but would regularly refer to other people, places, and things of her fantasy world that were more important to her.

These are attempts to gain some control of the external environment. The cupboard and the magic kingdom were escape valves, used whenever life became too grisly to endure. Unfortunately, for children like overweight Ben, fantasy and reality sometimes became indistinguishable: "The monster is right behind you, looking at me with his fangs, saliva dripping from them. He follows me wherever I go. Sometimes he peeks in the window or lays in wait behind the staircase. He goes to school where I do and he comes for me at night. For a while, I thought he was just pretend. But he is here so much anymore, that I really believe he is real now," the child reported.

The fight or flight impulse in children is strong. Since there is no one person to blame for the homelessness, it is more common for children to flee. But it is impossible for children to run away from homelessness. This could be why so many children escaped to other worlds. Homelessness's chaotic effect on the emotional state of children can be seen in the story by Yanali, a fifteen-year-old New Hampshire homeless girl:

A Short Horror Story

It was night time in the fairgrounds. Everyone had left hours ago. The fun and music was far and over. Now it was just another happy memory for the people who had been there. Now the place was dark and gloomy. The carnies were all in their campers and trailers sleeping off the hard night. The air was a chilling coldness. And the wind rushed through the trees every so often, as if whispering to the creatures of the night. The sky was pitch black. No stars to guide weary travelers, no moon to give light to the helpless. Not even a cloud in the sky, to reassure you that the dark sky isn't a massive hold ready to devour the earth. It was the sort of night that makes you feel like the sun was never going to rise again. And for some that was good. And for others that was bad, for they would eventually become the victims of the evil that goes on in the night.

Far off on the other side of the fairgrounds two teenage boys run through the main gate. One runs for his own life from the other. The one being chased finally stops in a dead end, cornered and no way to get out of it. He was going to have to face his enemy. The other boy slowly walks toward him. Now he was only a few feet away. The one who had been running gets ready to defend himself, but before he raises his hand, the other boy leaps at him like he was flying. They both end up on the ground. The other boy struggles and fights to get free. But it was a lost cause. The boy had tremendous strength. He reached for his victim's throat and began to strangle the life out of him. After a few minutes, silence fell over again. The boy looked up at the black sky with a twisted, evil look of satisfaction in his eyes. Then he got up from the ground, and grabbed the dead boy by the ankles. He drug him under one of the trailers nearby. There he bit open the skin of the dead boy's arm and feasted upon his blood.

Middle-class children usually write tales with happy endings. This child saw no happy ending. Her view of the world was a result of the chaotic life that she led. Surely her views are not unique among homeless children.

In summary, homelessness causes a variety of emotional and social problems for a child. The environmental chaos creates social chaos, which in turn creates internal, psychological chaos. A child may be able to survive the physical chaos, but the impact of the emotional chaos will not go away when one gets a roof over one's head. Homelessness alters the way children in small towns come to think about themselves and their communities.

five

Kids Can't Think When They've Got No Place to Sleep

It doesn't matter if you are a city kid or a country kid—when you are homeless, the cards are stacked against academic success. Schools are not designed to deal with transient kids who have no stable home base. Academic progress is built upon a pyramid, with certain concepts being learned before others are attempted. Every semester skills are acquired that enable the student to take more advanced courses. It is difficult to succeed in such a system if one frequently moves from school to school, or even state to state.

However, schools are still the backbone of the rural community. School is the one social institution that comes into contact with every child in the community. Teachers are in the unique position of being able to observe what goes on in the lives of their students. Teachers come to know multiple generations of families—where the parents work, how much they make, what the family does for recreation, what role they play in the community, and what kinds of problems they have. When students have academic problems, ideally the schools can call upon parents to help identify the sources and solutions for the problems. When children have problems at home, the problems cannot help but enter into the classroom. Therefore, rural schools have not just an academic relationship with the child but a partnership relationship with the entire family.

By viewing the strengths and weaknesses of all the children and families, educators can identify where the community is headed. It is not surprising, then, that my initial contract to study homeless children and families came from the state Department of Education. School personnel knew there was a homeless problem in their small towns. Educators also admitted that while the school was the major institution to identify and help children at risk, school structure and policies also contributed to the children's academic problems.

JENNIFER HERRON

If a child is tired, sick, and hungry, how can he do well in school? If a child has no place to do homework and no resources for class projects, how can she be competitive? More than any other group, homeless children count on education to transform their futures. Schools in rural areas have become havens for homeless children because they provide the only constant in these children's uncertain lives (Vissing 1991; Luloff, Zaso and Vissing 1992). They give children ongoing relationships with teachers and peers who can be role models for a better way of life. School is a warm place to stay during the day, a place where they can get a free meal at noon. Homeless and nonhomeless students alike told me that students are judged at school according to their academic and social performance—not on their housing status (Berger 1990).

But it is not always easy to get homeless children into school. And once they are enrolled, helping them to get there—and stay there—is difficult. The chaos that accompanies homelessness is directly transformed into assaults that children experience in school.

Homeless children must overcome a variety of barriers interfering with their educational process (Stronge 1992). A report of the National Association of State Coordinators for the Education of Homeless Children and Youth (1993) showed that almost 300,000 school-age children experienced homelessness; of those, 28 percent did not attend school. Sometimes homeless children are denied access to education outright (National Law Center on Homelessness and Poverty 1990a), but in most cases the children slip through the cracks of the educational system (Westchester Initiative for Homeless Children 1993).

Despite efforts of the McKinney Act, homeless children are not always allowed to enter the doors of schools across rural America. Residency requirements bar homeless children from school in more than 60 percent of the states—many of which are rural (National law Center on Homelessness and Poverty 1990a). Because of the difficulties homeless children have had getting admitted into school, in most states there is a special unit of the state department of education to "confront the inhumane suffering caused by the system that is theoretically supposed to help homeless children" (Kozol 1991; McKinney Act 1987). The assault on the mind experienced by children in rural Maine, New Hampshire, and Vermont is not much different from that experienced by urban children studied by Kozol.

Obstacles that prevent homeless children in rural areas from being admitted to school include the lack of residency status and the inability of homeless students to provide proof of age, health, or education records (Eddowes and Hranitz 1989). Failure to provide appropriate guardianship requirements excluded homeless children from school in 40 percent of the states (National Law Center on Homelessness and Poverty 1990b). Before they can attend, children must provide documentation of health status and proof of immunizations to the school. This information may be difficult for the homeless family to obtain, since they may have lost the records or forgotten the dates and types of immunizations received. Records from previous schools are supposed to be sent promptly, but small town schools with small staffs may not send the information quickly.

In 70 percent of the states, homeless children have difficulty getting records transferred (National Law Center on Homelessness and Poverty 1990a). This record retrieval process is complicated when families fail to give accurate information for the tracking of needed documents. As one counselor explained: "These mothers come in—they're so frustrated and they've got enough on their minds. They don't know where the Social Security numbers are, and all of these silly things that the schools require. It is hard to have all the immunization records. We can bend the rules, but we can't break them."

While a child can typically enter school without having academic records in hand, most states require proof of immunization within thirty days. This means that if one cannot retrieve the documents, the child must get a new battery of shots.

All children are supposed to enter school with an address, phone number, and emergency contact, according to school personnel. But at the time of enrollment, many families in housing distress may not be able to give basic information such as a telephone number or address. If they are living with friends or family until they get on their feet, addresses may change many times during the course of the year. Often the parents falsify information in order to get the child enrolled in school. To have a telephone means that one has a place to live and income to support the phone bill. Therefore, sometimes phone numbers are fabricated as well. A school secretary told the following story:

> Because the mother was afraid we wouldn't let Eddie come to school if he was homeless, she make up information. We didn't even know they were homeless until the child was sick. We called the phone number that was on the admittance form, where they didn't live anymore. We were sent from person to person and got numbers that were no longer in service. Since we couldn't track down where the child lived, we asked the child where his mom was. The child didn't know where to even look for her, because she was out each day trying to find work and places to sleep. Typically she met him after school to take him where ever they were going for that night. So we had to keep him at school sick until we could find her at the end of school.

Homelessness seems to have one of two effects on students: the lifestyle causes some to be late to school or miss it regularly; others seldom miss because they view the school as their one lifeline.

National studies have indicated that anywhere between 220,000 and 750,000 homeless school-aged children exist in this nation (U.S. Department of Education 1988; National Coalition for the Homeless 1987a), although it is possible that these figures are way too low if the Columbia Study (Link 1993) is correct. Estimates of their school attendance rates range from as low as 43 percent (National Coalition for the Homeless 1987a) and 57 percent (Maza and Hall 1990) to as high as 70 percent (U.S. Department of Education 1989). Attendance rates decline for all students as grade levels increase (Rafferty and Rollins 1989). The older students get, the more likely it is that they are trying to work while they go to school.

One single mother who was relying on the benevolence of friends to help her out, reported, "We stayed with people who were so noisy that they were up to the wee hours, so we couldn't sleep. They said they would bring us into town early, but they were asleep and wouldn't get up, so we had no way to get the kids to school."

Older students were subject to the same kinds of problems when they stayed with others. "There is simply no control over what will happen during the night. Schools think everyone has it easy, going to bed early for a good night's sleep and then getting up for breakfast. Life is just not like that for us," a young man reported. Other students worked at fast-food restaurants or as janitors, often at late hours. Even those students who worked earlier shifts found it difficult to do the homework and get to school on time. "Sometimes it is easier not to go to school if you can't get your homework done than it is to show up and not have it," said Tina.

School administrators reported that the reasons that homeless students miss school were more acceptable than reasons that non-homeless kids skip school. "Homeless kids by and large want to go to school, but they have lots of survival issues to deal with. This is unlike the kid who has everything, and who just decides to blow off school. I have much more sympathy with the homeless kid," said a principal.

There are other reasons that homeless students in rural areas may not make it to school. Transportation to school can be a problem in rural areas, especially if buses don't run nearby. Stephanie reported, "If I miss the bus by even a minute, I am out for the day because it would take me hours to walk into town to school. It's not like we have taxi cabs out here—and even if we did, who could pay for one?"

Since public transportation is virtually nonexistent in rural areas, private transportation is the most used way to get kids to school. However, homeless people may not be able to afford a car—or insurance and gas. Once a car breaks, there may not be any money to fix it. And whoever owns the car wields great power over the lives of those who do not, as one teenage girl pointed out: "I didn't have anywhere to live, so I moved in with Bobby. He lives outside of town, and I depend on him to take me places. If he decides not to go to school one day, then I can't go either. If he doesn't want to take me in to work at [a fast-food restaurant], then I don't get to work that day. I worry a lot because I am afraid that I will get bad grades or get fired because of my transportation problems. I can't really complain to Bobby, because if he gets mad and kicks me out, then I have no place to go."

Sometimes communities refuse to send school buses to areas where there are known homeless, in hopes of forcing the homeless to move elsewhere. For instance, in one New Hampshire town the homeless lived in the campground because there they could find the most affordable housing around. But if people lived in the park year-round, the park owner would be forced to pay higher property taxes—and school fees that would enable school buses to be sent for the students. So he would close the park at strategic times during the warmer months, such as September and May, in order to force the homeless out and avoid the campground's being classified as a residential area (Schroepfer 1993).

In many communities, if a student moves to more affordable housing right over the district line, the student is legally supposed to attend the school in that new community. But as counselors pointed out, "It makes no sense for kids who have been attending one school to quit and begin attending the school in the next county merely because they decided to live across the border. Most of these kids float here, there, and everywhere—so the school is their only constant. If they want to make arrangements to get to our school, why should we force them out?"

This pattern is not unique to rural areas. Rafferty and Rollins (1989) found that urban homeless students are absent from school more than nonhomeless students. She found that homeless parents and children confront a host of bureaucratic problems that undermine efforts to ensure school enrollment and regular attendance. She also noted how all schools fail to allow students to attend their "home" schools where they have been attending if they move outside the school boundaries.

If a student moves frequently, it is an indication of housing displacement that may be caused by financial distress and homelessness. In one small town, there was over 100 percent turnover within a single school year! Children flow in and out of school systems for a variety of reasons. But schools in rural areas do not keep records on why children leave schools. As one elementary school principal mused, "I have two hundred students in my school and have had sixty kids turn over from September to December." Given this high transiency rate, and knowing his student population, he can easily figure out why this occurs. "People here are getting by as best they can. They have cut everything they have to the bone. They don't buy clothes, they don't spend money on recreation, and their food stamps limit how much food they can buy. The only place for them to cut back is to find cheaper and cheaper housing." Therefore, people move to other areas in hopes of finding cheaper housing and in hopes that there will be better job opportunities.

A third of the homeless rural students had attended a different school in the past year. It appears that rural students attend somewhat fewer schools than do urban students: Rafferty's study indicates that three-fourths of the students transferred to a different school at least once since the onset of homelessness, and a third transferred to more than two schools. Younger students were found to be more transient than older students as their parents moved frequently in order to find work. Older students moved less frequently to different school districts because they were more willing and able to put together alternative living arrangements. Teenagers often preferred to float from friend's home to friend's home in order to attend their school rather than pick up and move elsewhere with their parents.

Homeless children want to come to school (Rafferty and Rollins 1989; Douglass 1995; Vissing, Schroepfer and Bloise 1994). Homeless students in New Hampshire sometimes missed school, but they more frequently arrived late. "They may come in late because they have work or transportation problems that interfere with their getting here at 8 A.M., but they usually show up," said one principal. Homeless students were reported to be regular attendees, according to most principals. "This is the one place where they belong. They have friends here. It is warm, and they are guaranteed a hot meal. School gives their otherwise chaotic day structure, and it gives them dreams to hold on to. So if you ask me if they have attendance problems because of their homelessness, I would say no. On the contrary, I would say that their homelessness keeps them attending regularly."

The students agreed with this view. "I love school. I don't want to graduate. I've got friends here and good things to do with my life. Why would I want to miss?" said Lindsy. Kim reported that her parents moved out of town, and she decided it was better to live with several different friends through the end of the year because "the most important thing in the world to me is graduating from this school."

Homeless kids could give up, they could drop out. Many students with fewer obstacles do just that. "The homeless kids who stay in school are real survivors," according to one school nurse. Instead of taking full-time, low-paying, unskilled labor jobs, or getting pregnant and quitting school, these teenagers have decided to stick with school at all costs.

> I think the homeless kid is a motivated kid. These kids are resilient; there is a stick-to-it-ivness to them. They are motivated for one reason or another. In spite of anything going on out there, they have decided that they are going to hold on and make the most of themselves. I would tell you this right now, these are nice kids. They're not wise guys, they're not bashing anyone down. They're not aggressive people. They're holding jobs, they are taking care of themselves. I would put my money on a homeless kid more so than lots of other kids who have more going for them that they don't use.

Time and time again, school personnel in rural schools across New Hampshire asked the same question—how do homeless kids cope with all their personal problems and manage to walk through the school doors every morning with their heads held high? One school nurse, a year away from retirement, observed: "I think that they are heroic. If you can survive the way that these kids are surviving, I mean, that has to have some kind of heroics back of it. It's got to have some kind of strength, something special. They don't give up."

I found that many children were not destroyed by their homelessness. While the lack of housing and its accompanying lifestyle was more than inconvenient, somehow the children were able to manage it. They had not fallen into chaos. They could have dropped out of school but didn't. They came to school regularly, although they were tardy or absent on occasion because of their unorthodox lifestyles.

Children who work to support themselves and their families, who often have no safe, warm, or consistent place to sleep, deserve credit for making it to school regularly. Their grades, though not the best, are as good as can be expected, considering that they are often hungry and cold and have to deal with problems that many adults have never experienced. As a school nurse mused: "If I had to manage all they do, I couldn't pull it together to do all they do. But day after day, they hold their heads up high as they walk through the front doors of school. They manage school, housing, food, jobs, friends, lovers, family—on adolescent shoulders, with adolescent skills. They deserve every bit of help we can give them—and in no way should be condemned."

Many heroic students were interviewed in the course of this research. Some of them have gone on to college or vocational school. Others have joined the military, and some have found jobs. Still others of them could not find work and did not have anyplace where they could go where they felt they belonged. This latter group of heroic students could easily be transformed into "lost souls" unless they receive help.

Homeless students are at a disadvantage when it comes to producing quality work. Older students may have outside jobs that interfere with doing homework. Younger students may be expected to watch younger siblings or to go with parents from place to place after school. These children do not have home libraries and may not be readily able to access the public library. Homework assignments may be geared for a more stable, middle-class student population. They may require either technical or conceptual resources that are unavailable to the rural homeless student.

If a child lives in a crowded living environment, either at a shelter or in an apartment with others, he or she may have a hard time finding a quiet place to think or a suitable surface on which to write. If a child is cold, hungry, or worried, he or she may find it impossible to give the necessary attention to school work. When the importance of academic success is compared with getting a place to sleep and food to eat, it is reasonable to expect that school work should take the back seat (Maslow 1970). "And it should!" said one principal. "If a kid has to decide on whether to spend time dealing with where they are going to stay, how they are going to get something to eat, how they are going to find money for this or that, family problems, problems with peer group and sweethearts, worrying about if they are sick or pregnant, or whether to do a paper on the fall of the Roman Empire— school will come in last. The school has got to face the realities of kids' lives."

Homeless students have a harder time getting good grades than students in stable homes. As a result of the structural and personal problems, almost half of the homeless students in most studies are at least one grade level behind (Bassuk and Rosenberg 1988; Shaffer and Caton 1984; Bassuk et al. 1984). Rafferty and Rollins (1989) found that of homeless students who took the math achievement test, only 28 percent scored at or above grade level, compared with 57 percent of nonhomeless students. These results are consistent with Shaffer and Canton's (1984) findings that over half of the sample of homeless 10- to 17-year-olds were more than one standard deviation behind on their reading achievement tests.

These figures were in line with what I observed among the New Hampshire students. Several high school students were nineteen and twenty years old and still had a year of high school to go. Many had fallen behind in school, especially if they had moved frequently. Educational standards vary from one district to another, and what is an acceptable standard in one place may not be in another. School work at one grade level may be entirely different between schools, making it difficult for the new student to compete. Academic expectations may vary dramatically when one moves across state lines.

The New Hampshire data indicated that falling behind was the norm; students had scored much better in the past when they were not homeless. "My kids are C students now, but they were always straight-A students before. Being homeless takes too much out of us, there's too much going on for them to concentrate right. We don't have the time or money to help them like we used to," said one mother. A cycle can develop in which students fall behind, feel uncomfortable about their failure, and soon don't want to go to school at all (Gewirtzman and Fodor 1987).

The structure of schools—with required classes at set hours— may be functional for schools, but it is dysfunctional for those who are homeless. High school students may have specific types and numbers of classes that they must take in order to graduate. Especially for transient students, courses may not be directly equivalent, which puts students behind in their graduation schedule. Schools are not designed with students who must also work full-time in mind. The inflexibility of course scheduling, where required courses are only offered at select times during certain terms, makes it difficult for homeless students who work to obtain the needed courses in the appropriate order. As Melinda noted: "It has been very hard to stay in school. I need money real bad, and I can't work enough hours and go to school. I have so many things to worry about that it is hard to concentrate in school. I am always wondering where I'll be staying tonight and how I can get enough money for food and everything I need. It is hard to think about eighteenth-century literature when you've got these kinds of worries."

It is important to note that Rescorla, Parker, and Stolley (1991) found that in a study comparing homeless 3- to 12-year-olds compared with nonhomeless children, the groups did not differ significantly from one another on most measures. The finding that the school-age homeless children's ability, achievement, and adjustment were essentially the same as domiciled poor children gives credence to the fact that all poor children need help, not just the homeless ones. They note that preschool homeless children exhibited slower development and more emotional behavioral problems than did their domiciled peers.

In a few cases in New Hampshire, homelessness actually gave a boost to educational attainment. Jamie stated, "I work two jobs and do my homework whenever I can. I am going to college. I am an honor roll student. But it takes everything I've got to keep my grades up. But maybe I wouldn't have worked so hard if I didn't realize what lay ahead of me if I didn't."

Bernie, age thirteen, showed me his Educational Achievement Certificate with pride. He was put in a class for slow kids and became the class's outstanding student. Next fall he will be in class with the regular kids. Pretending to be cool about his award, he told me that I should keep his certificate in order to remember him. "Aw, it don't mean that much," he said.

The accumulative effects of chronic health and developmental problems, exacerbated by stress and frequent moves, are almost certain to contribute to a higher rate of special education among homeless children. Most of the New Hampshire students had learning problems that required special educational services. However, few of them obtained the help they needed, reflecting a national trend. The National Law Center on Homelessness and Poverty (1990b) found that in 55 percent of the states, homeless children are denied comparable access to special education services.

In order to receive official special education services, a student must be "coded," or assessed to meet particular criteria. The school that codes the child will become fiscally responsible for the special education services of that child—even if the child moves out of the district! Therefore, there is a disincentive for a school to diagnose a child as in need of special education services. This is especially the case for homeless children who may not be living in the district long anyway. As one counselor noted, "Even though the kids may need services, we are subtly discouraged from coding them. Let someone else get stuck with the tab is the usual attitude for little schools with small budgets."

Unless students are officially coded, they cannot receive special education. There are many homeless students who need help but do not meet the official criteria. But as a teacher pointed out, many students who are not homeless also need ancillary services. "I see little difference between the needs of my homeless students and the needs of students whose families are poor, students who have family troubles, students who are living high-risk lifestyles. They *all* need help—not just the homeless kids. Sometimes I get so angry because everyone wants to help the homeless kids, and the other kids who need the help just as much get forgotten! What are they going to do—wait until they become homeless and *then* offer to help? That is ridiculous."

In rural schools where everyone knows everyone else, having ancillary services that do not negatively label students as "slow" would be helpful. Two teenage sisters complained bitterly about the "special" services that were available in their school: "If they put us into classes with the retards, then everyone thinks that we are retarded too. If they put us in class with the regular students, we have a hard time keeping up and then we feel dumb. No matter what, we end up feeling dumb."

Many times, children need just a little extra help and attention to make up for the deficits caused by homelessness. As the mother of an eight-year-old girl who had been in six schools over a ten-month period pointed out, "I think what she really needs is to stop going to a different school every month. She didn't have this learning disability before we lost our home. What she really needs is a permanent home and extra help with her reading and math" (Rafferty and Rollins 1989). This was clearly the sentiment of the majority of homeless students in New Hampshire. They were not stupid; they needed help.

In rural areas, even the children learn early not to be too pushy, and to do for themselves. When students were asked why they didn't get teachers to help them, their sentiments were well-expressed in the statement of one sophomore girl: "I know I need help with my school work, and I want help. But teachers don't want to stay around as long after school as I need them to. They have homes and families and work for tomorrow to prepare. I need so much time that they can't help me in class, so I just keep on as best I can."

Homelessness interferes with a child's ability to learn. Homeless children who are in school should be regarded as a workable, salvageable population. They have not dropped out, even though they could have done so. They survive overwhelming personal adversity. They experience things that many adults cannot fathom that assault their ability to learn and do well in school. While the rural schools have assumed leadership roles in their communities in advocating for homeless children, the schools cannot do it alone. The McKinney Act states that not only are homeless children to attend school, they must have an opportunity to succeed. Yet this act receives such low appropriation levels that most states only have token dollars to respond to the educational needs of these children (National Association of State Coordinators for the Education of Homeless Children and Youth 1993), and the Act fails to fully support substantial prevention programs, as well as other needed services (Alker and Derricoutte 1989). The problems that cause homelessness occur outside of the classroom, and the solutions for rural homelessness are beyond the scope of the school.

six

Reaping What You Sow: Economic Crises in Rural Areas

Homelessness in rural areas cannot be understood without looking at the rural economy—which cannot be understood without looking at the national economic picture. Rural homelessness is a microcosm of national economic and political developments.

American society is currently experiencing a lengthy economic recession—one of the most depressed times since World War II—and this transformation of the economy has directly resulted in both urban and rural homelessness (Blau 1992). There are allegedly many different causes for the current economic crisis on the national level.

Many experts agree that homelessness as we know it increased as a result of the federal spending programs developed by the Reagan administration, whose policies both caused and exacerbated homelessness (Hombs and Snyder 1982; Piven and Cloward 1982; Katz 1989; Block et al. 1987; Ehrenreich 1990; Newman 1988). Yet others do not hold the Reagan administration responsible for the creation of our national homelessness problem. Some authors (DiIulio 1991) question whether homelessness is an economic issue and report that homelessness was increasing in the late 1970s and early 1980s when poverty was supposedly shrinking. Approaching the problem of homelessness from a broad public policy perspective, Lang (1989) argues that the American political economy permits community development patterns based on racism and self-interest. He challenges the belief that homelessness is entirely owing to the Reagan administration's budget cutbacks. Instead, Lang suggests the need for reform in our housing and employment policies by reviewing how competing socioeconomic paradigms make it difficult to enact meaningful and effective social programs.

While homeless people of today are victims of a gutted labor force, the economic conditions are quite similar to those experienced by earlier generations. From fourteenth century troubadours to the trap-

YVONNE VISSING

pers, miners, and cowboys of early America; the hobos of the depression; migrant workers; skid-row denizens; free-spirited hippies; street people; and finally homeless children and families of today, Miller (1991) illustrates that homelessness occurs as a result of the social and economic events of the day. He argues that with a constricting economy, there is every reason to believe that homelessness will increase.

Blau (1992) alleges that homelessness is caused by heightened international competition; a buildup of the U.S. military-industrial complex; the decline of the capital-labor accord; a growing regulatory movement in the private sector; and pressure surrounding the declining rate of business profitability. As a result of these trends, the 1950s belief that the United States would be the world's great economic power has been shattered. Worldwide allegations that "Captain America, you're falling" (Kinks 1979) made even those less knowledgeable about the intricacies of the economic system realize that as a nation, we were in serious economic trouble—even in rural areas (Conger and Elder, 1994).

The corporate response to these troubles was to become "mean and lean" in all aspects of business life, whether that meant in production, product cost, or the treatment of personnel (Blau 1992). This attitude filtered into the public sector, which included government, health care, education, welfare, and all social services. "Human" service organizations became obsessed with cost-benefit analyses in order to survive. The raison d'etre shifted in this environment. Staying afloat during the economic storm became just as important as the public good served by various agencies.

Chief executive officers and chief business officers were brought into health, education, and human service organizations. All too often, they brought with them axes for cutting not just programs and services but also staff morale and the organization's sense of community. Staff members received minimal cost-of-living increases, if raises were provided at all. Workers were expected to do more and more with less and less. Higher client loads, larger classroom sizes, and increased production demands were met with decreased resources, fears of layoffs, internal competition, and decreased staff morale. The organizations became mean and lean not just to the clients but to the very people who worked within them.

Blau asserts that the conditions for the contemporary upsurge of homelessness were facilitated by deindustrialization and the growth of a service economy. While some groups of the population would obviously feel the "pain" of this transformation, "enough Americans were confident of their own impunity to believe that the victim of this pain could only be somebody else" (Blau 1992, 39). No one was protected from potential termination—not those who worked on the factory line, or service workers, or clerical and sales personnel, and not even the administrators themselves. Ultimately, large numbers of workers from all walks of life were at risk of losing their jobs—and homelessness became a short step away not just for the always-poor population but for the middle class as well. Communities, when faced with tightened budgets and the unlikelihood that the federal government would expand programs to soften recession impacts, cut basic safety net programs (Shapiro and Greenstein 1991a). This put not just the lower class but also the middle class at risk of homelessness.

The recent economic transformation resulted in income polarization. Numbers of the "truly needy" increased, while middle-class workers found themselves at risk. Income disparities between the wealthy and other American has widened significantly. Income inequality is greater today in the United States than in other Western industrial countries (Shapiro and Greenstein 1991b).

The Congressional Budget Office estimated that between 1980 and 1990, the income of the poorest tenth of U.S. households decreased by about 10 percent, to an average of $4,695. However, people at the very top of the economic pyramid benefited considerably from these economic shifts. The top 5 percent of the population increased its income by 45 percent (Shapiro and Greenstein 1991b; Greenstein and Barnick 1990). The 1990 capital gains income accounted for 32 percent of the income of the richest 1 percent of the households, but only 1 percent of the income of the bottom 90 percent of the population (Greenstein and Barnick 1990).

The richest 1 percent of the population had an income that increased by 75.3 percent, to an average of $548,969. As a result of this trend, the top 1 percent of the population of U.S. households—some 2.5 million people—have nearly as much after-tax income as the 100 million people combined who constitute the bottom 40 percent (Blau 1992). There has been a 126 percent increase in the number of millionaires in the last decade (Danziger 1986). Census Bureau figures understate the gains of the rich because Census data do not include capital gains income and because the Census Bureau does not record any salary as higher than $299,999 (Center on Budget and Policy Priorities 1990).

As a result of these economic trends, income in the United States is no longer bell-shaped, with a huge middle class and small upper and lower classes. Instead, our economy has become a two-bump curve, of educated haves and uneducated have-nots.

The United States Department of Labor estimated that in the 1990s the following economic trends would occur: Women will fill half the jobs, and the number of minorities in the workforce will rise to one-quarter. Education will increasingly be the factor that distinguishes the "haves" from the "have nots." The labor force will be 70 percent larger by the year 2000, but growth in business will decelerate. High-tech, retail, and service industries are projected to grow, while manufacturing and mining will decrease, as they have been for two decades. Growth will occur in areas involving computers, health, and management, all areas requiring higher education. Similarly, growth will occur in low-paying service and retail jobs, with pay at or near the minimum wage (Coates 1990).

This skewed income distribution drastically affects the middle-income groups. The proportion of middle-income people has fallen. Census data shows that in 1989, the middle 60 percent of U.S. families received only 50.8 percent of the national income, the lowest percentage recorded since the Census Bureau began collecting this kind of information in 1947. Since the poorest fifth of the population received just 4.6 percent of all U.S. income, these data meant that in the aggregate, the bottom four-fifths of all U.S. families were receiving less than ever before (Blau 1992).

Nearly one in every five Americans who worked full-time did not make enough money at the end of the 1980s to keep a family of four out of poverty, up sharply from the 1970s. These U.S. Census Bureau figures reflect the shift from a nation that improves the lives of almost all working people to a nation in which many people are left behind, even when they do work. People in rural areas are hit just as hard as people in urban areas, as Sheldon Danzinger, a University of Michigan economist who is an authority on poverty, notes: "It's not just in the inner cities where people are having trouble" (Gosselin 1992a).

Sixty percent of American families earn less than $42,040 a year, while 80 percent earn less than $61,490. The Joint Economic Committee of Congress revealed that in 1983 the top .5 percent of American households owned 35 percent of the wealth held by families, up 10 percent from twenty years previous. If personal residences are included in the accounting, the top .5 percent holds 45 percent of all private wealth in the United States. Increasing 38 percent in the preceding twenty years, this figure stood at the highest concentration ever recorded (Blau 1992).

When one compares the average income of wealthy and low-income families over the past forty years, the incomes of the wealthiest fifth of the population has more than doubled. However, in the poorest fifth of the population, families are doing worse than they were twenty years ago (when the War on Poverty was under way). The difference in children's lives—and subsequent differences in lifestyle and opportunity—between the poorest fifth of the population and the richest fifth cannot be overstated.

Minimum-wage incomes used to provide enough money for the bare essentials. Thirty years ago, one could work at minimum wage and still have enough money to rent or buy a house, put clothes on the backs of one's family, and set food on the table. However, since 1960, minimum-wage standards have been thoroughly inadequate in keeping people out of poverty. One could work more than full-time at minimum wage and still be far below the national poverty level.

Yet there is still the notion that if people work full-time—even at minimum wage—somehow they should be able to support their families. The minimum wage needs to provide a minimal standard of living (Shapiro and Greenstein 1993). Many homeless rural parents I met worked full-time at minimum-wage jobs and could not earn enough to pay for food and housing. As a college student reported: "I went to work at the ski resort over Christmas break to earn a couple extra dollars. I didn't expect to find middle-aged men working there for minimum wage. I have a Spartan lifestyle, but if I could barely support myself on it, I don't see how they could take care of a whole family on what they make working full-time."

What the student saw was a slice of reality. Though the poverty rate was $11,570, the 1992 annual salary of a full-time, minimum-wage worker before taxes was only $8,880! The minimum wage amount has gone down, after adjusting for inflation 22 percent since the 1970s. There are today more than 8.5 million households with incomes of less than $10,000 (National Coalition for the Homeless 1993). They are all at imminent risk of homelessness.

When considering the role of taxes in the economic equation, the National Priorities Project (1992) asserted that "the rich get richer, and everyone else gets poorer," thanks to the tax formulas used by the federal government. They allege that in the past eleven years, the richest 2 percent got tax breaks totaling a $1.1 trillion loss to the federal treasury—which is an amount equal to the federal deficit accrued during that time. One can thereby argue convincingly that the $1.1 trillion that has not come into the treasury because of tax breaks for the wealthy is equal to the entire increase of the federal deficit in the last fifteen years. Controlling the growing deficit has become the federal rationale for cutting education, job training, and health and human service programs. Without a strong infrastructure, people get pushed closer toward homelessness. They note that 95 percent of Americans now pay higher tax rates than they did in 1978. From 1977 to 1992, taxes were increased for everyone but the top 5 percent, who earned at least $130,000 a year. While the income of 80 percent of Americans either declined or remained the same, the big-time gainers in the top 1 percent of the population more than doubled their income from $314,000 to $676,000. Their after-tax income gain is even more dramatic—a 136 percent increase from $202,000 to $477,000. The average tax cut for this individual is $83,457, ten times the average income of the individual in the lowest 20 percent. A "flat tax" will only increase economic disparity.

Therefore, the wealthiest 1 percent (about 2.5 million Americans), together will make $678 billion before taxes in 1994, $92 billion more than the 100 million Americans with the lowest incomes. The $2.4 trillion of income made by the top 20 percent is greater than the total income of the remaining 80 percent. Taking into account the net worth or the value of personal assets (house, car, bank accounts, and so forth) minus debts (such as mortgages and credit cards), the distance between the rich and poor becomes even greater. The richest 1 percent account for over 38 percent of net worth in the United States, over one and a half times that of the lowest 90 percent of the public, which only owns a little over 24 percent of the country's net worth. Most unequal is the distribution of net financial assets, such as stocks, bonds, and business assets. The richest 1 percent owns 55 percent of these assets, and the lowest 90 percent own only 10 percent. The top 1 percent of the country has nearly as much after-tax income as the bottom 40 percent of the American population (Greenstein and Baranick 1990).

The federal tax schedule has also illustrated the declining worth of children, if one considers the dependent deduction allotted for children. From 1948, the dependent deduction fell from 40 percent to about 5 percent in 1984. If the 1990 dependent deduction were raised to the same percentage per capita personal income as in 1948, it would equal $7,781.

While there have always been people who were not as well off as others, there has not always been an official, identifiable category of people known as "the poor." Nullifying the gains of the 1970s War On Poverty, by 1986 the poverty rate was 18 percent in nonmetropolitan areas—50 percent greater than in the metropolitan population (Newman 1988; First, Toomy and Rife 1990).

The federal government's official definition of "poverty" refers to a family of three in 1992 whose total income was less than $11,570. In fact, 47 percent (6.8 million) of those children who qualified as officially "poor" in 1992 lived in households where incomes were less than half the official poverty level (National Coalition for the Homeless 1993).

The government first established poverty thresholds in 1965 to provide the minimum income necessary to survive and maintain a nutritionally adequate diet. During the War on Poverty, target groups were identified who needed special assistance if poverty was to be eradicated.

What resulted was a new category of identifiable "poor." Guidelines have allowed gatekeepers to provide services for certain people and to exclude others. While many people are poor, they may not be considered officially poor because they fail to meet some criteria for inclusion. This has resulted in millions more people on the fringe, who are not "poor," but who certainly are not doing well.

The measures used to construct the official poverty levels are outdated because they are based on spending patterns from the mid-1950s. Although federal experts who originally designed the poverty thresholds recognized that they would need to be revised in response to changing household economics and rising living standards in the society, no major revisions have occurred. Families today spend a smaller share of their incomes on food and more on housing and energy than they did in the 1950s. Thirty years ago, large numbers of women did not work outside the home and require paid child care, as they do today. An up-to-date poverty line would be considerably higher, according to economic analysts, who assert that an updated figure for a family of three would equal $15,195—two-thirds higher than the official government level (Johnson et al. 1991).

Life below the official poverty line is relatively harsher than it was thirty years ago and more isolated from the experience of middle-class Americans. For example, the poverty level in 1959 was equal to 57 percent of median family income. If that relationship had remained constant, the poverty line for a family of four in 1989 would have been $19,820 instead of $9,885, and the child poverty rate would have been approximately 30 percent. This means that nearly 13 million children live below the poverty line and do not have their most basic needs met. The National Commission on Children (1993) reports that young people are increasingly vulnerable because of funding allocations. In 1991, although direct public spending on children totaled $295 billion, the poverty rate for these young people is 50 percent higher than it was two decades ago.

According to the National Coalition for the Homeless (1993), 25 million people lived below the poverty index in 1980, but twelve years later almost 40 million people lived below the poverty line. While the poverty rate for young families with children was 20 percent in 1973, it had risen to 40 percent by 1990. No progress was made in reducing poverty in 1989, while gaps between rich and poor people hit their widest points in more than forty years. In 1991, an estimated 9.2 million workers fell below the poverty line (Shapiro and Greenstein 1993).

New Census data shows that 35.7 million Americans were poor in 1991, a larger number than in any year of the 1970s and 1980s (Greenstein and Jaeger 1992). This increase was particularly great for children under six. The National Center for Children in Poverty (1993) reports that 5.6 million children under the age of six live in poverty and that the 24 percent poverty rate for children under six is higher than the rate for any other age group in the United States. This poverty occurred in once middle-class households in every region of the country. Using linear trend projection to forecast poverty rates the Center on Hunger, Poverty, and Nutrition found that if child poverty trends continue as they did over the period of 1970-1991, the rate of child poverty will climb to 28.5 percent over the next twenty years (Cook and Brown 1993).

The future is now in many rural areas. For instance, nearly 40 percent of all people in Washington County, Maine, live beneath the poverty level of $12,700 annually for a family of four. What is happening in rural areas that makes poverty and homelessness likely?

When only poor minorities in urban areas were homeless, there was much less public concern about it. Homelessness among those groups came as no surprise to the American public. As long as homeless was kept behind inner city and ghetto lines, it was regarded as "their" problem—and not "our" problem. But as middle-class, white,

Å

employed, two-parent families in suburban and rural areas experienced economic woes, new concerns about homelessness developed. As neighbors in small communities become homeless, "us" and "them" drifts closer together.

What are the problems which have been experienced in rural areas as a result of the national economic trends? Reversals in both farming and industry have seriously affected the economy of nonurban areas. Growth in service industries, greater international competition, transportation deregulation, losses in the consumer market, and reductions in local earnings and tax revenues are but a few of the social and economic changes that have increased rural poverty.

Displaced farmers, laid-off factory workers, and the working poor are but a few of the rural homeless who are living temporarily with friends or relatives, camping in parks, or living in their cars. One is not aware of their existence when driving through the scenic countryside. Rural areas that were already economically disadvantaged experienced federal funding cuts and policy changes that further disenfranchised them in their competition for resources. The tightening of the housing market resulted in escalating rents, while home ownership has become an economic liability for many in rural areas.

Homelessness is regarded as essentially an economic problem in rural as well as urban areas (Patton 1987; Rossi 1989). The failure of policymakers to appreciate the extent of the rural economic crisis and the degree to which a majority of rural counties are especially vulnerable has contributed to the tendency to perceive homelessness exclusively as an urban problem (Patton 1987).

Parts of rural America are facing their worst economic crisis since the Great Depression. The growth of rural homelessness is complicated by major social and economic changes in rural communities during the 1980s as a result of changes in land use (agriculture, lumbering) and the restructuring of the national economy (Flora and Flora 1989). During the early 1980s, poverty rates increased at a more rapid rate in rural areas than in urban areas. By the end of 1980s, reports began to surface that rural homelessness appeared to be growing as rapidly as that found in urban communities—even faster in some communities where there has been great economic distress (Patton 1987).

Farm foreclosures have been taking place at a staggering rate: 650,000 farms have been lost since 1981, and another 200 farmers give up this occupation each week. Low-wage, labor-intensive rural manufacturing has lost over half a million jobs since 1981 as a result of foreign competition. Timber and mining energy industries have experienced downturns. The rural unemployment rate now consistently exceeds the urban rate, a reversal of the historical trend. The rural poverty rate is now at 22 percent, the highest level in two decades (Sinclair 1987; Sherman 1992).

Unemployment in rural areas is now higher than it is in metropolitan areas, and at least 1.6 million rural residents during 1990 searched for work but were unable to find it. The Economic Policy Institute found that displaced rural workers not only are more likely than their urban counterparts to lose their jobs as the result of economic upheavals, they also suffer longer periods without work. Even when they succeed in finding a new job, they still typically suffer a loss of earning of 12.3 percent, contrasted with a loss of 5.2 percent for those in metro areas. Rural pay is lower in every field, and the rural-metro income gap is at its largest in years. Earnings of young workers started lower in rural areas and fell faster, doubling the metro-rural earnings gap in eight years (Sherman 1992).

Because I conducted my interviews with people who lived in New Hampshire, I felt it was important to understand the social and economic context in which they lived. I learned that "the recession started earlier in New England and is more severe in New England," according to Andrew Sum, director of the Center for Labor Market Studies at Northeastern University (DeParle 1991). "What New England is suffering is fundamentally different than the rest of the nation and deeper than any decline we've felt since the Great Depression," reports associate director Paul Harrington (Gosselin 1992a).

The hardest hit areas are the rural areas, which have no industrial base. There, the children and families are the poorest of the poor. Rural communities most at risk for developing economic problems that lead to homelessness are those which have not diversified their economic base. Two out of every three nonmetropolitan counties are dominated by a single industry. Counties whose economy is dominated by a single industry have found themselves in distress when the industry fails. Those areas already plagued by persistent poverty offer displaced workers few job alternatives (Patton 1987).

A report jointly issued several years ago by the National Coalition for the Homeless (1986) and the Des Moines Coalition for the Homeless examined economic problems in rural areas. Farming and local industry have been particularly affected. The report asserts that the magnitude of the economic crisis is almost impossible to measure because it has so many ramifications. Not only have farm workers and the industry suffered, so have a variety of other segments of the community. Storekeepers, service workers, and the entire area all lose income when the major employment bases of the community are feeble. While the homeless do not generally come from the ranks of laid-off industrial workers, the homeless are often the people whose marginal jobs—in supermarkets, restaurants, bars—disappear without attracting much notice when unemployment hits the middle-class work force (Mowbray 1985).

In New Hampshire, more than 20,000 manufacturing jobs were lost between 1985 and 1991. Industries especially hard hit have been computer, electronics, and communications; paper; shoes and textiles; and construction. While New Hampshire gained 138,000 jobs between 1981 and 1989, 70 percent of these jobs were in the service and retail trade sectors, in which employment wages are low, jobs are often part-time and temporary, and there is little security and few benefits.

In New Hampshire, more people work second and third jobs just to maintain the current standard of living. The Department of Employment Security found few openings in the well-paying manufacturing sector during 1990 and 1991.

The five largest banks and two major utilities in New Hampshire went bankrupt in the early 1990s. The banks lost $1 billion in 1990, which is more than the annual state budget. Unemployment has quadrupled, from 2 to 7.2 percent. State and local governments have run out of money, resulting in a $200 million shortage. Property taxes, which finance local governments, have doubled in ten years. Supporting schools, which are 90 percent dependent on the local property tax, zhas stretched many communities to the breaking point, resulting in decreased aid for education. Health care has become too expensive to afford, costing 2.4 times what it did in 1980; 140,000 residents have no health insurance at all, and another 140,000 are underinsured.

The state's child poverty rate increased by 50 percent in 1990. As a result, the state saw a 111 percent jump in AFDC requests between 1989 and 1991, the highest in the nation. Twenty-four percent of the children in the state are estimated to be chronically hungry or at risk of being hungry. The number receiving food stamps increased in nine months by 41 percent, from 16,000 in 1990 to 22,000 in 1991.

The state lost $1.3 billion in federal spending by the early 1990s. The most significant cuts were in housing, economic development, children's services, and the environment. General revenue sharing was cut $215 million, affecting firefighting, police, schools, and infrastructure improvement. Economic development assistance was cut 59 percent, or by $39 million. Job training was cut 51.3 percent, by $217 million. Community action and antipoverty funds were cut 62 percent, by $253 million, while the energy conservation funds were cut 44 percent, by $24 million. Education lost $9 million because the New Hampshire State Board of Education elected not to comply with Clinton's Goals 2000 program.

Forty percent of the state's bridges are deemed substandard, while the number of "poor" and "very poor" roads have increased 33 percent over the past 20 years, to 41 percent being substandard (National Priorities Project 1992).

The people I interviewed had often moved across the state lines to "see if the grass was greener over there." Vermont, Maine, and Massachusetts too suffer in this depressed economic climate. Those who moved across the state lines found experientially what economics knew statistically: since 1968, New Hampshire has lost 14,000 shoe jobs, but there have been similar losses of 25,000 in Massachusetts and 17,000 in Maine. In all of New England, over 273,500 manufacturing jobs have been lost in the last two decades. New jobs require more education than muscles, and wages for jobs as chambermaids or restaurant help have not kept up with inflation and are often part-time without benefits. By the year 2000, Vermont is projected to create 18,900 new jobs in retail trade and the "service sector" that pay an average wage of $6.09 an hour. As discussed earlier, this minimum income makes it impossible to support a family. There will be only an estimated 2,900 jobs in manufacturing created in the next decade—jobs that pay $13.75 an hour.

People on minimum-wage jobs often receive no health, insurance, or retirement benefits. The Census Bureau reported that 35.4 million Americans had no health insurance in 1991, an increase from 34.7 million in 1990. About 29 percent of all poor people had no medical insurance of any kind in 1991. By contrast, 11.7 percent of people above the poverty line and 14.1 percent of all Americans said they were uninsured (Pear 1993). As a result of the economic crisis, insurance and benefits to the people frequently get cut. Workers are often asked to pay more out of their paychecks for the same benefits in order to offset administration cost. This presents greater financial and health distress for rural people, as in Vermont, where 45,000 Vermonters have no health insurance at all (Vermont Department of Education 1990).

It is difficult to live as a rural laborer in this precarious economy. In coastal Maine, for instance, where clamming is a traditional form of labor, clams are harder to find. Between 1979 and 1989, the annual clam harvest in Maine decreased from 5.1 million pounds to 2.3 million pounds. Women with hands that move almost faster than the eye could find work in fifty sardine canneries in 1950. Now they have just eight from which they must compete to find work. Haddock and cod, once plentiful, are so scarce today that there are limits on how often fishermen can go out to catch them.

Farm work declines as farms become house lots. Jobs are lost when cows feed themselves with computerized equipment. This year there are only a third as many jobs for hired hands in Maine as there were in 1964, with a loss of ten thousand jobs. Loggers need expensive equipment, from $500 chain saws to $70,000 logging skinners (Patton 1987; Anderson 1992).

As many traditional rural jobs, in farming, lumber, fishing, and unskilled labor—have been lost, they have either not been replaced or been replaced with jobs for which the bulk of workers are not qualified. The top ten job openings in New England in 1991 were for retail salespersons, janitors and cleaners, bookkeeping clerks, cashiers, general office clerks, nurses, waiters and waitresses, store clerks, secretaries, and manager-executives (National Priorities Project 1992). The majority of these occupations will be at, or only slightly above, minimum wage and are located primarily in larger towns and cities—not in smaller rural areas.

When rural people who have minimal skills lose their jobs, it is not easy for them to find another. First, living in communities where everyone knows everyone else can work for—and against—one in finding work. Second, there is a saturation point of employment in rural areas; when it is reached, there simply are not other jobs that are available. Third, this means that one must commute to other towns to find work—and this may mean distances that are prohibitively far for people who live on the edge with marginal transportation. Perhaps most important, people who have been able to make it for long periods of time find that their lack of education keeps them from getting jobs that will make them upwardly mobile. As Kim noted: "I quit high school because I needed money and had to go to work. It never occurred to me that not having graduated from high school would keep me from getting work, until I got laid off. I can't get any job until I get my GED. Without my GED, I cannot work, but if I cannot work, I can't pay my rent or any of my bills. I've got to go back to school; it is the only way I'm going to make it."

According to the national trends, education will be the key determinant between the haves and the have nots. Yet among the rural poor there is often a lack of money for schools, conservative educational programming, and a disrespect for education unless it results in a job. The better educated a person, the better the opportunities for finding work. Educational success by all students is a concern of educators and employers alike. Academic problems for rural children are a local manifestation of national trends.

Since the publication of *A Nation At Risk* in 1983, America has been grappling with how to "fix" the educational system. The task force that wrote this report concluded that the disappointments many people have voiced do not necessarily reflect a reduction in the quality of our teachers, schools, or principals. Our schools are simply out of step with the larger social and economic realities of our global economy.

They found that the educational system's current performance—in quality and quantity—is far from adequate. There are higher grade retention rates for blacks and poor students. The reading, science, and math levels of black seventeen-year-olds are about the same as those of white thirteen-year-olds (Children's Defense Fund 1990, 1995). Rural schools, which have fewer technical and monetary resources, have difficulty preparing students in the same way as wealthy, urban schools. Preparation of students poses major problems for employers who need to build a strong economic base (New Hampshire Governor's Task Force on Education 1990; Business and Industry Association of New Hampshire 1990).

This theme is repeated by Ernest Boyer, president of the Carnegie Foundation for the Advancement of Teaching, who believes there is a new attitude about the educational system in the United States: that the system is beyond repair. Not only has it failed, but it needs restructuring, according to educational specialists, in order to keep pace with increasing demands for excellence (Kozol 1992; Linehan 1992; National Association of State Coordinators for the Education of Homeless Children, 1993).

Equal education, as it is provided to boys and girls, is a myth, according to a 1992 American Association of University Women study, researched by the Wellesley College Center for Research on Women. While public schools may be theoretically based on "equal education" to all students, Kozol (1991) and others (Coles 1967) have found "savage inequalities" to exist for children in American schools. Children born into wealthy families are privileged to receive high-quality education; children born into poor families all too often experience poorer quality schools and teachers, lack of instructional resources, and environments in which it is difficult to learn. As the AAUW study reports: "The invisibility of girls in the current education debate suggests that girls and boys (and students of different social classes) have identical educational experiences in school. Nothing could be further from the truth. Whether one looks at achievement scores, curriculum design, or teacher-student interaction, it is clear that rurality, socioeconomic status and gender make a difference in the nation's public elementary and secondary schools" (Baily 1992).

It is not as if those words have gone unheeded by school administrators. Everyone knows that something needs to be done to make the educational system work better, especially for children at risk. However, while many of the programs sound good, the programs are not as successful as one would hope, owing primarily to inadequate funding.

American students' performance in reading, math, and science still lags behind students in many other developed and developing nations. The high dropout rates and lack of basic skills and knowledge needed to get a job even among those who did graduate indicate serious problems for the rural students. Fewer than half of American seventeen-year-olds who are in school possess the skills and basic knowledge required for college and many entry-level jobs. Fewer than half can understand complicated literary and informal passages that are typical of high school work. About half the students can compute with decimals, fractions, and percents or solve simple equations. Many are so limited in their command of written English that they are unable to communicate a reasoned point of view (National Commission on Children 1991; Taylor 1988).

Assessments of twenty school systems around the world rank American eighth graders tenth in arithmetic, twelfth in algebra, and sixteenth in geometry. Americans tie for science scores with students in Singapore and Thailand for fourteenth place. Among advanced science students, Americans are last in biology (National Commission on Children 1991).

The task force for *A Nation At Risk* found that the cumulative four-year dropout rate in public schools is approximately 25 percent. Business leaders report that an estimated 25 percent of high school graduates are not qualified for entry-level positions. While by age twenty-one, 83 percent of youths have a high school diploma or equivalency certificate, dropout rates approach 50 percent in some cities. Rural youths are more likely to be dropouts than those in metro areas and are less likely to return to school later (Sherman 1992). This fact puts rural youth—especially females—at risk of subsequent homelessness.

The social and personal costs of school dropout and academic failure are enormous. In 1988 high school dropouts were twice as likely as high school graduates and five times as likely as college graduates to be unemployed. Students with weak basic academic skills are more than nine times as likely to have a child out of wedlock and more than twice as likely to be arrested as their academically successful peers. Young people without basic educational skills and knowledge are five times more likely to receive public assistance than their better-educated peers. More than 80 percent of inmates in the prisons are high school dropouts, each costing taxpayers an average of twenty thousand dollars a year (National Commission of Children 1991).

Poor academic performance and failure to complete high school result in a growing disparity between the qualifications of students' and skill requirements of available jobs. Many of the jobs in today's and tomorrow's economy will require moderate to high levels of education and skill. It is estimated that college will be a prerequisite for one-third to two-thirds of the new jobs in the year 2000 (National Commission of Children 1991). But students cannot go forward without a solid foundation—a foundation that must start before they ever enter school.

Head Start, the program to enhance preschoolers' ability to be competitive in the classroom, has been a demonstrated success. Children who attend Head Start have been found time and time again to be more successful than their peers who did not attend the program.

As a result of poverty and poor prenatal care, the number of children in rural areas with developmental, learning, or emotional problems has escalated. Programs such as Head Start can help children on the margin over the hump toward success. But such educational programs only work when they are available and utilized—which are both problems in rural areas.

Specifically, Head Start promotes gains in IQ, improves children's self-esteem and motivation to achieve, improves social behavior, and has a positive influence on children's health, motor coordination, and development. It encourages parent participation and makes community institutions more aware of and responsive to the needs of low-income families and children. Head Start graduates are less likely to fail a grade in school or require special education services.

However, less than 27 percent of the children eligible for Head Start are provided the opportunity to attend. While the 1990 Congress passed an act designed to serve all eligible children by 1994, the current funding would take until the year 2171 to achieve that four-year goal (Edleman and Ladner 1991; National Commission on Children 1991). Getting children at imminent risk of homelessness into Head Start is even more difficult in rural areas where there are fewer resources, longer distances to travel to get to the schools, and populations who may not be aware of the importance or availability of Head Start programs.

It is important to note that despite the successes of the Head Start program, it can be argued that money would be better spent to attack the problems that made Head Start necessary in the first place— problems like poverty, discrimination, and economic depression. If all people were able to earn a decent wage, and if good child care were nationally available at a reasonable cost, children would be better equipped to meet the demands of school and work.

In rural areas, the schools cannot pay for everything students need because of the high costs of education today. It is even more difficult when schools serve a small population that is spread over a wide area. The fixed costs associated with school building operation and maintenance are high when expressed in per-pupil terms because of the small student population. Busing also increases rural school costs, when there are wide areas to be served. Yet there are traditionally low fiscal capacities in most rural areas to support educational costs. Because of their low revenues, rural communities spend less per student than do metro communities, even though local rural governments reserve a considerably larger proportion of their limited budgets for education. Schools spend less, which means that they cannot give as extensive an educational experience to rural students. Special needs programs are harder to fund at appropriate rates. Rural children are structurally at risk of receiving a poorer education—especially when they are financially poor or homeless (Sherman 1992). "Inadequate education not only limits opportunities for women, but jeopardizes their children's—and the nation's—future." (Baily 1992).

Given their lack of funding, rural schools—especially those that rely on property taxes for funding—are in great jeopardy for the future. A fund-raiser for an innovative school system in rural New England said:

> We had the most creative school program of anywhere in the region, and perhaps one of the most innovative in the nation. It was a program especially designed to help *everyone* in the community to improve their education. We wanted to assure that preschoolers were ready to learn, that children in school learned twenty-first-century skills. We wanted to make school so attractive that students did well and wanted to stay in school. The school was also going to be open to the community, so that unemployed people could learn trades to get them jobs. We wanted to develop an "everybody wins" school. But the school district and the community could not afford such an expensive school. We talked to funders and federal bureaucrats. While there was much support about this great idea, none of them would put up the money it required. Each of them had other priorities—and most of them were politically based. It was exceedingly frustrating to watch the school fail—not because of a poor design, not because of a lack of interest—but because of politics and money.

Rural areas experience a double whammy of a declining economic base and an educational system that is not designed to help students— hence local communities—grow and prosper. It is not the fault of those people who become homeless that such complex economic and educational problems exist. Indeed, it is not the "fault" of the community itself. Social and demographic trends have compounded economic trends, which have resulted in the residents of small town America being more at risk of homelessness than at any time since the Great Depression. National trends and crises have filtered down to small communities, where now even those who were once immune from social ills come face to face with the realities of homelessness. Restructuring the economic condition of the community may be the most productive way to prevent and eradicate rural homelessness. But restructuring the economy is difficult; it is hard enough to provide affordable housing and social services for those who are homeless.

seven

Lack of Affordable Housing in Rural America

Just as the economy negatively impacts job and educational opportunities for people in rural areas, national political and economic decisions also impact the availability of affordable housing.

In the simplest context, both rural and urban people become homeless because there are more people who need inexpensive housing than there are cheap housing units available (McChesney 1988). It is easier to simplify the solutions for homelessness by asserting "all you gotta do is find them a place to live" than it is to understand the complex relationship between the economy and the housing industry, and how it has promoted rural homelessness.

Construction has evaporated in many rural areas because values collapsed amid the farm failures and small town plant closings of the past decade. Meanwhile, existing houses are getting older, which means they require more repair. As families make less money, they may no longer be able to buy homes or pay for routine maintenance. Families may move from houses to apartments to mobile homes as they attempt to find more affordable housing, with more overcrowding within them (National Coalition for the Homeless 1987a). As the needs of the family escalate and incomes dwindle, finding decent housing at an affordable price has become "as difficult as pulling a rabbit out of a baseball cap" (Kilman and Johnson 1991).

Prices for home owners and renters alike have skyrocketed to the point of making secure housing almost impossible to afford. Families are less likely to own a house today than they were twenty years ago; the income group hardest hit are the poor and near poor families (Mihaly 1991). With declining incomes and increased costs of living, it is difficult for a family to buy—or even rent—a house. As banks have experienced their own difficult economic times in recent years, they are scrutinizing every mortgage application. People who may previously

YVONNE VISSING

have been given home mortgage loans now find themselves confronted with a complex application process, only to have their requests rejected.

Housing affordability problems have occurred as a result of changes and trends in American family life over the past twenty-five years, which has led to increased economic vulnerability of single-parent households. According to Mulroy and Lane (1993), four factors contributed to homelessness: (1) a resource squeeze, created by housing affordability problems, that precipitates the loss of permanent housing; (2) residential mobility, which destabilizes families; (3) discrimination in the housing market, which constrains housing choices; and (4) multiple stress burdens on single mothers who must be providers, shelterers, and caregivers, further demoralizing an increasingly fragile family system. The loss of inexpensive, decent rental housing is also a problem that contributes to the rise of rural homelessness. This, coupled with a systematic pattern of stagnation and decline in the quality of the existing housing stock in rural areas, will only increase the amount of homelessness seen especially among single parents and the elderly in rural communities (Schwartz et al. 1988).

The cost of housing is a growing burden for rural families—one that makes it unlikely that they can afford their own home. The percentage of young families with children that owned their homes in 1980 was 47.4 percent; by 1991, that percentage had dropped to 31.5 percent (National Coalition for the Homeless 1993). Three-quarters of the rural poor pay rents that exceed federal standards of affordability (30 percent of income) (Sherman 1992). Families cannot survive spending as much as 70 percent of their income on housing alone. One in nine rural house-holds—or two million homes—pay more than one half or more of their income for housing (Sherman 1992). More than 5.1 million low-income renters either spend more than half their incomes on housing or live in substandard housing, according to HUD (National Coalition for the Homeless 1993).

Single mothers are more likely to spend over half their income on housing. These figures substantiate what I observed among my rural homeless families—that most homeless families were headed by a single mother, who could not afford rent or housing payments on their limited income. How has the federal government addressed the problem of rising housing costs on low income?

While there are many reasons that the homeless cannot find reasonable housing, Tucker (1990a) asserts that the federal government's housing policies are ultimately to blame for the escalation of America's homeless problem. The federal government has largely abdicated its traditional role to provide low-income housing to rural people that would help people pull themselves up from poverty. Without a remedy to these problems, homelessness in the American countryside will shortly become as rampant and visible as it currently is in American cities (Patton 1987).

While some argue (DiIulio 1991) that during the Reagan administration, outlays on housing subsidies for low-income households more than doubled, housing vouchers were introduced, and 165,000 new units of public housing were developed, the majority of information questions or refutes such claims. During the 1980s, the Reagan administration sought to infuse its housing policies with a market orientation. Reagan's commission on housing assumed that the genius of the market economy, freed of the distortions forced by government housing policies and regulations that swung erratically from loving to hostile, could provide for housing far better than federal programs. They recommended free and deregulated housing markets with minimal government intervention. Government, they felt, would retain a continuing role in providing housing to the poor, but in reality this did not occur (Blau 1992). Federal policies have increased the likelihood of homelessness in rural areas in the following ways.

Federal housing assistance was reduced during the 1980s. In 1981 the Department of Housing and Urban Development had budget authorizations of 32.2 billion; by 1989 they had been slashed to 6.9 billion, a reduction of 78 percent. Since 1980, federal housing programs have been cut more than 75 percent, from $32 billion to $7.5 billion, a decline of 80 percent after adjusted for inflation. This results in many Americans having no place to call home. For nearly half of all homeless children, these findings also mean that these children have no place to go to school and a reduced means for social support (Weiss 1988).

The federal government abandoned its fifty-year commitment to build public housing and drastically cut other housing programs. In 1979 Congress authorized 55,000 new units of public housing. In 1984, it authorized zero, and it has averaged less than 7,400 since then. That drastic reduction in public housing construction during the Reagan years contributed to the increase in homelessness. The federal government, which had produced more than a million new other housing units in the periods from 1976 to 1982, was producing only 25,000 units annually by the end of the Reagan years. The number of new households helped each year fell from an average of 316,000 new households in fiscal years 1977–1980, to 82,000 new households in years 1981–1988—a decline of nearly three-quarters (Blau 1992).

According to the federal report on "The State of the Nation's Housing," the failure to produce additional low-cost housing units between 1980 and 1989 contributed to a total loss, since 1974, of over one million units with rents below $300 per month. States (which were experiencing their own federal cutbacks) subsequently reduced their financial contributions to the poor. Transitional living programs that provide shelter, support, and education to young mothers meet the housing needs of only about 5 percent of homeless teen parents and children (Gornstein 1990).

For each dollar the federal government spends, about one cent goes for housing, which is one-third the necessary expenditure prescribed to address the critical housing needs of homeless and low-income people (Dolbeare 1991). The Center for Community Change (1993) found that many low-income renters are paying up to 70 percent of their income on housing. High rent burdens drive many poor people into substandard and overcrowded housing and homelessness. As families move into overcrowded, doubled-up housing and find that those situations do not work, many are forced to leave. Most of them return to the shelters or move from place to place (Levenson 1992). The low-income housing crisis will worsen as rental housing costs rise, as more people live below the poverty line, as unemployment continues, and as subsidized housing ages.

Changes in the private housing market, cutbacks in federal spending on low-income housing, and local rent-control ordinances have all contributed to the rise of homelessness (Jencks 1994). Rural states, which had been experiencing other financial difficulties, were reluctant to tax their residents further in order to alleviate one group's housing distress, at the cost of creating housing displacement for those who were just squeaking by.

Despite a decade of cuts in federal housing funds, one of the largest federal subsidies is that of housing tax breaks for the wealthy. More than 80 percent of taxpayers have incomes less than $50,000. It is difficult to buy or maintain a house on that kind of salary, which forces people into renting from property owners.

One of the biggest benefits to home owners is the property tax and mortgage interest deduction. This deduction is an important taxpayer saving each year, and it creates a huge loss in federal revenues. Over the next four years the tax deduction is expected to account for a total of $231 billion. Those making $100,000 and up (only 3 percent of the population) claim a third of the deduction—often for luxury second homes and mansions—for a total of $11.6 billion in 1990. Those earning the least need the most help affording homes, yet they claim little of this tax benefit. Ironically, what is spent on subsidies for the wealthiest Americans almost equals the amount allocated for the entire 1990 federal housing budget (National Priorities Project 1992). There is, then, a huge incentive to own real estate.

The housing market has never met the housing needs of the poor, according to Blau (1992). He asserts that government intervention alone allows even some of the poor to obtain housing, for left to the mercies of the real estate industry, few poor would be able to secure housing. Hence, blaming government intervention for the failure of the real estate market misreads history. The real estate market was simply never designed to assist the poor.

Historically, there have been no strong political or economic forces to encourage the real estate market to make inexpensive housing available to needy people. There has been no strong push to support a public housing sector in general, and certainly there has been no systematic attempt to mainstream poor people into settled neighborhoods. When such efforts have been contemplated, the real estate industry has been consistently successful in limiting the endeavors.

There are many ways that the real estate market helps keep the system in check, and the poor out. For instance, the market has facilitated the skyrocketing prices for land and houses that have occurred over the past decade, with house costs rising as much as 400 percent in New England during that time. Poor and middle-class people's incomes have not gone up nearly that much in comparison.

Government controls, exclusionary zoning, and market restrictions also drive up the cost of housing beyond that which most people can afford (Tucker 1990a). Even if property is available within the family, people are no longer so free to put up their own trailers or shack on it because of tightened land use and building restrictions (Fitchen 1991).

Stricter enforcement of building and fire codes has also resulted in the closing of many previously occupied buildings. Some places in rural areas where people could live for cheap have not met public health requirements and have been closed. Similarly, buildings have been closed or razed owing to high maintenance costs or have become targets of vandalism and landlord abandonment (Patton 1987).

Even when the government has made housing monies available, they were often misappropriated, according to Blau (1992). Between two and four billion dollars was "stolen" from Housing and Urban Development (HUD) by private contractors and real estate vendors. HUD lent well-connected developers millions of dollars worth of Section 8 funds designated for the poor. Although housing money has been intended for the poor, many rehabilitated homes ended up being occupied by members of the middle class (National Coalition for the Homeless 1987a).

The real estate market influences homelessness in yet another way. In the past, many rural poor people had the security of owning a place to live or having parents who owned a place. But this security is being replaced with the precariousness of tenancy, as more of the poor people in rural areas today have neither land no relatives with land (Fitchen 1991). Joe told me how: "My dad had to sell the family farm, because we couldn't afford to keep it going anymore. We had bills, and the equipment, the feed, everything cost so much compared to what we made that when he got an offer, he sold it. But now our home, our land is gone, we can't get it back, and we can't afford another." As Joe found out, hanging on to your house may be difficult, but the costs of buying a new one may be out of reach.

Because of the deplorable economic situations in rural areas, homelessness hovers on the horizon for more and more people. In New Hampshire, housing prices have doubled in the past twelve years, but incomes have not. Only 5 percent of New Hampshire renters can afford to buy the average house, since the average weekly income of a renter in New Hampshire was $475 in 1990. This is only half of what bankers say they need to pay for a median-priced house in the state (National Priorities Project 1992).

Those people who make the most money are a very small percentage of the total population, yet the majority of houses are in the price range of over $125,000. At the other end of the scale, almost 65 percent of the state's population can only afford a house under $50,000, and yet there are virtually no homes available for them (National Priorities Project 1992).

From 1979 to 1989, the median-price for a house in the state shot up from $48,000 to $124,000—twice as fast as incomes increased. A full 42 percent of the state's renters cannot afford a down payment. Foreclosures are at a sixty-year high in many parts of New England (National Priorities Project 1992).

Owning and then losing one's home is bad for everyone. It is bad for the bank who held the mortgage. It is bad for the community and the state. And it is worst of all on the family, who has lost not just a place to stay but self-esteem, history, security, and a place to build a sure future. One mother of three told me:

> We owned our own house, do you hear? It was pretty, we had space for everyone and everything. We had neighbors, and we lived like you and everyone else. But then my husband lost his job. I couldn't make ends meet on my job. I don't have much education, and I can only get [service jobs]. So we lost the house. I can't begin to tell you what it felt like, having to sell our stuff at the yard sale and move out to an apartment. It was hard on all of us—the kids, my husband, and me—all for different reasons. We even had to get rid of our dog. Losing that house was the beginning of the end for us. Not just did we lose the house, we lost self-respect, and a lifestyle that made us like everyone else.

The beginning links in the chain of events for prehomeless families were owning a home, economic distress, losing the home, and then moving into a rented apartment.

When people cannot afford to buy a house, renting becomes a viable option. But even the number of available low-cost rental units has declined as the demand for them has increased. Landlords and home owners could demand—and get—whatever price they wanted. A single mother of three said: "We could not afford a place to rent. All of the rents were at least $500 a month, and those were not even for very nice places. Then they wanted another $500 for a damage deposit, plus first month's rent. Who has an extra $1,000 they can shell out at one time? The only way we were able to even get a place was thanks to the Salvation Army, who has a special program where they will help people one time with their damage deposits. If they didn't help, we would have stayed on the street."

Things are rough for home owners and renters alike, but they are especially bad for very-low-income renters who have less than 50 percent of the median income. In New Hampshire, 35,000 households, a quarter of all renters, have very low incomes. Almost one-third of the state's renters can't find housing they can afford. Paying more than 30 percent of their income for housing puts a serious strain on low- and middle-income households, who may have to forgo food, medical care, or heat to keep a roof over their heads. In Vermont, it can cost more than $1,100 to move into an apartment. This includes the security deposit, first month's rent, and utility deposits. The average two-bedroom apartment in Vermont costs $640 per month, and an annual household income of $25,600 would be required to afford it (Vermont Department of Education 1990).

As the Sakes family found out, where they lived was a clear sign of their housing distress, and it was increasingly difficult to find good places to live that were affordable: "After we sold the house, we rented a house in town. But the landlord increased the rent, and we simply couldn't afford it. So we moved into a condo by the landfill. But the rent was okay, and we didn't mind drinking bottled water. Then my husband lost his job, and we had to look for an even cheaper place to live." The place where they ended up had cardboard over the windows.

Rural areas and small towns have fewer rental units and cheap houses, especially in the less populated areas. Also, many areas, such as those in the mountains, are ill-suited for housing construction. In central Appalachia, for instance, only 5 percent of the rural land is suitable for housing construction.

In small towns, special interests often control the land—and making it available for low-cost housing is not their priority! In one small town, almost all of the property is owned by a handful of residents, who control what will—and will not—be built there. Local politics may forbid certain types of constructions to be built in a community. Some rural areas are largely controlled by mining and mineral interests, which prevent the land from being used for housing development. Therefore, land that could be used for housing in many rural areas becomes both unaffordable and unavailable.

In rural areas that rely upon the tourist industry, rural property is purchased by wealthy urbanites for vacation homes or as retirement property. Tourist industries purchase other desirable properties on which they build ski resorts, restaurants, hotels, condos, and the like. The result of these purchases is that once affordable land can no longer be purchased by middle- and low-income people. The prices—and the taxes—have often made the purchase of land and homes prohibitive. This often forces those who can no longer afford housing to the campgrounds during the summer and to rentals the rest of the year.

Poor people who have more resources can stay in more secure but still not deluxe accommodations. Trailers, single-room occupancy units, motels, low-income apartments or houses, stripped-down houses, mobile homes, or other "creative" accommodations (such as doubling up, staying in campgrounds, staying in cars, or building shelters in the woods) are places that often become "home." These types of living accommodations were the most frequently used by homeless people and those on the edge of homelessness.

Because rural areas have a limited amount of rental property, and because of the close-knit nature of interaction between residents, most landlords know one another. Once a tenant is identified as "unreliable" about making payments, it is easy to become officially or unofficially blacklisted. Landlords are less concerned with the tenant's personal problems than with making a secure income from the rental property. As one landlord pointed out: "Things are tough for everyone. I don't want to rent to loafers who can't pay their bills. I got my own bills to pay."

While this position is easily understood from an economic point of view, it does not consider the point of view of the tenant who was doing the best she could to pay the bills: "I try to feed my kids and do the best I can. When it comes to paying the rent or feeding my kids, I will feed my kids. I want to pay the rent—don't think for a minute I don't. I do. But there is only so much money to go around, and I hope the landlord who has more than we do will understand and give us a break if we are a little late paying. If they had to choose between paying rent or feeding their kids, they'd feed their kids too."

Housing quality in rural America is actually worse than in urban America, according to statistics on rates of housing inadequacy, and worst of all is rental rural housing. A decade ago, over a quarter of renters in nonmetropolitan areas lived in inadequate dwellings, and conditions are worse today (Apgar and Brown 1988).

Poor, rural housing may not contain indoor plumbing, insulation for warmth, or safe heating systems. Window panes are frequently replaced with plastic, wood, or cardboard. Abandoned cars and refrigerators as well as unsightly debris pose health risks. Driving through the backroads taking photographs of ramshackle houses, I found one home that looked so dilapidated that I thought it could not possibly be inhabited; yet, the door opened, and a young man stepped out and waved hello.

Just as urban renewal came forth in urban areas to clean up ghettos and provide room for public housing developments, public housing has also come to the larger towns within rural America. But rural areas that have prided themselves on independence and lack of government intervention have not been overly receptive to having low-income housing developments in their communities. Public housing has become politically legitimate in the United States only by accepting the concept of "less eligibility"—meaning that the conditions for the poor should be no better than can be afforded by the lowest paid worker. This has resulted in conspicuously poorer housing being all the housing available for the poor. Blau (1992) asserts that under the principle of less eligibility, public housing could not compete with the real estate market, and it could not succeed in providing good housing to the poor. This stricture caused public housing to be blamed for many problems that were not of its making. It could not be attractive, and when it was of decent quality, the supply had to be limited. Thus public housing was not easily received in rural areas that wanted to avoid the urban stereotyped structures that supposedly housed within them a variety of urban problems.

According to Michael Harrington (1984), the housing policy of America has sought the integration of the poor with the poor—which is to say, the segregation of other Americans from the society at large. Segregated by class, race, and location, and easily identifiable as a distinct architectural style, public housing got the problems inherent in carrying out the task assigned to it. And when, in the early 1980s, the Reagan administration used these problems to reduce its subsidies, the cutbacks combined with an escalation of costs in the private sector to create a crisis of affordable housing and homelessness (Blau 1992).

Federal appropriations for rural housing were slashed by two-thirds between 1981 and 1991, while the need for housing assistance soared. Three of four poor rural households receive no federal, state, or local rental or home mortgage assistance. This puts them at high risk of becoming homeless (Sherman 1992). In 1981, federal funds assisted more than 217,000 new households to obtain housing through Section 8 programs. By 1989, fewer than 85,000 new households received assistance (Coates 1990). Federal subsidies to poor people have always played a relatively minor role in the national housing market. In fact, only 5.6 million of all households in the United States (or slightly more than 6 percent of the total) benefit from direct, public subsidies.

The public sector in most Western European countries is considerably larger than in the United States, amounting to one-third of the housing market in Britain and slightly less than 40 percent in France and Sweden (Blau 1992). This puts the United States as one of the lowest contributors to public housing of any industrialized nation— and rural areas become the lowest supported areas.

Another dilemma facing homeless people in small towns is the wait for subsidized housing—which can take years. The wait for subsidized housing in New Hampshire and Vermont is typically three years. As one family reported:

> We are from here [New Hampshire], and we moved away to New York
> to find more secure work. But things there were no better. We heard
> things were better in Vermont, so we moved there. But there was no
> work there either. We lived there for a while and applied for subsidized
> housing. The houses are better there, and if one can get work, the
> chances of getting benefits are better than they are here. But we found
> out that it would take three years or more to finally get into an apart-
> ment there. So we moved back here to be near family until the day we
> move up in the list and can qualify for housing there.

After the three years, the family found themselves still way down on
the list and have decided not to move to Vermont now but to make a
go of it the best they can in New Hampshire.

Homeless people are poor and typically need help securing housing until their crisis is past. It may be possible for some single mothers
to qualify for subsidized housing, but it takes a long time to make the
system work, according to this mother:

> I got burned out of my place and asked and asked for their help to get
> housing. I was given form after form to fill out, and they were compli-
> cated. The next time I would stop by, I would find that it wasn't pro-
> cessed because I forgot to fill out a box, or there was another form yet to
> be completed. Every time, it was something else for why I couldn't get
> housing this week. In the meantime, we were living in our car, at the
> shelter, or wearing out our welcome with family or friends. While they
> were messing around with their damn forms, we were on the street.
> Only because I was insistent and went over their heads to get help did I
> ever get housing. And then, they [the housing office workers] got snotty
> with me because I dared to go over their heads. It was as if because I was
> homeless, I deserved to wait, and had to act grateful for them doing
> nothing to actually get my kids off the street.

Two-parent families found that it was harder for them to get subsidized housing. In some cases they could, but because often the fathers worked part-time jobs in which they made some money—but too
little to support their family—the family would not qualify for aid. A
shelter worker reflected on one two-parent family with three children
for whom she tried to find housing:

> These were wonderful people. They just met up with a series of unfortu-
> nate circumstances. I let them stay the maximum amount of time I could
> here at the shelter. After that, I had to ask them to leave, despite each
> parent doing all they could to find work. It seemed that because they
> were married, they missed qualifying for all sorts of aid. It bothered me
> so much, having to kick them out, even though we were both doing all

we could. At first they thought they were getting to stay in a cottage at a church camp, where they could be groundskeepers. The kids were excited about having room to run, and I told them if they got it they could have my dog. They needed something to hold on to. But that job fell through. They were devastated. For a while they stayed in a summer rental, but it was not insulated and had no heat. So when cold weather came, the pipes froze and they had to find someplace else. Then they stayed with friends for a while, but that ended up in hard feelings because of too many people in too little space for too long a time. I hear they have moved about a half dozen places in the past four or five months. Both parents keep looking for work, but can't find more then part-time, temporary work at low wages. I heard things were pulling apart for them. I do not know where they are at now or what has happened to them. I just know they could have made it with the right help.

There are three residential patterns of rural poverty: open country residential clusters, small villages, and trailer parks (Fitchen 1991). Homeless and poverty-stricken children and families in New Hampshire were consistently found in these three areas. Community research about the homeless and near-homeless has revealed that there is a great deal of movement from one small town apartment to another, from one village to another, from trailer part to trailer park, from trailer park to village, to open country to village again, and so on. It is usually the lower-income people in these settings who are doing the most moving. Their moves tend to be circumscribed within a fairly localized region, usually within a few adjacent counties.

Generally, young adults appear to be the most mobile in rural areas, for they are the ones dealing with the most difficult situations of poverty and stress, trying to support themselves and their children on inadequate employment or meager welfare.

In New Hampshire, the only area in which most families could cut back on their expenditures was in housing. Food costs had been cut to the bone, they did not buy new clothes or cars, and money for recreation was virtually nonexistent. As one principal of a rural elementary school pointed out, "Parents move in order to find cheaper housing, thinking that will ease their economic problems. But it does not ease their burdens enough, so they continue to look for even more affordable housing."

Rural residential mobility, especially among the homeless, is on too fine a scale and is too recent a phenomenon to be documented in any census or other statistical material (Fitchen 1991). In order to find more affordable housing, crossing county or state lines is common. Yet every such move may result in the unexpected loss of services. Moves across county lines require a great deal of paperwork, trips to the county seat, delays and confusion in transferring assistance such as AFDC, welfare, food stamps, or medicaid. Some forms of housing rental assistance are not transferable. Moves across school district lines cause problems for children staying in school or learning in the curriculum of the new school.

Fitchen (1991) alleges that the higher numbers of urban poor who move to rural areas (especially in small towns closer to metropolitan areas) is becoming a national trend. Such in-migration increases the likelihood of rural homelessness because it uses the existing service delivery system beyond its capabilities. When poor people move to rural areas seeking cheaper housing and a better quality of life, the outlay for service and welfare costs is on the receiving community. This also reduces the cost for the community from which the newcomers came. "This trend is nowhere sufficiently documented or studied," according to Fitchen (1991, 148).

Housing problems that plague urban areas also create homelessness in rural areas. However, there are more options available in urban areas than in small towns. Rural areas have fewer places of residence—and fewer social service resources to help people through times of distress.

eight

Getting the Rural Homeless the Help They Need

It is difficult, if not impossible, to get homeless people in rural areas the help they need. Rural areas are poorer, have fewer professionals and services, and consist of residents who are more resistant to using formal organizations in times of crisis. Once homeless, families run into economic and bureaucratic mazes that are impossible to manuever. While help is "supposed" to be available, time and time again, rural families and children experience insurmountable barriers to receiving aid. Personal problems, economic distress, and a lack of affordable housing can be addressed when there is a human service delivery system that "works." However, for many rural people who are at imminent risk of homelessness, the system just doesn't work. My respondents learned that it was often a waste of time for them even to ask for help. As one mother reported, "there were always loopholes" that made her family ineligible for receiving aid. And when they did qualify, "it takes so long to get the help that you could die in the meantime," one father told me.

A person needing services who is poorly educated, new to a community, disabled, or lacking in interpersonal skills will have difficulty successfully utilizing a fragmented human service system. It is convenient to blame the homeless for having personal characteristics that made them somehow at "fault" for not using the system "right." But as a human service administrator with a postdoctoral degree, frequently I could not find information or resources that I thought "must" exist. There is no central depository of information about all of the programs that one might use; there is no uniform qualification criteria for accessing services; there is no single place or person to go to in order to find out the whats, hows, whens, and wheres of the service delivery system. This is true for professionals and recipients alike. So while the homeless sometimes do not know how to find the help they

FRED BLOISE

need through the web of services that could benefit them, not accessing resources was more a matter of system failure than personal failure.

Why are rural services often inadequate in providing comprehensive services to homeless families? What I observed in New Hampshire reflects a national pattern of human service delivery in small towns. The Center for the Study of Social Policy (1991)[1] alleges that the overriding problem is that a myriad of services have been created at the federal and state level with no direction for them, or capacity to manage them, as a *system* at the local level. For instance, no one is in charge of local community services for children and families. No one oversees the totality or has the responsibility for overall outcomes. Instead, many agencies oversee a limited number of services. What results is a system of multiple, disconnected program strategies. Differing philosophies and perspectives about families, housing distress, and economic problems prompt agencies to operate in very different and sometimes contradictory ways.

This means that those who need services must go to many organizations located in different places, where they must provide the same intake information countless times to professionals who do not talk to one another. The rules and guidelines are different in every location, and each agency responds differently to the client.

Most communities do not have clear policy directions about what should be done for people at imminent risk of homelessness. Community leaders allow each organization to decide the who, what, when, why, and how of service delivery. Most organizations react to situations within their own single-agency vision. Seldom is there a network of community visionaries who lead the agencies in a singular direction for action and policy within the community. The fragmented service system has no effective way to respond to new and emerging child and family problems (Center for the Study of Social Policy 1991).

While there may be fewer homeless people in rural areas, their human service needs are just as acute as those experienced by urban dwellers. Yet, the resources are not always present to provide the variety of services rural people need. In many rural communities, the entire spectrum of community and human services operates under increasing stress. Problems grow worse when money, staff, and institutional capacity have not grown as rapidly as the needs. Time after time, I witnessed the impact of this fragmentation on the lives of the homeless. Rural areas acutely feel the shortages of preventive services, promotional services, family services, mental health treatment, health care, rehabilitative services, crisis and respite services, educational programs, and transitional services (U.S. House 1990; Fitchen 1991). Those who sought and those who provided services all felt frustrated about the system failures. However, the providers consistently demonstrated a need to defend and justify the system inadequacies. As a result, rural areas have looked to programmatic developments that have been successfully used in urban areas in order to help them grapple with social problems that have migrated to their villages.

But adopting urban program development and decision-making models may not have been in the best interests of small town communities. "Perhaps the most significant trend in human services in recent years, an insidious and far reaching trend that has especially major impact on rural areas, is the application of economic rationality and a balance sheet mentality to the provision of services" (Fitchen 1991, 154). Because the cost-effectiveness model judges a program's worth not in terms of what it does for people or communities but in terms of how much it costs per person served, it aggravates the effect of the higher costs of rural services. This contributes to the increasing centralization of services, and as a result leaves some rural populations underserved.

The "cost-effectiveness" model and "efficiency" emphasis—which has been promoted both within the business sector as well as in the government itself—has been used within the rural human services as if they were businesses, not care-giving institutions. It is more costly to serve small, dispersed populations of poor people than large, concentrated ones. Because of the higher per person cost and the smaller number of persons to be served, decisions are made at the federal, state, and local levels that "we simply cannot afford to serve those in rural areas" (Fitchen 1991, 157).

This shift has resulted in a variety of negative impacts on distribution of services for low-income residents in rural areas: (1) the small town neighbor-helping-neighbor model has been replaced with an impersonal, money-oriented business approach; (2) many people will not know where to go for help if help is not available nearby; (3) if the geographic distances are too far or too difficult, people will not seek help even when services are available; (4) cost-containment efforts have resulted in the setting of standards or qualifications for entitlement, which end up limiting who can receive services. These small town changes have been imported from the business of government. As a result, the nature of interpersonal communication around helping those in need has changed, the number of people who were just squeaking by has decreased, and rural poverty has increased.

As national economic crises filtered down to small towns, and as federal housing policies directly influenced the housing shortage in rural areas, federal funding decisions affected local human services. Just as the federal decision to declare War on Poverty reduced rural poverty, the problems experienced in rural areas during the 1990s were born a decade or two earlier because of federal decision making.

Under President Reagan and President Bush's new federalism, federal support of local communities declined. Using 1980 as a benchmark, researchers showed how federal spending for human services decreased by 66 percent and loan guarantees by 41 percent. The Budget Reconciliation Act converted seventy-seven categorical human service grants to nine new block grants. Sixty programs were eliminated. In 1987, general revenue sharing was eliminated with equally dramatic results. Cuts in local services were dramatic, and states were forced to adjust to declining federal support (Butler 1992).

The federal government does supply substantial aid to rural areas—but it is focused primarily on agriculture, to the exclusion of more broad-based support. The dollar share of federal funding that goes to rural areas is approximately equal to the proportion of rural people in the U.S. population. However, farm programs receive nearly half of the nonentitlement funds going to rural areas. Those engaged in farming number only 2 percent of the nation's population and less than

9 percent of the nonmetropolitan population. More than 70 percent of federal spending in rural America is actually a redistribution of income to individuals in the form of transfer payments, such as farm subsidies, Social Security, and welfare, rather than a grant of funds directly to rural governments or to nonprofit organizations (Butler 1992). If farm programs and entitlements are excluded, less than 10 percent of the remainder of federal funding goes to rural areas of less than twenty thousand people. Only 5 percent of federal spending on human resources goes to rural areas, despite the fact that they house over 16 percent of the population. As agriculture continues to decline or disappear as the economic base in rural communities, there is an increased need to provide a variety of human services to those who live in rural areas (Sherman 1992; Flora et al. 1992).

In their book on *The New Class War: Reagan's Attack on the Welfare State and Its Consequences,* Frances Fox Piven and Richard Cloward discuss how the Reagan administration and its big business allies declared war on the unemployed, the unemployable, and the working poor. While Reagan's administration cited "fraud and abuse" as reasons for fiscal cuts, "the real budget cuts were not directed against these problems. They were directed against the recipients of welfare state benefits" (1982, 6). In particular, this meant single women with children—the largest group of the rural homeless.

As a result of federal appropriations a decade ago, Congress slashed $140 billion from the social programs between 1982 and 1984—more than half of it from the income maintenance programs that provided low-income people with cash, food, health care, and low-cost housing. Then they cut $45 billion in 1983, and $30 billion more in 1984 to "achieve a balanced budget." No balanced budget resulted. What remained was an institutional system that could no longer adequately serve the poor, the minorities, and families—especially those in rural areas. The increases of homelessness, drug use, and crime, can be legitimately attributed to the programmatic cuts a decade before. The Bush-Reagan legacy is that of destroying the infrastructure that supported the backbone of society—families and children.

These decisions were not made because national leaders were unaware of the crises experienced by parents and children. These cuts occurred *after* recognition that American families were in trouble. More than a decade ago, Congress enacted legislation to guarantee support for children in troubled families. This support was to take place in homes within the community—a model that was ideal for rural areas. Children and families were to be provided basic and supplementary services that are essential to their survival.

Rural areas are microcosms of the national agenda. Under the new federalism, it was no surprise to find a social service backlash that was particularly problematic for women, children, and rural areas (Faludi 1991). As an example of the ramifications of this backlash, consider the experiences of the United States Select Committee on Children, Youth, and Families. They wanted to know: Are children receiving quality services when they are entrusted to the child welfare system? Can troubled children and families rely on human service agencies to help them cope with the host of new and complex problems which threaten their stability?

"Our findings are alarming," reads the report (U.S. House 1990). The report describes agencies in crisis and services that fail families and their children. The promise extended a decade ago was not kept, and children are paying the price of this failure. Chief among their findings is that today's social and economic conditions are hurting large numbers of American families. Our current child welfare, mental health, and juvenile justice systems must now deal with problems that they were not created for and are ill prepared to address. Mounting child poverty, child abuse, and the devastating impact that alcohol and drug abuse are having on families propel children out of the home at an escalating rate. Children are subject to be removed from their homes because of their families' problems, which come to the attention of authorities when a family has no place to live. Other children run away to flee untreated domestic problems.

Congressional leaders found, in many cases, effective services are in short supply, "skimming the surface of the need." Regardless of the system—welfare, health, education, child protection—the lament was the same: where services exist, they were generally ineffective, inappropriate, or inefficient. The range of services is frequently limited, with critical services being unavailable or unattainable. There was very little coordination among the systems that are mandated to serve families, and there is usually no plan to determine which agencies should be responsible for service to a particular child. Consequently, families are unserved, underserved, or served inappropriately. The National Law Center on Homelessness and Poverty (1993) found that homeless families are increasingly trapped in a system of emergency care that offers little chance of escape. Insufficient services and programs that have a negative effect on family unity abound in place of humane, effective programming. In another study (Meade 1993), it was found that 75 percent of clients had their benefits terminated before the end of the first year. This phenomenon, when unrelated to financial eligibility, is known as churning. It occurs because of computerization failure, or

over-quick termination of appropriate clients. A lack of service coordination and integration hinders the success of homeless families
(Molnar, Hartman, and Klein 1988).

While there is little doubt that economic and social trends are fuel-
ing a collapse in children's services, the U.S. House of Representatives
found that many aspects of human services remain in our control. But
they found that federal oversights were great and funding of such
services was weak to nonexistent. There are too few resources in the
service systems designed to meet the increasingly complex needs of
children. Too many of the services that do exist are uncoordinated, inefficient, and ultimately ineffective. These deficiencies waste money
and give rise to inadequate care and potentially dangerous situations
that jeopardize hundreds of thousands of children.

Still, the acknowledgment of child and family distress in mainstream and rural America has not resulted in fiscal action. If anything,
the failures of the system have become justifications for not providing
more support to those programs that try to help those in imminent risk
(Limbaugh 1993).

Consider the range of ways that the political process has inadver-
tently facilitated the rise of homeless rural children and families: Funding for child welfare systems that provide prevention and reunification
support has not yet reached the 1980 authorized level of $226 million.
While the number of youths in juvenile facilities increased 27 percent
between 1979 and 1987, funding for the federal Juvenile Justice and
Delinquency Prevention Act has declined from more than $100 mil-
lion in 1979 to $66.7 million in 1989. Aid for Dependent Children
(AFDC) was reduced by $3.6 billion. Food stamp benefits were reduced
for 20 million people. An analysis of the 1987 benefit levels of AFDC
prepared by the Center on Social Welfare Policy and Laws found that in
forty-one states the combined value of AFDC and food stamps is below
75 percent of the poverty level, and there was no state in which the combined value even equals 100 percent of the official poverty level (Taylor
1988). AFDC benefit levels are now far below the poverty level in all
states, and the gap between benefits and the national median income is
widening. In almost every state, the full monthly AFDC benefit is insufficient to cover housing costs. The annual cost of living increases in food
stamp benefits have not offset the loss of AFDC benefits (Center on
Social Welfare Policy and Law 1993). AFDC grants are too low for families to find affordable housing. The ability of poor people to find adequate housing has drastically declined over the past decade.

According to federal data tabulated by the Center for Law and
Social Policy, one eligible family in twenty is getting the child care as-

sistance promised. This means that many former AFDC mothers are spending a large portion of their meager wages to pay for day care, leaving their children in the care of people who are not good care providers, or leaving them to fend for themselves. Many others still on AFDC are dissuaded from taking paying jobs because there is no one they can rely on to watch their children. In California during 1990, 25,474 families went off AFDC because the mother took a job, but only 875 got child care assistance. In Ohio, 6,840 graduated from welfare to paid employment, but only 197 received child care benefits.

The federal welfare reform law, the Family Support Act of 1988 (or JOBS program), was to provide additional federal support for state education, training, and employment efforts for AFDC families. The program began in late 1989, and its scope, quality, and effectiveness depends primarily on the willingness of each state to invest its own matching funds in programs that address recipients' employment and training needs. It was billed as a liberal-conservative grand compromise in which liberals agreed to demand that welfare recipients able to work must take jobs and conservatives agreed to become more generous with money to lubricate the transition. The Family Support Act established training programs and even authorized giving welfare recipients subsidized jobs. But only 430,000 of the nation's 4.6 million welfare recipients were enrolled three years after the program's inception. Of those that did participate, less than 5 percent got on-the-job experience. Many recipients, such as parents of young children, are exempt. And for those who aren't, states prefer education programs to actual job training (*Wall Street Journal* 1993). The Job Opportunities and Basic Skills program has possibilities of truly helping the needy, but while participants feel that being in the program was a positive experience, afterwards they are still met with barriers to employment and transportation and child care problems (Stricki 1994).

Even remedial programs are not as successful as they need to be, and they are seldom found in rural areas. The Job Training Partnership Act (JTPA) was to improve basic academic and vocational skills of disadvantaged youths and adults, but current funding is adequate to serve only 5 percent of the eligible population. The program's current allocation formula fails to direct funds to the geographic areas where they are most needed—and it does not focus on rural areas. Its emphasis on short-term results discourages most communities from developing truly comprehensive training efforts that could be more effective in helping families permanently escape poverty (National Commission for Employment Policy 1990). While the Job Training for the Homeless Demonstration Program (JTHDP) has been relatively successful in some areas, future job training programs will need to provide a wide array of services, including housing assistance and follow-up support (Employment and Training Administration 1994).

The Job Corps has a good record in training young high school dropouts with poor employment prospects, but it has funding to serve only 40,000 of the 750,000 adolescents who drop out of school each year. The Job Corps is another program more often found in urban areas. In depressed areas, or in rural areas where private sector employment is scarce, even the most ambitious programs are likely to have little impact. Poor families in rural communities are particularly likely to be bypassed by these new initiatives because the federal law does not require states to operate such programs in remote areas.

Even programs that are clearly successful have not been met with federal financial support. WIC's essential food for infants program and Head Start have been cut and do not serve all of the people who could benefit from such programs.

The decline in federal support to rural areas has led to increased state demands to promote economic development (Fitchen 1991; Flora et al. 1990). But state policy cannot substitute for an effective national rural policy. The people in small towns can only be taxed so much to increase state appropriations. After a while, they simply have no more money to provide to the state kitty; local money cannot substitute for federal dollars. The rural human service delivery problems are largely a result of problems foisted upon them by a federal, professional audience. But some delivery problems are homegrown.

Little towns have a formal and an informal infrastructure that can be mobilized to assist those in need. A major reason that rural officials do not see the homeless in their towns is that they are kept invisible through the help of informal helping networks. Most people prefer to do for themselves for as long as possible. Therefore, many people who are in extreme housing distress are never identified by agencies who could help them.

Rural residents have a long tradition of pride, preferring self-help and reliance upon relatives, friends, and neighbors over professional intervention. This self-help orientation effectively disguises the magnitude of the rural homeless problem. If there are no professionals to help those in distress, then those in distress will never be identified as homeless and in need of services. If people prefer to help each other without seeking formal help, it can be perceived that no such problems exist in the community.

In rural communities, the "we take care of our own" value orientation stems from times when rural people depended upon one another in order to survive. The rural ideology of self-care was exemplified across America during the Great Depression of the 1930s. My grandparents, for example, were not adversely affected during the Depression because they grew their own produce and raised chickens and cows. Often, less fortunate friends, relatives, and acquaintances would drop by at dinner time, knowing that Grandma Grace wouldn't let them leave hungry. They always had an endless stream of extra hands to help them mend a fence or harvest a field or tend to the children (who actually took care of themselves). Grandpa Mel gave some fruit trees to one man, who used them to create what is today the town's largest greenhouse. It cost Grandpa nothing, but it gave the man a chance at dignity and self-sufficiency.

In 1992 *Readers Digest* published a story called "Kindling Spirit" that illustrates the attitude. A granddaughter wrote her remembrances of her grandparents during the Depression. Their central Pennsylvania farm brought "an unending flow of men out of work," and instead of giving handouts to the needy men, they always pointed to a stack of firewood and asked that the visitor move it to the other side of the fence as a way of earning his meal. "Grandma says she doesn't remember how many strangers they shared a meal with during those Depression days—or how many times that stack of wood got moved," the author wrote. More important than the food they shared was the dignity the couple allowed the men who had done honest work for their meal.

Services can be provided in ways that give dignity and integrity to the recipients. Perhaps that caring spirit is easier to convey when one regards others as neighbors. But in many rural communities, not everyone is considered a neighbor. Sometimes, people cannot help those in need. The informal network of help that is provided by family and friends keeps afloat thousands of rural people who are in housing distress. The professional human service system assists many people, but many others fall through the cracks and do not get helped. While the people I interviewed told me stories about the assistance that they had received from "wonderful, caring people," I heard many more stories about how they had been failed by those who could have helped them.

Who constitutes a neighbor is no longer clear, as the rural sense of intimate community has eroded. People who don't know one another well don't just "drop by" for a handout, the way they did at Grandma's table. Bringing strangers in to eat with the family no longer occurs in rural areas. With urban violence encroaching on rural areas, people outside of one's intimate network who pop in unexpectedly now are a source of suspicion and fear (Hassinger 1982). As small towns have been identified as utopias by those fleeing troubles or urban lifestyles, longtime residents now find that they do not know their neighbors well. There are "strangers" living next door. Newcomers are not readily accepted and are looked upon with suspicion until they "prove" themselves. As Becker (1963) notes, "outsiders" are treated differently from "insiders," who are thought to be more "like us."

But the feeling of neighborliness is also declining among people who know each other. Over the last two decades, changing technology has eliminated the need for routine community building efforts, such as harvesting, house raising, and lumbering. Machines will now do what people used to do for one another. The intimate relationships of people helping people appear to be declining in rural areas as a direct result of technological advancements. The corner store has been replaced with supermarkets, and it is harder to find a sense of familiarity with one's mail carrier, salesclerks, or mechanic.

Even so, data on rural households suggest that demands placed upon friends and families have actually escalated in the 1980s and 1990s (Fitchen 1991; Flax et al. 1979). But it is hard to be your brother's keeper when you are barely keeping your own head above troubled water. As a father of three who had housed his sister-in-law and her family for two months stated: "It is not that we won't take care of them [homeless relatives]; we simply can't. The house is too small to accommodate my family, much less two families. And I can barely put food on the table for my own. What am I supposed to do, make them sit in the other room and stare at us while we eat and they don't?"

Frequently help is denied not by hard hearts but because the requests exceed that which the imposed-upon family can provide (Conger and Elder 1994). Just because people ask more for help from the informal network does not mean that help will be delivered, as Sally found out: "I tried everything I could to make it on my own without asking for help. First I asked my family for help. They gave me what they could, but after a while, they could give no more. Then I asked my friends to help us. They too helped for a while, but most of them were not much better off than we were. I went from friend to friend, moving down the list of people who might be able to help, finally asking people I barely knew. At last, the only thing left to do was to ask total strangers for help."

Human services have taken on a changing role in rural communities. The key to understanding relief-giving programs is in the functions they serve for the larger economic, social, and political orders, for relief is a secondary and supportive institution. Formal, large-scale human services have not been part of rural culture. Families and friends helped each other, or charity was provided through churches.

Highly formalized human service is a relatively new phenomenon in rural areas. Because this formalized type of service relies on professional expertise, urban newcomers to the community wish to assume caregiving positions. Because they are strangers to the community and they rely on an impersonal mode of interpersonal exchange, relief programs are sometimes not used even when they would be beneficial.

While professional assistance may be helpful, Piven and Cloward (1971) assert that most social welfare activity has not greatly aided the poor; indeed, many "social welfare" programs have ridden roughshod over the poor instead of aiding them. For classic examples of this point, consider how New Deal agricultural subsidies resulted in the displacement of great numbers of tenant farmers and sharecroppers, or how urban renewal schemes deprived poor and minority peoples of their urban neighborhoods. People are told that the programs will help them, but in actuality, many human service programs do more for those who fund them than for the recipients. In rural areas, decisions about what social and health services to provide are often made by governmental leaders, not human service experts. There are almost 39,000 rural governments, including those for towns, townships, municipalities, and counties. Eighty-six percent of these serve populations of less than ten thousand. Fifty percent serve populations of less than one thousand (Butler 1992). Given small budgets, local leaders decide how to allocate monies for needed services.

In theory, the services provided by local government are determined by the needs and demands of citizens in the local community. In reality, the types of services that a local government provides are often mandated by the federal and state government. Local communities cannot choose whether to provide clean air and water, or schools that incorporate special populations. These mandates are developed from federal and state initiatives (Butler 1992). This leaves the leaders to make difficult decisions about whether to fund human service programs—programs that can be regarded as extraneous, in that they do not stem from any official mandate.

As rural jobs are lost, tax revenue declines—but demand increases for community services such as job training, welfare, counseling, and housing (Butler 1992). This puts greater stress on local citizens to help, meaning that local leaders may have to decide which programs to have and which ones to avoid, and at what levels of funding. What an "opportunity," according to one town selectman: "With this piddly pot of money, we are supposed to choose whether to fund a new school, fix the potholes in the roads, buy a new police car, support the health clinic, fund drug abuse prevention programs, . . . and help the homeless. All these things are important, but when you are forced to choose, you've got to choose the services that will help the most people."

Rural leaders believe that the homeless should be helped. But it would be convenient if they lived, and were helped, somewhere else. It has been easier for communities not to see the rural homeless. If they don't see them, then nothing will have to be done for them. The good will of many small towns is severely strained, as leaders wrestle with their consciences and depleting budgets. There is also the concern that once homeless services are provided, the town will become a magnet, drawing homeless from all over the region (Kilman and Johnson 1991). One city welfare director pointed out how:

> I feel we have done a good job to help homeless families. They come here and know they will be treated right, and that they will get help—as much as we can, anyway. But the [community leaders] tell me that I shouldn't do such a good job, because now homeless people from all over the region come to our town because the word is out that we will take care of them. So my helping hand has become a double-edged sword. The people love me and the politicians hate me. I'm told to leave well enough alone, and they threaten to cut my budget—because if there is less money, then I can serve fewer people. Then the word will get out that my town isn't a good one for homeless people, and maybe they will stay in their own towns instead of coming here.

This not-in-my-backyard (NIMBY) orientation goes along well with the perception that rural areas have somehow escaped the problems found in urban areas. For instance, in Iowa a study was conducted to determine the number of homeless. In one small town that had the largest number, this finding was vehemently denied. "Homeless people are on the street. We don't have that problem," said the president of the local bank. Similarly, in another small town, town officials shunned the idea of a homeless shelter because "we are a wonderful place to live. It is hard for me to see our homeless the same as those in a big city" (Kilman and Johnson 1991a:1).

Rural families and children who are homeless want to take care of themselves; they do not want to live on the dole. But sometimes short-term assistance is needed; national welfare statistics indicate that most people who have to go on welfare receive assistance for less than two years (U.S. Department of Welfare 1994). Between 1988 and 1992 in New Hampshire, food stamp caseloads increased 70 percent; Aid to Families with Dependent Children (AFDC) went up 130 percent, and Medicaid increased more than 400 percent (Duncan et al. 1993). When parents are in trouble, and their kids become hungry and homeless, interviewed parents said they had no choice but to "swallow their pride" and ask for help. Family, then friends, were first asked for help. But for most, this informal network was not able to help them to fend off the problems that eventually would lead to their homelessness.

It was difficult for all of the parents I talked with to seek professional assistance for their problems. Asking an agency professional for help is a rite of passage seen as signifying the transition from having manageable troubles to being unable to make it on your own. For rural people who have worked all their lives, applying for welfare is more than embarrassing. It can be a humiliating, stigmatizing event. People who provided monetary aid to the homeless did so in a way that made the recipients feel that the money was "doled out as if the money was coming straight out of their own pocket." Asking for help, one woman recalled, made her feel like a "beggar to total strangers who can pat themselves on the back because they helped some 'loser' like me."

In order to keep their personal troubles from becoming public problems, rural people prefer to ask friends, relatives, ministers, doctors, or teachers when they need help. While small towns seldom have formal social service systems, they do have highly developed informal referral networks that can be used to assist people in need. It is "kinder and gentler" for people to ask folks they know—who probably know about their troubles anyway—for help than to ask total strangers for assistance.

Asking for help destroys people's feelings of integrity, especially when those who are providing the assistance make them feel that they are not as good as those who do not have to ask for help, the rural parents told me. When asking for help, one is often forced to play "true confessions" with the person providing the help, as one mother reported: "I just asked for a place for us to stay so I could get things together. I didn't ask for them to do anything else. They [shelter workers] decided that if we were to stay, I had to tell them all kinds of personal information. We didn't feel lots of it was any of their business, or had any relevance to why we were there. The kinds of stuff they asked us should have had little to do with putting us up for a couple of nights."

Asking for help got to be a game, some parents told me. If you gave the right answers, you could get help. If you gave the wrong ones (answers the staff didn't like), then you were "out on your ear." Moreover, you were supposed to act eternally grateful for the help, as indicated by a forty-two-year-old man with a wife and seven children who found there is no free lunch, even when you are homeless:

I went from agency to agency, and from church to church, asking for help. These places all want to know about your work history, your money, troubles you got into when you were twelve, your sex life—anything to find dirt on you. When I got mad about the questions and the waiting list to get emergency help, they told me if I didn't want to cooperate, I could just leave and get nothing. The churches all expected me to love Jesus and become regular churchgoers at their church if they gave me clothes or food. They would give help once, but if you don't show your face on Sunday morning, there won't be no more help. Guaranteed. Nobody gives something for nothing; everybody wants something in return.

And while seeking aid is supposed to be confidential, in small towns often it is not. One social worker told me: "Everybody in town knows what our office does. We are, fortunately or unfortunately, located right in the middle of town. So if anybody sees you walk through the door, they know why. The gossip is out on the street before you are."

The behavior of the homeless sometimes contributed to their not getting help when they went to the agency to ask for it. Most of the time, in serving the rural homeless, professionals were confronted with quiet, well-behaved, passive individuals who were grateful for whatever kindness that was given to them. Once in a while, however, the frustration became too great. After biting the bullet to ask for assistance and finding themselves shot down, the homeless may disintegrate into emotional outbursts, crying, or cursing. Sometimes their "unacceptable behavior" may be reasons cited for failing to give them more services. But as one nurse indicated,

If you and I were in the same situation, I would do more than curse and pound my fist on the desk. Given the situation they are in, the homeless people have a right to be upset. They are human beings. So many agencies fail to treat them with respect and dignity. We try to help them keep their integrity here. Just because they are homeless doesn't mean that they should be treated with any less courtesy and assistance than would the bank president. If we treat the homeless person differently than we would the most influential person—then it really is our problem, not the person who is homeless.

Those who work with the homeless are, by virtue of having jobs and homes themselves, one-up over their clients. In rural areas, many professionals are from more urban environments and have a greater difficulty relating to the lifestyles of the rural homeless (Flax and Wagenfield 1979; Patton 1987). As Boxill notes, even those who were once homeless who now work as providers can hold power and authority over them, which can disrupt human relations.

Rural communities are much more likely to provide assistance to local folks than to people who are just passing through town. Transients requiring assistance can be easily given the short shrift. Why are outsiders not given the same kind of support as local residents? One shelter director reported:

> Before I came to this job, I thought it was awful that transients were given short answers and bare minimum services in order to encourage them to move on to urban areas. But now, I see that there are not enough beds, there's not enough low-income apartments, there are not enough jobs, there is simply not enough of anything to go around for all the people who need help. So we have to make decisions about who is a priority. People from town, or who have family in the area, or who have job skills or who have families—these folks are our priority. People who are not from here, who have little possibility of supporting themselves, are not folks we are going to put at the top of the list for services. It would be better for many of them to relocate to other places where there are better options for them. So I now find myself doing the same thing that I once condemned, because it is the only thing that can be done to serve the most people in the most constructive way for the community.

Some small towns encourage transients to move on by giving them bus fare to the nearest city, arresting persons until deportation can be executed, rousing persons from where they stay, and providing few, if any, helping services. Nonurban places may be hostile to homeless outsiders (Roth et al. 1986). As one homeless man pointed out: "I have been homeless in big cities and in small ones. And I've got to tell you, the worst place to be homeless is in little towns. They've got nothing, and they treat you the worst. Without a doubt."

The homeless in rural areas avoided using social service professionals for as long as possible. Professionals are often urban immigrants who know little about the community, people, or their way of life, and are subject to suspicion and distrust (Vissing, Salloway, and Siress 1992; Vissing, Salloway, and Siress 1993; Farley et al. 1982; Flax et al. 1979). Seeking professional intervention may be regarded as a sign of personal failure or that one's personal life has become unmanageable (Vissing, Salloway, and Hudson 1991).

As previously noted, in rural areas there is a poor network of information. It is hard to know whether there are no services available that would help or they exist and are just very difficult to find. As one professional man told me, "It is an absolute maze to find out if, or where, the most basic services exist. It is total frustration to work with inane rules, callous workers, and folks who are not the sharpest crackers in the can."

When the homeless did seek services, I found that they often sat back quietly, waited their turn, and were not forceful about demanding their rights and services. They were not belligerent or rude, unless unreasonably provoked by insensitive staff members. However, this polite approach did not necessarily work well when the agency did not want to serve another poor, displaced person. Consider this case of a young man who was a diabetic who sought help from a social service agency:

> Randy was referred to the social service agency by a health agency. He went early to the morning appointment and waited. The counselor had appointments open, but Randy did not know how to make it clear to the receptionist what he needed. He just sat and waited. At lunch he asked where the counselor was, and she had gone out for lunch. Having no money and no lunch, he waited, believing that when the counselor came back that she would see him. But she began seeing her regular clients. At the end of the day—after sitting there quietly—he learned that she had gone home for the day. Having had nothing to eat all day, he was on the verge of a diabetic attack, when a nurse who was leaving for the night happened to identify what was happening to him and helped him.

Homeless people may not know what questions to ask, or how to fill out paperwork correctly. When they do not use the system "right," they are often penalized. Consider the experience of Joanne and her children, as they sought services:

> Joanne had her children taken away and placed in foster care because she had no place for them to live. When she applied for subsidized housing, she was told she would be contacted whenever something became available. The mother would stop by the office periodically, and she was consistently told that she would be contacted when the time came. The housing authorities finally sent her a letter, informing her that she could now get subsidized housing. She was notified in the letter that she had to be at the housing office at a particular time and date. The mother never received the letter, since she had multiple places to live since the time of her registration. Not knowing about the appointment, and not being told of her status when she stopped by the office on one of her periodic visits, she missed the meeting. As a result, she was taken off the list for housing. Weeks later when she did get the letter, she came and asked for her housing. She was told that she had been removed from the roster, and

that she would have to reapply for housing—and wait her turn again. This was particularly distressing for the mother, who had learned that during the time her thirteen-year-old daughter was in foster care that she became pregnant. The mother felt had her daughter been with her, she would not have become pregnant.

A nurse talked about making the system work for the rural homeless: "It means more than giving them the name of an agency to contact. It means sitting with them and making the phone call. It may mean taking them to the meeting. It may mean going in with them and interfacing with other professionals on their behalf. It may mean sitting down with them and filling out forms and helping them to figure out answers to questions. It is time consuming. But it is often the only way that many of these families will secure the services they need."

But this kind of advocacy is not always met with delight by other professionals. As one provider contemplated, "I know they [the other agency] cringe when they hear that I'm coming over with one of my people. I know if I didn't go with them, they wouldn't get help. While some professionals in the community like working with me, others resent me because they cannot pull the wool over the clients the same way they can for clients who are there by themselves. So many times you have to know about existing services, or use the right buzz words to trigger the other guy to refer the homeless to the right services."

Professionals who work for the homeless often feel frustrated, because they know that there are too few resources available for everyone to get what he or she needs. "When you squeeze out scarce resources for one client, you realize that another client gets bumped down the list who needs that service just as much," said one social worker.

There are a variety of structural factors that keep people who are at imminent risk of homelessness in rural areas from receiving the help that they need. These factors are not interpersonal but are owing to conditions beyond any individual's control.

In rural New England, the homeless, poor, and needy face a dire shortage of all human service providers. "The primary care infrastructure is falling down around us," according to John McCormack, director of Cary Medical Center in Caribou, Maine (Hohler 1992). In many rural areas, it is common to find communities where there is no human service network at all—only a gas station or grocery store. Even when there are services, they tend to be poorly funded and inadequately staffed. In a review of health care for the rural poor, Summer (1991) found limited access to health care, which resulted in poor rural residents using health care services less frequently than poor urban residents.

When federal health programs, such as the National Health Service Corps, Community and Migrant Health Centers, and the Medicaid program are available, these programs do not function as well in rural areas as in urban areas. In a study of mental health service delivery, it was found that barriers for service for the homeless are not the same in rural and urban areas. There was a lower tolerance in rural areas of people who did fit into the existing system of care, which sometimes has led to their confinement (Belcher and McCleese 1988).

Even relatively low numbers of homeless individuals and families can easily overwhelm a rural community's sparse resources (Patton 1987). According to one welfare director,

> We are expected to take care of an increasing number of clients with fewer and fewer resources. They have cut our money to the bone, and more people are in trouble. Our waiting list is unacceptably long. Even when we finally get people into the office, it takes forever to get them the services they need. People in crisis need help *now*. The system is not designed to provide immediate gratification. It can take weeks to get food stamps, months—or even years—to get into subsidized housing. They come here as a last resort. If it takes so long to get them back on their feet, what do they do between the time they come here and the time we can get them back on their feet? It is that gap in between that is the worst.

The lack of services and professional helpers exists for all human services, be they in mental health, physical health, or social health. For instance, there are few mental health professionals in rural areas; only 3 percent of the nation's psychiatrists practice in rural areas. Although the law establishing community mental health centers mandates rural services, only 13 percent of the funded centers claim to serve people in primarily rural catchment areas. Those centers are poorly staffed, offer fewer services, and are few and far between. In a federally sponsored review of all community mental health centers, only 17.5 percent of the rural centers were rated as adequate. Barriers in mental health services in rural areas limit their use to as few as 5 percent of those in need actually being served (Rosenblatt and Moscovice 1978).

In rural areas, there are fewer physicians available than in urban centers, and one may have to travel considerable distances to find a doctor. Because there are fewer doctors in rural areas, it is difficult to find one who will accept new patients. If a doctor has few openings for new patients, those openings may be reserved for patients who have good insurance. Medicaid and medicare require that many complex forms be submitted in order to get reimbursed. Even then, the rates for reimbursement are often lower than regular insurance companies pay.

"Basic health care has grown dangerously elusive in rural New England," according to Hohler (1992:a1). "The problem is severe. Isolated, rural populations are being ignored or poorly served, and unfortunately, the trend is not promising," according to the associate dean of medicine at the University of New England (Hohler 1992:a1). Nearly 413,000 rural New Englanders are at risk, according to "Lives in the Balance," a report issued by the National Association of Community Health Centers. Of those at risk, 220,000 are considered medically underserved because of physician shortages or poor health brought on by impoverishment. With 31 percent of the U.S. population, rural America has 12 percent of the doctors—one doctor per 2,400 persons, five times fewer than found in urban areas. More than 135 rural counties were found to have no doctor at all (Farley 1992). From 1980 to 1988, 161 of the nation's 2,700 rural hospitals had been forced to close, and 600 more were on the brink of closure (Fitchen 1991, 155).

Even though most of the homeless children interviewed were often sick, "we can't afford to take them to the doctor, so we wait and hope they will get better," the parents report. However, the lack of preventive care typically exacerbated the illnesses into serious, preventable disorders. When professional help becomes essential, "we go to the emergency room." For a variety of reasons, primary health practitioners are not typically available for homeless children and families. Homeless families may be newcomers to an area or may not have a family physician. Given that the homeless usually have no money or insurance, providers may opt not to serve them. Public health clinics may not be available in rural areas. People may have to travel many miles to find such a clinic, only to learn that they live outside of the catchment area and do not qualify for service. If clinics exist, they may serve younger children, leaving older children without any sort of health care coverage.

The lack of professional service providers puts an even greater demand on the few professionals and resources that do exist in the rural area (Farley 1992). Teachers, ministers, and police departments in rural areas are under even greater demand to provide a variety of human services (Reynolds, Bank, and Murphree 1976). They provide services that are outside of their job functions—and outside of their area of expertise—because no other social service system exists for people in need there. Rural workers find themselves expected to be all things to all people, because they may be the only professionals in the area who can be contacted in times of crisis. As one social worker in the only agency for a sixty-five-mile radius noted,

> I am really a nurse who has become a social worker because there was no one else here to do it. I work with old people, children, families, and single men. I do the fieldwork, the paperwork, the administration, the budget, and the public relations. I have been learning how to program the computer and how to put together a slide show. In rural towns like mine, we do not have many professionals who can help us. We do not have consultant money to hire specialists to assist us. So we are forced to learn how to do all the things that need to be done. We become jacks of all trades.

I learned that many teachers, nurses, and social workers go way beyond the call of duty to help children on the margin. For example, a school counselor told me, "One Friday afternoon a high school student presented herself at my office, indicating she had no where to stay. I called thirty different agencies across the state, and not one would take her. Most of them wouldn't take kids. The places that would were full. So after checking with all those places that they tell you to call if you need help, there was no help for this homeless girl." This type of experience was recited again and again. Most homeless adolescents "know there is no help out there for us, so we have to manage things ourselves."

Managing on your own may be the only alternative if services are far away and you don't have any transportation, I learned. Since there are fewer services in rural areas, those that are available are expected to serve large areas. As previously noted, a single agency can serve a half dozen counties; people who live at the far edge may have to travel hours to get to the service.

Since homeless people may not even be able to afford cars, it is unlikely that they will have reliable transportation to take them long distances to obtain services. In rural areas, the probability of transit systems—or even taxi services—are low. This forces the homeless to ask yet another favor of their friends—to take them into town—or to use their own feet to go sometimes great distances.

In many parts of New Hampshire, not only are distances between services great but the roads themselves are treacherous. Needy people may have to take an eighty-mile trek down winding, two-lane roads through the mountains in order to obtain help. This ride, especially on icy roads in the winter, may prove to be "more trouble than it is worth."

I learned that most little towns do not have shelters. The New Hampshire's Department of Mental Health funds thirty-four shelters throughout the state; this means that few communities have easy access to a shelter. Of those thirty-four shelters, only nine are emergency shelters, which will take in people on the spur-of-the-moment on self-referral. There are also three family shelters, four substance abuse shelters, and six domestic violence shelters for the entire state, and only three programs in the northern, mountainous part of the state (Powell 1994).

Those in need are forced to travel to larger cities or urban areas, such as Boston, for assistance. This process inflates the actual number of urban homeless while reducing the actual number of rural homeless.

One reason that many families do not receive benefits is their difficulty meeting the bureaucratic requirements. "The Bush Administration's Department of Health and Human Services developed written regulations that would make a Soviet appartchick blush" (Kuttner 1991). Every agency has its own criteria that a family must meet in order to qualify for services. Sometimes these are local rules, but often the restrictions come from the federal government. Federal regulations have exacerbated the nutritional problems of families in shelters. In 1986, the U.S. Department of Agriculture started enforcing a rule that required the cost of shelter to be considered as income to families, thus making many ineligible for food stamps. Thousands of families lost their governmental nutrition assistance and were forced to spend more of their scarce money on food, while trying to save for security deposits, new shoes, or doctor bills. For three years Congress blocked the process, but in 1990 Congress relented under USDA pressure and agreed to a compromise: the shelter cost is now counted as income. Generally, this has resulted in families losing most, but not all, of their food stamps. Even of those who use food stamps, only one in ten households meet the recommended dietary requirements. A federal government survey of 2,112 individuals in family shelters who were eligible for food stamps found that 49 percent were not receiving them (U.S. House 1989).

In a separate illustration, if a welfare mother signs up for the official state job-training program mandated by the 1998 Act, she can get the child care benefits—if she is one of the lucky ones. But if she shows initiative and gets a job on her own, she can be excluded from consideration of benefits. By quitting AFDC, an ex-welfare recipient is supposedly free of red tape, but to get the child care aid, she must continue to file regular AFDC forms or will be denied the assistance. A family that gets a child into Head Start will get its income and benefit package recalculated and can lose child care entitlement. If a stepfather is working but the mother is in school, that can trigger a termination of the child care aid. In short, when the mothers attempt to improve the lot of themselves and their families, there are systematic constraints against their doing so. If they fail to take action to work outside the home, they are branded as welfare leeches. There is absolutely no way for a poor mother to win (Kuttner 1991).

Two-parent households found themselves failing to quality for assistance because there were two able-bodied adults in the home. Parents reported time after time how single mothers could get aid easier than could two-parent households. Women were told—not by the professionals, but by people who had attempted to qualify for aid—that "if you have your husband leave you, then you will qualify. If he don't, you won't." The welfare director in one community reported that the government was developing aid programs for two-parent households but that "virtually no one could qualify. And if they could, the bureaucratic mechanism for processing their claims is not in place, so it doesn't do them any good anyway."

The regulations do not end once the homeless family receives subsidized housing, food stamps, or other aid. They are continuously monitored. While this monitoring is appropriate to ensure cost-benefits for both the recipients and the social service system, the violation of minor regulations can be used as a way to get "undesirables" out. For instance, when Mrs. Jones finally moved into a subsidized apartment, she taped over all of the electric plugs so that her children could not get hurt. The building inspector saw the tape and told her to remove it or she would be evicted for lease violations. The mother would not remove the tape, since the felt she would be putting her small children at risk. Besides, she was not damaging the apartment in any way, and she had signed a lease that gave her the right to make it her home. Her landlord disagreed, and their fight ended in the courtroom. Thus, getting aid is not the only problem—keeping it is also a concern.

Services designed to assist children and families and those who may become homeless are often just able to get by financially. While rural people may not hesitate to pay the grocer, plumber, or the lawnmower repairman, the idea of paying for social services is often met with significant resistance. People are used to an informal network of helping; it doesn't seem "right" to rural residents to pay for things that used to be provided free routinely. Also, the rural resident has a relationship with the grocer, plumber, and repairman. This relationship is more of an exchange between equals—or, at least of mutually willing participants. However, seeking help from professionals—who are likely strangers who have a string of "expert" qualifications—for problems that people are embarrassed by creates an uncomfortable exchange for the person in distress. When the outcome is not what people expected, they don't want to pay for services.

Similarly, communities may not want to support services that address problems that they really wish didn't exist. Also, communities simply may not have enough money to pay for all the services that residents may need; when this happens, social services typically take a backseat to "essentials" such as police and fire protection, education, or street repair.

From my experience working with boards of directors of various organizations who assist the homeless, children, families, or the poor, many such organizations live "hand to mouth." They are often not in much better financial condition than those they seek to help. Many organizations scramble to get enough money to survive for a year at a time. In order to do so, boards consider all kinds of possible funding strategies. Unfortunately, some of the options they consider to survive are not in the best interests of either the organization or those they seek to serve.

For many providers, the most logical step in helping the homeless is determining all the things that went wrong in their lives. This pathology model comes from the medical model, in which all sorts of social and personal problems have become regarded as illnesses. The solution for dealing with social diseases has been to treat the person who displays the problems (Conrad 1992).

Such an approach is practiced almost universally in the human service field. Yet, conceptually, we know that there may be nothing pathological about somebody who is merely unfortunate enough to lose his job and have no savings to buffer his family from hard times. "Treatment" may not be as important as prevention; "fixing" the individual may not be as accurate a unit of intervention as fixing the system.

But it is easier to blame the homeless for their lack of housing (Ryan 1976) than it is to look to see what their strengths are. Social workers I worked with found that it was easy to fall into the trap of seeing the "half-empty" glass instead of the "half-full" one, as the following story indicates:

As a social worker, I met Mr. Robinson, who had custody of his four children after his wife skipped town to live with her drug-dealing boyfriend. His developmentally impaired brother lived with them. In order to pay bills, he rented one of the three bedrooms out to a young man who was into drugs. The little girls slept on a mattress in one room, the dad and boys slept in the other bedroom, and the brother slept on the couch in the living room. There were no sheets on any of the mattresses, and a few dirty blankets were used to keep them warm. They had problems making ends meet, and there was little food in the refrigerator or shelves. From my first observation, this family had nothing going for them.

The initial impressions were so overwhelming that it was impossible for me to see anything positive about this family. But as I got to know them, I came to see them differently. This family had been homeless and moved from place to place over many months. When the mom left, the dad buckled down, found an apartment, had a steady job, and gave his kids a greater sense of security than they had experienced in years. The marital conflict was no longer present, and there was a greater sense of peace in the house. The children, who had few clothes or possessions before, were slowly beginning to accumulate items. Sure, the clothes were secondhand and the toys were used, but nonetheless, they had things now. The father went to work every day, thereby showing his kids the importance of a work ethic. Even though he didn't make much and had trouble making ends meet—they were getting by. He got the kids to school on time every day, and the brother was there to meet the kids in the afternoon. The dad no longer used drugs, and while the renter smoked pot, he kept it confined to his bedroom. The father had taken his family a long way from where he was. The love he showed his children and the diligence he took to assure that their basic needs were met was impressive. I did not see it the first time I met him. I was so into looking at what was wrong, I never stepped back to look at what was going right for this family.

Policies, programs, and procedures can all help—or hinder-a family's ability to keep from becoming homeless. The economic, housing, and human service institutions all influence the social conditions that determine to what degree rural people will live on the brink of housing distress.

The difficulties encountered are ultimately the result of no one being accountable on a local level for the welfare of families as a whole and for the results of the services rendered on behalf of them. Local governments do not have the money or authority to provide major services and have abdicated this role to professional agencies. Agencies act under their own professional and funding mandates, which are independent from local control. State agencies have taken responsibility for providing services but have done so in a highly categorical way, thereby providing often too highly specialized and narrowly restricted services. As a result, local government as currently organized cannot by itself resolve these problems and achieve the desired improvements in the lives of at-risk children and their families.

A cycle of rural poverty is created when there are few usable national, state, or local resources by which those on the margin can help themselves. The federal level determines which economic, housing, and human service funding and programs to address. Without a doubt, these structured institutional problems create rural homelessness.

But structural problems create personal problems that make homelessness even more likely. Instead of looking at the causes of homelessness as owing to either structural problems or personal dysfunction, the causes cannot be divorced from one another. We need to look at the coexistence of both in our understanding of what causes homelessness. Without this understanding, social programs to help the rural homeless are doomed to fail.

Some people who are in need refuse to ask for help. Others find that the help is not provided. Yet, somehow, that rural ethic of everyone taking care of each other still is present in the minds of those who live in small towns. It is particularly frustrating for those who believe that there will be help, and none is provided.

A disillusioned father reported: "On the books, the service exists. If you can get in for an appointment. If you can meet the almost impossible criteria for qualifying. If you can get the help when you need it. If you can stand the wait. Then you have to ask—once you've got it, does it even make any difference?"

nine

A Framework for Understanding Rural Homelessness

The stories told by the rural homeless children and families convey themes that can be merged into understandings about the causes and consequences of rural homelessness. This is an inductive method of building theory (Neuman 1994).

While there is no single type of rural homelessness, the duration of rural homelessness, and the time in which it occurs, can be predicted. These include episodic homelessness, intermittent homelessness, seasonal homelessness, and chronic homelessness.

The most common form of homelessness experienced among the rural people I interviewed was episodic homelessness. This form of housing displacement was not precipitated by one particular cause and could occur during any time of the year. Rural teens and families in this category had never been homeless before. They may or may not be homeless in the future. Episodic homelessness can be accidental (owing to fire, flood, or hurricane), situational (owing to divorce, a health crisis, or a fight with people with whom one is staying), or slowly accumulating in cause (owing to economic problems or domestic violence).

Regardless of cause, the loss of housing was unexpected and catastrophic for families who never imagined that they would be homeless. These families were typically stably-housed and employed, and they regarded homelessness as a devastating problem. These temporarily destitute felt shame and guilt over their homelessness because it violated the rural ethic of making it on their own. Episodic homelessness often separated families physically and emotionally. Approximately 45 percent of my subjects experienced episodic homelessness. Jenny's experience was not uncommon:

> I married Tony when I become pregnant during my senior year in high school. I never finished school, but with Tony working and my staying home with the kids, I didn't need to. But I guess things at home got boring

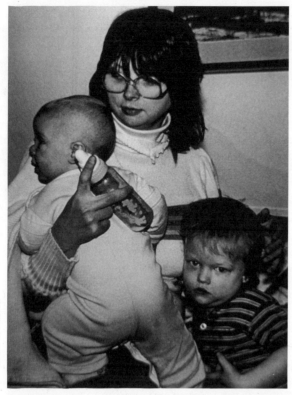

SCOTT CHARETTE

for Tony, and he found interesting people at work. He became involved with another woman and informed me that he was moving out. I didn't have any money of my own, and divorces are too expensive, so I never went to an attorney or filed for an official divorce. Tony was happy, living with this bimbo. I couldn't fight him, and he didn't want to come home anymore. When he left, so did my only source of income. He had always disapproved of my working, even as a volunteer. We didn't have many people you could call friends. Everything had revolved around Tony and the kids. Having no money, no friends I could ask for help, I lived in the car for two days and decided to go to the homeless shelter. They helped me get my GED and vocational training so I could get a job. They showed me how to get food stamps, housing, and counseling. I thought when Tony left it was the end of the world. Now I am able to take care of myself. I will *never* be homeless again.

Intermittent homelessness is a pattern of repeated episodes of homelessness that have become a routine part of the family's existence. Homelessness had happened before, and it could happen again—but no one is quite sure *when*. The intermittent homelessness that afflicted 35 percent of rural families was created as a result of the families' economic marginality.

As the economy became more depressed in rural areas, intermittent homelessness increased. Families fluctuated between times of financial stability and financial crisis. Part-time and temporary jobs, which provide no job security, were desperately taken when factories closed. Becoming accustomed to this variability, families found ways of dealing with it. When the bad times came, these families counted on relationships with people who could house them for a spell—family members or friends, who might end up on their doorstep for a similar favor at a different point in time. They are still integrated into mainstream society, and most of the time they are not homeless. They have some job skills that enable them to find work, even if the work is low-paying and temporary. Additionally, they have not lost all personal resources and still have attributes that give caregivers "something more to work with" than the chronic homeless.

Zack and Sue exemplify intermittent homelessness. They were high school sweethearts who never made it through the graduation ceremony. He dropped out in tenth grade, and she followed suit in the eleventh. Starting a family required that he "get out there and get to work." But Zack found it was hard to find a job without having finished school—and this impediment became more of a handicap over time. Sometimes he was able to find steady work and things were good. But just as they were feeling secure and starting to settle into a community, he would get laid off. "I've been laid off more times than a blanket on a bed," he sighed. They reported that Zack has been laid off each time not because he was not a good worker but because low-paying, low-skill jobs are the first to be cut. They estimate that they have been homeless five times during their marriage. Early in their marriage they stayed with family, but it was not good, so they never asked to stay with them again. They have lived in their car, in campgrounds, and in apartments, moving before they were evicted. They currently live in subsidized housing. "We have lived in six states hoping that the grass will be greener over there. But it never is, and we always end up back home again in New Hampshire. We work hard when we can find work. It is awful to want to work, to want to live like everyone else, and keep finding yourself unable to do it," reported Sue.

The lives for the intermittent homeless are complex, but the lack of housing is not as unexpected or as emotionally catastrophic as it was for those who experience episodic homelessness.

In rural areas, seasonal homelessness is a lifestyle for about 10 percent of my subjects. Their homelessness is predictable by event and time. For instance, migrant farmers know that homelessness will occur when the seasons change and they are forced to leave their summer dwellings. When families living in campgrounds find that September has rolled around, they know that the camps will close and the kids must start school again. Thus, they may search for winter rentals or other affordable housing until the spring. As Anne reported:

> We can't afford a house anymore. Even an apartment is out of reach, by the time you add up the security deposit and one month's rent. So we have found we can get by best by camping out during the warm months. It is cheap to stay at the campground, and we can make do fine there; there are bathrooms with showers there, we cook out over the grill, and can keep food in the cooler. When it is time for the kids to go back to school and cold weather comes around, then we start looking around for winter rentals. If you are lucky, you can get really nice places for not so much money. Then when spring comes and the people want their place back, we head back to the campground. We have done this for several years now, and overall it seems to work pretty well.

For folks who become local nomads, this type of homelessness is ordered, understandable, and predictable. There may be periods when they do not have housing—when they are between being evicted from the campground and finding a winter place to hole up—when short-term emergency housing is necessary. But given time and resources, literal homelessness is short-term.

Chronic homelessness is the most infrequent type of homelessness for rural families and children. Only 5 percent of my respondents experienced ongoing, chronic homelessness. Stereotypes of the chronically homeless are the skid-row bum and the bag lady. However, I learned that many children are becoming chronically homeless, living out their youths on the streets, usually with other children.

Chronic homelessness occurs when people have no place to live for extended periods. Though they have places to live from time to time, they end up back on the streets on a regular basis. For these people, homelessness becomes a lifestyle. People who fall into this category are likely to do so because they have become so estranged from mainstream society that they can no longer function in it. This long lasting homelessness is far more likely to occur among single people. Take for instance, the case of Charley:

My parents split up when I was little. For a while I lived with my mom, and then she couldn't take care of us and I lived with my grandma. She was old and couldn't really handle a bunch of little kids. So my brother got moved to my aunt's house, my sister was put with a family friend, and after getting bounced around to a couple of different places, I ended up in foster care. Talk about being a stranger in a strange land! It was awful being a foster kid. I never belonged there, I was always treated like the invader. So things didn't work out there, and then I got shuffled around from one foster home after another. By the time I got old enough to get out of school and be on my own, moving around and belonging nowhere was the only way I knew. I tried getting married—even had my own kids—but she and I just couldn't seem to make it work. When she left, she took my kids and made it real hard for me to find them. I traveled around, looking for them. Once I found them, they didn't want no part of their old man. Oh, I've lived in Boston, Portland, Manchester, you name it. And I gotta tell you—it is lots harder living in little towns than it ever was in the city. People in the city accept each other more—in this town, only them that was born here belong. I figure I'll be living somewhere else before too long—not that I want to. God only knows I would like to have my own place and be settled. But it just never seems to work out that way.

Chronic homelessness reflects an unorthodox, yet ironically ordered way of life. Folks in this situation were able to survive for extended periods of time without a home or the basic necessities. Yet they didn't starve to death, and they didn't freeze sleeping out in the snow. They seemed to know where to go for help, food, clothes, and a place to sleep, and where to get pocket money. There is, then, order in the midst of their disorder, complexity in the center of the chaos.

But the ordered existence, the strength and survival patterns of the rural homeless are often never observed. It is easier for those naieve in the topic of homelessness to attribute urban strereotypes to rural families and kids. As convenient as it is to target only one cause, rural homelessness is not the result of just a lack of affordable housing or personal dysfunction (Hutson, Mcloyd and Cull 1994). Rural homelessness is caused by a complex interweaving of social and individual factors. The four major factors—ideology, social infrastructure, demographic characteristics, and individual behavior—are all interrelated on both the national and local level.

In some communities, there is a social infrastructure that is able to address the basic needs of the residents and an attitude of helping present within the community, so that when individuals have problems, the problems can readily be addressed. In this context, people are not likely to become homeless. If one does experience housing distress, the community will be able to provide needed assistance so long as all of the factors are balanced.

Other communities may have weak infrastructures, populations whose needs exceed the communities' ability to support them. If a community believes that homeless people are different and should not be encouraged to stay, when people experience problems they may be given "bus therapy" to another town as a means of dealing with the problem of homelessness. This latter type of community is a bad place in which to be homeless, for it will perpetuate a variety of individual and social problems.

In most communities, some parts of the infrastructure work well while other parts do not; some people's needs are met while other needs go unaddressed. Some people may believe that certain types of homeless people should be helped and that other types should not. The relationships among the four factors and the creation of housing distress will obviously vary from community to community, or even within an existing community from one time to another because of changes in the local and national infrastructures.

As the political and economic institutions fail to provide the bare necessities of a way for individuals to support themselves, and as housing, educational, and social service institutions are unable to pick up the slack, homelessness becomes a realistically probable social outcome for people in rural communities.

Rural homelessness is caused, in large part, by the lack of affordable housing, paucity of jobs, inadequate wages, lack of social services, and poor education. The infrastructure of all major social institutions is crumbling, and all American citizens are adversely effected by it, directly or indirectly. Economic, political, educational, and health and human services decisions have, in some cases, actually created conditions that lead to homelessness. In other cases, the institutions have been ineffective in staving off the negative impact of social and demographic trends that breed housing distress.

It is clear from my research that rural homelessness is more of a "top-down" phenomenon than a "bottom-up" problem. Rural areas do the best they can to use scarce resources to support as many citizens as possible. But national social trends and economic policies create rural poverty and homelessness because rural areas are merely microcosms of the national picture. Small towns and villages are not prepared for, and are not fiscally able to deal with, a significant number of homeless families and children. When individuals can made a decent, regular salary and have affordable housing, they are not likely to become homeless. Unfortunately, small towns struggle to "take care of their own," and the resources are simply unavailable to serve all the people who now need help.

In earlier chapters I explored the role of economic, housing, and social service institutions in the creation of rural homelessness. I described how the institutions of the family, education, and health care were unable to ward off housing distress and its consequences. While each institution—political, economic, service, and familial—all contribute to the creation of rural homelessness, rural poverty is the factor that links each of them together. Poverty causes homelessness, and each institution has its hand in preventing, creating, and maintaining poverty.

Rural areas frequently have little economic diversity. Many are driven by a single factory, business, or institution. In communities without diversity, there are fewer social insulators that can protect the citizens in times of distress. When the paper mill closes down and the town loses its main business, the newly unemployed workers are not the only ones who suffer; the entire community suffers. When the factory workers become unemployed, they can no longer buy as many groceries. They postpone getting haircuts, and they fix the leaky sink themselves instead of calling the plumber. As a result, a variety of other businesses are forced to cut back or lay off personnel.

For people who are one paycheck away from homelessness, the results can be catastrophic. For a nondiversified community, an economic crisis is not just a personal problem but a communitywide catastrophe in which every resident is in some way affected. But if a community has several different resources, while the elimination of one may be upsetting, it will not destroy the social fabric of the community. Other resources will exist that may be able to soften the impact of the economic loss. Therefore, while the closing of the shoe factory left a few hundred people out of work, the rest of the community still worked at the local college, government center, or industrial park. The local economy does not have to deteriorate. Residents in the community who continue to work can still provide moral as well as financial support to those in need.

Diversified rural areas, then, can survive the loss of a few local resources. Strong institutions may be able to offset weak ones. But if the community is beset by national economic and social woes, then the national crises are imported into the rural areas. Mom-and-pop businesses, which existed to serve tourists, close when national economic problems make it difficult for people to travel. When people can no longer afford to buy nonessential items or services, those who made their living in their production are out of work.

In rural areas like New Hampshire, the sluggish economy has created a lack of affordable housing. Housing costs have increased 400 percent in New England and doubled in the last twelve years in New Hampshire. In the meantime, incomes have not increased. Eighty percent of the taxpayers earn less than $50,000 annually, and approximately one-fifth of that group is poverty-stricken. Most renters cannot afford to buy a home, and even renters have difficulties finding a place they can afford. As a result, bankruptcies, foreclosures, and evictions have skyrocketed (National Priorities Project 1992).

Despite a growing population, rural areas have received the least amount of new housing money. New public housing nationally has been virtually eliminated, and that which is constructed is in urban areas. This puts the rural people with the lowest incomes at greatest risk of homelessness.

Infrastructure failures, including economic and housing distress, can be managed if they do not permeate the entire social fabric and if one has access to a functioning informal network. But when there are communitywide economic problems, the informal support network fails. Everybody then has problems, and there is nowhere to turn for help.

Rural communities have been famous for "taking care of their own." But today the informal safety nets are increasingly fragile. The rural homeless find that the institutional safety net is not available to catch them either. Factors that influence the loss of the formal safety net include limited economic resources to provide needed services; limited financial resources to pay for the services; fewer professionals to access; lack of service diversity, in which one provider may be in charge of all local human services; geographic barriers; and organizational policies that reduce options for obtaining a variety of confidential help. These structural barriers to assistance promote homelessness.

While the presence of homeless children and families illustrates the failure of the infrastructures, most people are not homeless. Why? I suggest that either parts of the infrastructure still work in their local area or people are not adversely impacted by one of the other three causal factors, as described next.

Every town has its own unique configuration of residents. As we have seen, rural America can range from just a few people per square mile to communities up to fifty thousand people. This means that some communities consist of people who have known each other for generations, while others may consist of a more fluid population. Residents may vary widely by age, sex, family size, racial, ethnic, religion, income, and occupational skill. Some rural areas are wealthy and beautiful, with a well-developed political and social service network. Other areas are impoverished, with no infrastructure at all. Tourist regions may reek of wealth in the summer but house the marginally employed during winter months. Rural areas, and the people within them, are not alike (Fitchen 1991).

As the nation's composition changes, so changes the composition of rural areas. The changing makeup of the American people has placed increased demands on our social infrastructure. As previously noted, there are increasing numbers of single parents, decreasing incomes, increasing costs for all housing, declining two-parent income and support for families, and fewer jobs for the ill-educated. Such demographic changes are largely beyond small town control. Institutions respond to changes in the configuration of the population—and rural areas have been less prepared to meet the demands of a mobile, female-centered, economically depressed population.

Changing population composition means that communities must alter the number and types of services that they provide. Unfortunately, major changes may outstrip a community's ability to provide for all the needs of all the residents. Even rural areas vary widely by the age, sex, race, ethnicity, and social class of their residents. Communities have a range of sizes, resources, and standards of living. Demographic configurations influence the type of problems a community may face and its ability to solve them. It is hard for an economically strapped community to support the needs of many people who have personal problems.

Individual dysfunction is commonly blamed for the rise of homelessness. Individual factors may prevent—or encourage—the outcome of homelessness. This factor contains personal causes of homelessness, in which personal problems, such as relationship problems, poor education, ill health, substance abuse, emotional distress, and low self-esteem, make it difficult for a person to find secure work and housing. This factor also refers to how well an individual can access resources to fend off homelessness.

Homelessness is frequently portrayed as a personal problem. Situations such as divorce, school problems, illness, substance abuse, lack of interpersonal skills, employability, and poor money management may be caused by structural factors, but this fact is ignored by those who prefer to blame the victims for their homelessness.

A variety of personal problems can cause homelessness. So long as resources outweigh problems on the balance of life, homelessness may be avoided. But when the scale tips, even existing resources may spill. This makes it difficult to avoid ongoing homelessness, especially when the infrastructure is weak.

Personal problems increase mobility—and homelessness. If life is bad in one community, it is natural to hope that life will be better somewhere else. So people move from place to place, looking for the American dream. With fixed incomes, how can money be saved in times of economic distress? The rural poor do not spend much money on clothes, recreation, or luxury items. The amount that it takes to feed a family is fairly constant. The one expenditure that could be reduced, according to people interviewed, was housing. But increased mobility means a loss of support in times of distress, unfamiliarity with new helping programs, new costs, and increased stress. Instead of increasing stability, frequent mobility increases the chances of homelessness.

How much should homeless people be helped? Rural communities must address this question and take into consideration the number of people who are homeless, whether they are residents or newcomers, and whether they are worth helping or to be avoided. These decisions are influenced by the ideology of homelessness held in a community.

Ideology about the homeless and the role of helping others within one's community is also important in the presence of rural homelessness. The public holds ideological views about the causes of homelessness and what homeless people are like. Unfortunately, their views may not reflect reality. Personal experiences or media views may become generalized to explain all homelessness. This has been an especially big problem for the homeless in rural areas, who may have little similarity to the urban homeless. But personal beliefs in turn affect policy attitudes. This results in a problem when individual pathology is regarded as the cause, when in reality the homelessness is caused by structural and demographic patterns (Lee, Lewis, and Jones 1992).Two separate ideologies converge around the issue of how much a community should help the homeless.

On one hand, every community has a reputation for how much they take care of each other. Some communities have created resources to help others in need, and they regard those in housing distress as neighbors and treat them with integrity. Other communities are suspicious of people who are different and are not sympathetic to people who do not pull their own weight within the community. But by and large, the rural ethic of "we take care of our own" still typifies small towns. The "Kindling Spirit" is still present within many communities.

On the other hand, rural people have not escaped stereotypes of homeless people being analogous to alcoholic, mentally disturbed, skid-row bums. Research on homeless people is frequently skewed, equating them more with nuts, sluts, and perverts (Lemert 1972) than Joe and Susie America. The media and popular figures, such as H. Ross Perot and Rush Limbaugh, portray the homeless as almost subhuman. Even homeless people themselves know these stereotypes, feel stigmatized, and fight to maintain dignity.

Thus, there is ideological tension between these two poles. Balancing the desire to be a brother's keeper and the belief that homeless people are somehow "different" from "regular folk" plagues rural areas. Community ideology, available resources, and the ability to help others are all, then, highly interrelated. But the two factors that are most important in understanding rural child and family homelessness are personal problems and infrastructure problems.

Even though most rural homeless families do not become homeless because of mental illness or substance abuse problems, they do often have personal problems. Clearly, there is a relationship between personal problems and homelessness (Kaufman 1986; Schutt and Garrett 1992). Personal factors that encourage the development of homelessness include poor education or employment skills; being burned out of one's home; getting divorced and not having financial resources; having a personal history of family dysfunction; using substances to excess; having an unanticipated accident; being emotionally or mentally disturbed; having work-related problems; being socially isolated; and experiencing significant problems with one's partner or parent. However, structural/institutional problems such as the lack of affordable housing and jobs for the unemployed are better predictors of homelessness.

As an example of how personal problems result from structural problems, consider the Thompson family's experience. When Sal and Rob Thompson were laid off from the factory the same day, it wasn't long before they had financial problems. Frustrated over not having work and not knowing how to make ends meet, the couple began quarreling. Rob had an affair, and Sal began drinking. The children, who witnessed the effects of the unemployment, began staying away from home. The oldest boy was hauled in to the police station for petty theft and vandalism. This progression of more and more serious problems, which could have been avoided, is what Lemert (1972) refers to as secondary forms of deviance.

Few people in small towns who experience problems become homeless. In fact, most people do not. Not everyone who gets divorced becomes homeless, not everyone who has work problems becomes unemployed, not every alcoholic falls to the skids, not everyone who is from a dysfunctional home spawns a dysfunctional home with his children. Looking at the personal problems without looking at how they interface with structural variables can only result in an incomplete picture of the etiology of homelessness.

Somehow, most people in rural areas are able to find a place to live, scratch out a living, and take care of their families. Some parts of the country are even thriving in this time of economic distress. There are places where there is no housing shortage and an abundance of affordable housing. In certain communities there is economic growth, plenty of jobs, and a strong social service system. But even within these communities, there is hidden homelessness.

What differentiates those rural folk who survive hard times from those who fall into homelessness is the number and severity of their structural problems, and the presence of personal and social resources with which to resolve them. Problems increase as resources decrease. I concluded from observations that there is a direct relationship between personal problems and structural resources.

In the New Hampshire data, less than 5 percent of the respondents were accidental homeless. Approximately 15 percent were personal catastrophe victims. The remaining 80 percent of the homeless families experienced some form of structural problem that encouraged their homelessness. Of those, over half had become homeless only because of institutional failure. Though they frequently had economic, social, and psychological problems, the problems were not significant before some crisis for which there was no institutional assistance. Had the structural problems not occurred, neither would the personal problems. The remaining 30 percent had personal problems that could have been manageable with good institutional intervention, problems that became exacerbated by structural problems.

Many rural communities I met felt that if they "just had a shelter," then they would have successfully addressed their homeless problems. But there are different causes of homelessness; interventions must address the logical cause. Creating an emergency shelter will not make the homeless go away, nor will it alone address the source of their problems. While personal problems that facilitate homelessness require individual-level interventions, community-based problems require socially based interventions. There must be a variety of intervention types—some on the structural level and some on the individual level—if rural homelessness is to be prevented and the existing housing distress eliminated.

"Accidental" homeless people experienced no major personal or structural problems that led to their becoming homeless. Having a home destroyed because of fire, flood, earthquake, or hurricane, losing a job because of an accident at work that disabled them, or experiencing domestic violence that led to a sudden separation can cause a person to be homeless without notice. They did nothing to cause their homelessness, and without the precipitating accident, they would likely still be stably housed.

Beneita, her brothers and sisters, and her mother were doing financially okay after her father had left some years before. They didn't have much in the way of savings, but the mother was able to provide for all of the children's physical, social, and emotional needs. They were very happy, and things were functioning well for this family. Then one Christmas Eve they were awakened by smoke; a neighbor's apartment had caught on fire, and the entire building was destroyed. Having no immediate family in the area, the mother did not want to impose on friends and was referred to a local homeless shelter. The church immediately donated clothes and food. School children collected Christmas gifts so that their friends would not have to do without. Within three weeks the family was settled into their new home.

Because the accidentally homeless were functioning adequately up until the accident, their accidents are regarded as misfortunes. The entire small town may provide them with support and assistance, in line with the rural ethic of "we take care of our own." In such cases, the homeless are pitied, and they are helped. They are not thought to be bad or at fault for their misfortune. The accidentally homeless, then, are not negatively stigmatized. But children and families who become homeless unexpectedly do not constitute the bulk of homeless children. Most of the time, structural and personal problems are to blame.

"Institutional" homeless people experience structural problems that cause the homelessness. When a parent is laid off from a job and not able to find another because of a depressed economy; when wages are too low to pay for rents that are too high; when there is simply no affordable housing available—these institutional failures create homelessness. Institutional victims do not have extraordinary psychological or domestic problems that contribute to their becoming homeless. They have few personal problems. These people are mentally healthy and have no problems with substances or relationships. While being out of work and losing their homes may cause them distress, this reaction is normal and can be managed when they still have personal resources available. But when the system fails them, their resources disintegrate and their chances for homelessness increase.

As examples of the institutional victims who became homeless in rural areas, consider the following cases. A realtor in northern, rural New Hampshire ended up homeless. Gwen had been earning a fine salary and had bought a luxurious condominium and car as well as expensive jewelry and clothes. Then, suddenly, the market in her area went "belly-up." People no longer were buying homes, and her sales fell to zero month after month. She began living off her savings until things improved. But the economy did not get better; it got worse and worse. Soon she had spent all of her savings. She could not sell her car, coat, or expensive items because nobody else in the area had money to buy them. She lost her condo and found herself to be "the best-dressed homeless woman at the shelter." She did not become homeless because of any personal problem. She became homeless because the economic bottom fell out of her community, and she had no options for employment there.

Most rural folks who become homeless never live as high a life as the realtor. Most people are like Ralph and Martha—getting by, but not doing very well financially. Ralph was laid off because his business no longer had enough customers to support all the employees. His wife could not earn enough money babysitting to support their family. They decided to move to another state, where they heard there were more jobs. But upon arriving in the city, they found there were few jobs available and people from the area had the upper hand in getting them. They lived on their meager savings until they were depleted, then found themselves looking at having no money, no jobs, no friends or family nearby, and no way to pay for food or housing. Both parents were likable sorts who had junior college training and wanted to work. No one could blame them for their string of misfortunes. They were simply unlucky and couldn't make ends meet without a steady income.

The institutional victims are people we do not expect to become homeless. When their rural neighbors hear of their plight, a common response is "they shouldn't have become homeless." They shouldn't have—but they did. Like the accidental homeless, this group of individuals engenders sympathy and support from others who are also victims of a cruel economy. Because the homelessness is seen as the result of hard times that anyone could experience, homelessness is not regarded as personal failure. However, institutionally caused homelessness makes everyone nervous—because if it happened to one of "us," it could happen to "me." Therefore, negative stigma is unlikely to be applied to the rural homeless who are in this category.

"Personal catastrophe victims" are another category of the homeless. Sometimes people live in communities where there are enough jobs and where there is sufficient affordable housing. But some people seem to live from personal crisis to personal crisis. They may have family problems, substance abuse problems, or problems handling "reality." People in this category may have difficulty holding on to their jobs. They often have inadequate education or training. They may not be well-equipped to handle the types of jobs that they have been given. They may have difficulties carrying out instructions, or they may make continuing errors. For whatever reason, they just can't seem to keep things together.

Ultimately, the personal problems become so great that the available structural resources—like understanding employers or available social services—cannot help. As one employer noted: "I liked her a lot, and I knew she needed the job. But she kept on making mistakes, even after she was shown how to do her job correctly. There comes a point to sympathy—when people's personal problems become my problems, they just got to go".

A typical example of the personal catastrophe victim was Leigh. She lived in a community that had adequate housing, business, and social services available. She had been working at a dry cleaners when her husband walked out on her for another woman. Distraught, Leigh was constantly upset and told everyone she met about her problems. She began drinking and using depressants as a way to numb her pain. Customers would find themselves unable to get out of the door as she went on and on about the intimate details of her life. People began taking their cleaning elsewhere. As a result, Leigh lost her job—and then her home.

The victims of personal catastrophe are more likely to be seen as responsible for their homelessness. There is less pity for this category of homeless people because their personal dysfunction is used to blame them for their lack of housing. Deviant behavior—especially in rural areas—is not tolerated without stigma. Their personal problems are seen as signs of moral failure, poor character, personal weakness, and bad choices. Certainly such people are thought to need help from the rural community—but "we can only help so much. They gotta get themselves together." This category of homeless require help in order to "make it"—but not as much help as those who experience the double whammy of personal and structural problems.

When people's private problems are not adequately addressed, it is difficult for them to keep those problems from interfering in public areas of their lives. When people have homes, jobs, and a social support network, personal problems are more manageable. But when people have personal problems and lack structural resources, this is a formula for disaster. Structural problems cause their own sets of problems and exacerbate previously existing personal problems. This is the case for the "double whammy" victims. As a result of both personal and institutional problems, these people have few resources upon which to draw in times of crisis. There is no supportive employer, no savings to fall back on, few friends or family that can really help, and few agencies that will serve them. These people are in dire straits indeed.

Homelessness, in which the person loses everything, is most likely to occur in this category, as pretty blonde-haired Marty found out. Marty was eighteen, pregnant and unmarried. She had a miserable relationship with her parents, which had led to her hooking up with Ronnie in hopes he would love her and take care of her. When she announced she was pregnant, her parents disowned her and kicked her out of the house, and her boyfriend turned cold and distant. Not having graduated from high school, she could not get a good job. There were few jobs available in this rural community anyway; the only factory had closed down two years before, and there were few restaurants or sales jobs available. The nearest town was forty minutes away, and Marty did not have a car. These factors contributed to her becoming homeless and showing up at a shelter.

Victims of the double whammy require the most of the scarce resources that exist in rural areas. This group of homeless people could be pulled out of their homelessness but not without a strong personal and community investment. Because double whammy victims have identifiable personal problems, the community is more likely to blame them for their own homelessness rather than look at the structural causes. To look at structural causes infers that the homeless may not be responsible, and that the community might have something to do with the creation of the housing distress. This is too uncomfortable; it is easier to stigmatize the homeless person.

Homeless people's housing distress is directly related to four interrelated causal factors: social infrastructure, personal behavior, demographic characteristics and ideology of the residents. (See Appendix B) Even personal behaviors are frequently caused by structural factors. Therefore, rural homelessness is caused primarily by social factors, not individual pathology. This means that the most effective social interventions to eradicate existing homelessness and prevent future homelessness are at the community and institutional level.

t e n

Bringing the Community Together to Solve Homelessness

Lack of a uniformly held theoretical perspective about homelessness among rural leaders consistently led to fragmented action plans to help those in distress. I found that most leaders across rural areas want to help the homeless but do not know what to do. A speaker at a community group described her experience:

> The concerned leaders of the small town convened in order to "do something" for the homeless children in their community. Clergy, educators, social workers, the housewives of the city elite, professional women, and men who took off from their administrative positions sat around the table and brainstormed "what can we do?" They know they have homeless children. They believe that it is a problem. They want to do something about it. But what? "How do we help these kids to avoid problems that lead to homelessness?" they asked. . . . "Just tell us what to do and we will do it!" they implored. But there are structural limitations to what can be done. There are limited resources, barriers, and the protocol of the way things are done there. They knew that their attempts to help must succeed, because they will likely have only one chance to demonstrate to the residents of this town that they should and can do something for homeless kids. So what should, and can, they do?

Despite their laudable intent, they failed to prevent or eradicate homelessness. Too often decisions are made based on limited information and fixed resources. A commonly used strategy is to import urban models of shelters and services into rural areas with little thought as to their actual applicability to rural communities. In this case, well-meaning organizations grasped at a good idea here and something that might work there, but community leaders shared no uniform vision about rural development of homeless services. As a result, a fragmented

FRED BLOISE

"system" resulted. Without a theoretical understanding of the nature of homelessness in rural areas, it is almost impossible to develop a comprehensive strategy that will really help.

In his discussion of how social programs are the result of public reaction to homelessness, Peter Marcuse (1988) states that the initial outrage at extreme poverty amid the affluence of our society became neutralized in the absence of a quick fix for the problem. He argues that sweeping homeless people from public view is often the easiest and most readily available solution undertaken by communities. It is ludicrous to solve homelessness through the provision of temporary shelter, as the government and most communities have advocated. Only through an examination of homelessness's systematic causes in a community can an area develop the long-term solutions for homelessness.

Rural homelessness is here to stay unless a systematic action plan is undertaken. Small towns, the mainstay of the traditional American way of life, are at risk of becoming inundated with social problems that were once thought to exist only in urban areas. Acknowledgement of homelessness can be constructively used as a warning bell by rural communities to do something *now* in order to preserve their strengths and traditions. Little towns can still bring their residents together to address community problems like homelessness, poverty, disease, and crime. But if small communities do not actively pursue their wholesome ways of life, that part of their existence will deteriorate.

Preservation of the rural community is, in many ways, the preservation of the best of who we as a nation have been. People in rural areas must be given the opportunity and encouragement to live as neighbors—communicating, caring, and working together in active pursuit of commonly held goals. It is the position of this book that prevention is easier, cheaper, and better than denial, blame, and treatment. Communities cannot be preserved if those residents who are in need are left to address their problems alone.

From my analysis, no federal agency or independent organization is taking the lead to address rural homelessness. What they provide is, at best, piecemeal assistance for some of the people at risk of housing displacement and poverty. Rural communities have no choice except to "grab the bull by the horns" and rely upon themselves to address the causes and consequences of homelessness.

I propose that the best choices for rural areas are (1) to re-create the best of what it means to be rural, recapturing the rural ethic and transforming it into a model for the twenty-first century; and (2) to weave the existing resources into a safety net that works for, and with, the people they are meant to serve. In order for social change to occur, both our minds and our actions must become engaged.

In order to deal effectively with rural homelessness, one must focus on the local level. Realistically, communities cannot count on federal policies, programs, or funding allocations to address the causes or consequences of rural homelessness. They have no choice but to use their own resources to address the problems that cause housing distress. But this is difficult to do when the social fabric of the community is weakened.

"What has broken down [in rural areas] is [the sense of] community. The problem is not just the poverty, the lack of money, [the homelessness], but the fact that there is no sense of belonging or oneness. In these communities, there is no longer community, no longer a community to give the support—and the criticism—that people need" (Fitchen 1991, 129). The majority of Americans believe that adequate food and shelter are basic rights, that government should take more direct action to alleviate huger and homelessness and that tax increases to fund huger and homelessness assistance programs are acceptable. But the extent of people's willingness to support more spending on antipoverty measures was found to be influenced by three factors: the degree to which society rather than the individual was seen as responsible for hunger and homelessness; the degree to which hungry and homeless people were perceived to deserve help; and the extent to which respondents adhered to a communitarian rather than an individualistic ideal (Mellman and Lazarus Research 1988). Community caring for one another has historically bound rural residents together. It is the traditional attributes of rural life that deserve to be rekindled, for they lay the foundation for building a sound community infrastructure for all of its residents. And what are those strengths that need to be rekindled? They are simple, common sense behaviors.

1. *Communication with one another.* This is necessary on all levels—town, agency, neighborhood, and family. People cannot understand or feel a part of one another's lives if they are strangers to each other. Opportunities for interaction must be constructed. People in many rural areas still have regular dances at the Community Center or meet for potluck suppers at the church. These events may no longer be appropriate for many communities, but there are other ways to bring people together. Communities must be creative!

2. *Creating a sense of community where everybody belongs.* Viewing others as neighbors is vital. Belonging is an essential human need. If one does not feel as if he belongs, it is impossible for that person to become emotionally healthy—and impossible for his social contributions to be productive. "We have changed belonging from an essential and inherent human right (and need) to something we have to earn, something we have to strive for, which can only be achieved by the best of us", says Kune (1992). We have created a national mindset in which we must now *earn* our right to belong. The child who does not feel a sense of belonging to the community either will not participate or will find competing subgroups with which to affiliate. Some of the subgroups are in direct opposition to mainstream norms and values. If belonging is essential to the human spirit, then it is imperative to find ways of steering that need to achieve positive personal and social outcomes. Young and old, male and female, and people of all racial, ethnic, or religions distinctions deserve the right to be treated like valued members of the community (Etzioni 1993; Barber 1992).

3. *Creating a sense of empowerment among the members of the community.* The rural ethic is based on self-care. This approach safeguards privacy, because only those who know a person well will know the extent

of his or her distress. It also helps the individual receiving help to preserve his or her sense of integrity. Empowerment creates greater dedication among the players within the community, who find that what they do *will* matter—that they can implement decisions to improve the quality of life of both individuals and the community.

4. *Benevolent action.* If certain groups within the community have particular needs, there is a moral obligation on the part of a caring community to see that those needs are addressed. The informal network and charities traditionally assumed the role of caregivers for those in distress. Professional agencies are now an essential part of the rural infrastructure. Rural professionals/agencies must learn (1) to speak the language of the recipients; (2) to provide service in a humane, not stigmatizing, way; and (3) to be one-down, not one-up, in their style of interaction (Liebow, 1993; Vissing et al. 1994). Help must be given in a timely fashion, with respect for the realities of personal and geographic barriers of help-seeking in rural areas.

While these aspects of rurality are critical to maintaining the traditional rural lifestyle, the proposed actions cannot happen without three important factors occurring: (1) rural areas must make the moral commitment to do what it takes to reestablish principles of democratic concern for one another; (2) rural areas must develop a diversified economic base that enhances rurality; and (3) local areas need a unified system of organization for providing services to those in need.

Rural areas are small enough to reestablish democracy in action. Democracy means freedom of expression and respect for the equality of all. Democratic communities can put these principles into concrete action. Inherent in the argument for rural democracy is the belief that *all* citizens are valued. The entire community depends on each and every member achieving his or her greatest potential. This means more than just giving the individual his or her legal rights; it means helping people to feel as though they are essential to the well-being of the community.

Democracy, according to Barber (1992), insists on leveling as the price of equality. It aims always at leveling up, never at leveling down. It demands that slaves be emancipated, not that masters be enslaved; that suffrage be granted to the dispossessed, not taken from the powerful; that I win the exercise of my rights, not that you lose the exercise of yours. This means that all of us should have reasonable housing, and none of us should fear homelessness; that all children should receive the resources that would enable them to become productive citizens, not that all children should be denied having the resources essential to survival.

The homeless people of the community belong to it just as much as the most well-to-do. This is part of the reality of democratic equality. If children belong to the whole community, then both parents and society have an obligation to assure that their physical, emotional, and social needs are met. If the position is taken that children belong to all of us, then we have the social obligation to help each and every child as if he or she were of our own flesh and blood. In rural areas, the failures of each child become the failures of the community, while the successes of the child are the celebrations of both individuals and communities (Aiken and LaFollette 1980).

We cannot afford to sacrifice any family, because families are the main socialization unit for a child. We cannot afford to ignore the needs of any parent, should they fail in their mission to rear their children. If we do, we inevitably destroy our own future. When people's needs are not met by healthy democratic forms of community, unhealthy and antidemocratic forms are sought that will divide us instead of unify us (Bellah et al. 1991). Service to neighbors and community are not just the gift of altruists but the natural outgrowth of believing that we are one. Hence, we must help one another not because we are supposed to but because it is the right thing for everyone in a democracy to do. And it is the only way that we are going to survive (Community for Economic Development 1991).

Concern that improved treatment of homeless and at-risk children should be a national priority is voiced by liberals and conservatives alike. While there is agreement that the lives of children and families need to be improved, how to do so is a source of debate. Some scholars, such as Benjamin Barber (1992), assert that educational, structural, and interpersonal equality are the keys for upgrading the lives of families and children. The Research and Policy Committee of the Committee for Economic Development (*The Unfinished Agenda,* 1991) urges the nation to develop a comprehensive and coordinated strategy of human investment. They redefine education as a process that begins at birth and encompasses all aspects of children's early development, including their physical, social, emotional, and cognitive growth. Others, such as Amitai Etzioni (1993) allege that a communitarian movement that focuses on reestablishing moral values on the community level would allow for greater democratic involvement. The communitarianism movement is based on grassroots decision making within communities. It acknowledges that values are interjected into community decision making, and it is hoped that discussion of what is best for the community will lead to benefits for the individuals within them. But this has to be in conjunction with changes in the large institutions and structures—such as the economy, which create our good society (Bellah et al. 1991). However, there are those who believe that such a movement is a neoconservative one in which there are dangers of a community agreeing on standards that are contradictory to individual interests (Winkler 1993). Some fear that the foundations of democracy will be undermined if communities fail to adequately represent all beliefs and groups of people.

Issues of democracy, opportunity, caring, and homelessness are all interwoven (Bedard, 1992). But most experts agree that our nation is condemning much of a new generation to lives of poverty and despair. Therefore, it is imperative that rural areas develop a stronger economic foundation.

It is much more difficult to gain a sense of community, communicate with others, and act benevolently when the economic base of a community has eroded. People are not keen on taking care of others when they have difficulty caring for themselves. Lack of jobs produce low self-esteem, no money with which to buy necessities, and no tax base for supporting town services. A community can care for one another best when there is a flourishing economic base.

The transformation of the American economy has had a profound effect on most rural areas. Community-based economic development is desperately needed among rural communities that have lost traditional industries such as farming, mining, fishing, or logging. A broader view of economic development is needed, a view that includes human development, education for creativity, regaining and understanding popular knowledge and history, and democratic decision making. As a result of this investment in developing human resources with local residents, the residents themselves will be better equipped to rebuild their own communities (Gaventa and Lewis 1991).

Many rural areas have addressed their economic needs by courting urban industries to locate in small towns. When urban business moves to rural areas, all too often the results are more negative than positive. Natural resources may be depleted, as pollution increases. Frequently the manpower needed to operate the business requires skills that are not present within the local community. As a result, people from urban areas are recruited into the small towns—when locals thought jobs would materialize for themselves. The money used to build the rural business satellite comes from urban investors who have little interest in improving the quality of life for the local community. And when economic woes come and the business lays people off or closes entirely—the local area is left with more problems than before the company arrived.

Rural areas need a diversified economic base that enhances the local attributes rather than detracts from them. Rural investment—financially, physically, and emotionally—can create a solid, long-lasting business environment in small towns. Consider rural businesses such as Ben and Jerry's Ice Cream and Stoneyfield Yogurt. These businesses are built upon rural traditions of quality and use local resources. They hire local people to work in the relatively pollution-free factories. Such businesses hire local workers trained to manage the work-tasks. They also help build up the local and state economies, giving back to the community and making profits all the while. They create an "everybody wins" situation.

Vermont and New Hampshire have a long tradition of maple products that use local resources, personnel, and investment. While they are not megabusinesses, they have provided a stable income for many generations. Local craftspeople and woodworkers make stable incomes while producing high-quality merchandise.

The key to economic diversity in rural areas is not the importation of urban business but the cultivation of small-scale, mom-and-pop businesses that allow for creativity and productivity. While it may benefit some communities to import urban businesses, communities may suffer when the businesses experience problems. Small-scale businesses can empower people of the community to help each other and to realize that their individual efforts are important to the overall survival of the community. Economic empowerment will logically lead to other forms of empowerment in the community and enhance the willingness of residents to help one another. Economic empowerment can result in less need for social services.

Local governments are plagued with a myriad of fragmented local, state, and federal services that are coordinated and evaluated by no central unit. As pointed out by the Center for the Study of Social Policies (1991), no one is ultimately responsible for the overall outcomes of government, health, education, or social services in the community. As a result, people in housing distress routinely fall through the cracks, never getting the services they need. There are seldom clear policy directions available to the local operating units as a framework within which resources can be invested. Agencies and local governmental units do not necessarily work toward common goals that cut across organizational boundaries. With fragmented goals the system has no effective way to respond to new and emerging child and family problems such as homelessness. As one provider told me:

> In my area, there are two organizations involved with the homeless, five which concern child well-being, seven that serve families, a couple of others which address housing, a bunch more that are devoted to financial assistance . . . everybody is doing something different for the same

groups of people. Most of the time they don't work together. They don't have the foggiest idea of what the other is doing. For one federal grant, several of them were actually competing with one another! No surprise, none of them got the money. Who would fund an area which obviously doesn't work together?

It is important to develop a network in every community so that every need is somehow addressed by a some unit or organization. Each unit must know about what the other units can and cannot do. This networking is not just an interagency matter; it is an issue in which all agencies and community leaders should take part. If the community does not provide access to a comprehensive range or services, the residents cannot be protected from ills such as homelessness.

Perhaps once small town governments alone were able to address most of the problems of the community. But today, local governments cannot. Local government no longer plays a significant role in providing services to families and children. Professional and state agencies have taken responsibility for providing services related to children and youth in a highly categorical way. The solutions that each promotes address specialized problems and target populations. As a result, too-highly specialized and narrowly restricted services have emerged, making it all too easy for homeless people to slip through the cracks. Lack of financial resource and commitment to all residents has forced community leaders to debate "When is enough?"

Rural individuals and communities go through a similar process in deciding that they have a problem about homelessness that needs to be addressed. The problem of homelessness has been building slowly, incrementally, and methodically for some time, not just for individuals but for rural communities as well.

There is a point at which communities, like individuals, identify that the chaos is getting out of control. Chaos and complexity theories help to identify when individuals—and communities—must act.

In my experience, at first rural communities deny they have such a problem as homelessness. Then, when it is clear that there are homeless people even in *their* community, it is easier to provide piecemeal services and blame the victims for their homelessness. At this stage, homelessness is regarded as a personal, not a community, problem.

Many rural communities never move beyond these stages. Denial of the problem and blaming the displaced people for their lack of housing are common reactions in many small communities. These strategies are psychologically—and politically—useful, because if there is no homelessness, nothing has to be done about a problem that really doesn't exist and if homelessness does exist, it is caused by personal pathology and is created by defective individuals—not a defective community. Thus, no community intervention is required. One must only "treat" the homeless person—or encourage him to move elsewhere. The chaos of homelessness is identified, and maintained, as an individual-level problem.

But when homeless people don't go away—and more and more are identified—a community is more likely to identify that they have a problem about homelessness that needs to be addressed. It is at this point that they can look systematically at what the community is—and is not—doing that influence homelessness. When people recognize that homelessness is not just a personal problem but a community problem, community resolutions can be sought to address it. In the rural areas I observed, sometimes this meant creating a task force of community leaders; other times shelters, food pantries, or soup kitchens were developed; in other cases, grants were sought to develop more comprehensive programming to bring in new business or to construct more affordable housing units.

The critical point when a community decides to act—or not to act—is of particular concern. Identification of a problem is typically accompanied by a need to do something about it. A crisis engenders emotional commitment to begin problem solving. If the identification occurs early enough, there may be enough existing resources that can be mobilized within the community to actually do something about the problem. Out of the chaos of homelessness, then, can be born creative ideas that will not just address the problem of homelessness but enhance the entire well-being of the community.

If one misses the naturally occurring "moment" in which something must be done, it may be difficult to mobilize the resources in the future. The catastrophe may become too great to be solved. Poverty, crime, homelessness, and all the accompanying ills may become normative because they have escalated so high that people feel that there is now nothing they can do to bring the community back to equilibrium (Canellos 1991). If the community had acted preventively earlier, if they had taken action at naturally occurring critical points, then the chaos could have been manageable. Instead, the chaos has evolved into catastrophe. Once catastrophe occurs, it is hard to bring the community—or individual—back to where they were before the chaos began.

In short, the rural community that identifies that there is a problem of homelessness ultimately makes one of three decisions. The decision the community makes will influence the future of homelessness in rural areas. The choices are:

1. Communities can take action to *eradicate* the existing homelessness and *prevent* future homelessness from occurring. This means comprehensive programming and shoring up the strengths on which the rural communities were originally based. This option requires moral, political, community, and financial commitment. It will result in building an infrastructure whose benefit will spill over into all other areas of life.

2. Communities can do *something* to make life at least a little easier for homeless people. Piecemeal services will result in some people being helped while others are not. This is a "you can't change the world" position, in which a little improvement is seen as better than none.

3. Communities can accept that homelessness is here to stay and allow rural homelessness to become a normalized part of the rural fabric. But once homelessness becomes an acceptable part of the rural community, one should logically expect that other related problems will come to stay as well.

Rural communities are making decisions about how to manage housing distress. Some communities are still in the denial stages of the problem; most are implementing fragmented services, while a very few are attempting to build a comprehensive system of support. Many other communities wish that homelessness would just go away. As a result, they do nothing. But to do nothing is still to choose a course of action—one that can inevitably lead to the normalization of rural homelessness.

Other communities are engaged in an active program of community renewal. Other communities would act, if they knew what to do. It is unlikely that the federal government is going to become the major advocate for the rural homeless. The problem is, for good or ill, dumped in the laps of local communities. As discussed earlier in this chapter, economic diversification is essential. Development of a communitarian spirit is crucial. On a different level, communities must develop safety net programs that can benefit the whole community. The next chapter will provide pragmatic courses of action that can be undertaken by rural communities to "do something" about homelessness—and benefit themselves in the process.

eleven

Doing What It Takes

Books, reports, guides, articles, and opinions about "what to do about homelessness" abound (Homes for the Homeless 1994; Kirst 1991). Most of them do not specifically target rural areas, however. This has made it difficult for small towns to know exactly what to do and how to do it. For instance, the U.S. Conference of Mayors (1993) recommends that the federal government pave the way for a new approach to homelessness by funding housing, income, and social service programs. The Interagency Council on the Homeless's federal plan to help end homelessness (1992) includes nearly two hundred implementation actions being undertaken by the council and member agencies. Some of these efforts including improving coordination among the various levels of involvement, increasing support services, and new strategies for homelessness prevention. The Partnership for the Homeless (1989) asserts that a national agenda to address homelessness must include a comprehensive strategy, including providing employment opportunities, reducing the affordable housing gap, instituting and implementing welfare reforms, and providing comprehensive support services.

But most of the materials do not identify how to implement community development or homeless prevention programs in communities with a not-in-my-backyard (NIMBY) response. Community opposition to groups such as the homeless should be expected and thus any effort should integrate community relations as a significant part of the planning process (Dear 1991). This makes it necessary to lobby for rural homeless programs at the local, state, and federal level. Advocates do have access to information that can help them be more successful. The National Low Income Housing Coalition (1992) has developed an advocates resource book to help lobbyists for the homeless. They describe federal programs and summaries of how they operate, who benefits from them, and how they might be improved. Some of the programs described include HOME, Community Development Block Grants, and the Low Income Housing Tax Credit. They also provide information

CLAUDIA KAERNER

about how bills become laws and the authorization, budget, and appropriation processes. This organization supports a "Two Cents for Housing Campaign," which would double the amount of money currently appropriated for low-income housing. The National Housing Institute and American Affordable Housing Institute (1991) has compiled a list of major homelessness prevention programs that work and are cost-effective, replicable, and easily developed. One can find general lobby information that pertains to the national plight of children through the Children's Defense Fund (1992).

Organizing for social change is an art that should not be underestimated. Fundamentals of direct action organizing in rural areas include developing strategy, selecting tactics, developing leadership and public speaking skills, designing workshops, managing financial and legal matters, and grassroots fundraising. In order for the rural community to engender support for community development and homelessness programming, media can be used to educate about homelessness and advocate for those who are in housing distress (Ryan 1991). Lee and Link (1991) found that there is a connection between frequent and sympathetic media coverage of homelessness and the public's perception of it as a serious problem requiring action. Advocacy for the homeless consists of different stages, such as publicity, litigation, demonstrations, and education. While past homelessness advocacy efforts have been successful nationally, advocacy for the homelessness also has social trends working against it. Any advocate for the homeless—and especially those in rural areas—must be aware of the steps and pitfalls of advocacy (Hombs 1992).

It is a challenge to build community organizations in rural areas that are receptive to the needs of the poor and homeless; however, with savvy planning, it can be done (Bobo et al. 1991). Building caring communities is do-able and realistic, as the towns of Franklin, Plymouth, Manchester, and Rochester, New Hampshire, and others demonstrate. While many towns could be profiled here, I have selected two that used different strategies to address the needs of high risk children. Rochester was beset with a variety of problems, as described in the story by a homeless girl in "My Wild Gypsy Life" (see the Appendix A). Consider how one small town has begun to make itself more caring for the poor and homeless as it helps the entire community. We were contacted by Anne May, a community organizer in that community, to help her "do something" about a rundown, problem-filled neighborhood. Once that neighborhood had been a source of pride for the community. A few oldtimers remained there and wanted to turn the community back into a decent place to live. So Anne put flyers at all of the homes and shelters and used the media to publicize a community organizational meeting. Anne, my husband, and I helped the seventy or so people who attended the meeting to identify their problems, prioritize those they wished to tackle, and determine how they would go about solving them. At first, local residents like Norm were resistant, "nonbelievers" of change. But by the end of the meeting, Norm and company were excited about what *they* could do to improve their neighborhood.

Over the course of only three years, see what has happened: Rochester now has six community coalitions, each overseeing special neighborhoods in town. Now the six neighborhood groups hold joint coalition meetings. They share information, ideas, resources, and are building an infrastructure that is transforming the entire community. Because of their success, now outside business and groups call them, wanting to help. "At first we had to beg businesses, the media, and even the town council to come to our meetings. Now they regularly show up as part of the group, and they ask *us* what they can do!" said Anne. Even civic groups from nearby towns ask if they can invest their efforts in Rochester rather than their own communities, because "we prove we will act. Everybody wants to get in on a good thing. Successful helping is contagious."

The actions these neighborhood coalitions take, each seemingly insignificant on its own, together change these "backwater neighborhoods that have been passed by." Community organizers first change the tone of the community; *then* people change their perception about the community, each other—and themselves.

Initially, there must be opportunities for the neighbors to communicate with each other and to decide what they want to do. "These gatherings have a tone which honors the diverse elements of the community—kids and grandparents, greaseballs and doctors, police, and everyone in between." At the meetings, people "feel free to ask any outrageous question without getting stamped on." In short, everybody is treated as if he or she belongs. Off-the-wall ideas are sometimes unworkable, but show creativity. "It is important to build an atmosphere that fosters creativity, then honors it—and that's a big reason why people keep coming back," says Anne. "Some people are loose cannons, but if nonconfrontational roles are used with them, and they are allowed to have their say, then the principles of honoring diversity are preserved. We prove that everyone is important by the way we treat them. The neighborhood becomes an emotionally 'safe' place then because everybody knows they are accepted."

This approach holds that everyone has unique skills that he or she can bring to the community. Some people know how to use their hands, while some use their heads. Everyone knows something different that can be used as a resource. Alignments and networks must be built, in which members feel that they "own" the group. Building communities will not work with outsiders coming in to tell the residents what they ought to do; it can only work when the insiders of the community reach out to one another.

Leadership that gives away ownership, not keeping it for themselves, is critically important. The coalitions must be built in the spirit of true partnership. For instance, Norm has become a wonderful, insightful leader. He is not looking for a title, he is not doing it for honors, he is not into ownership of the group. He is someone who does what needs to be done because it is the good and right thing to do and who will work for it over the long haul. Norm regularly gets people together to process what works and where efforts go astray. A cyclical process has resulted, in which Norm empowers the group, which supports Norm to be more creative, which creates opportunity to empower the group. He and Anne are positive people who can transform negative situations into positive ones. Negative leaders who want to control create groups that don't work.

It is important to have fun and fellowship interjected into the business of changing a community. Neighbors get into good discussion and problem solving during the meetings. The meetings always end with dessert and coffee; there is something about breaking bread together that brings people into a sense of communication and concern for each other. Humor must also be present. One way that Anne found to lighten up a potentially busy or dull meeting is to "make what you are doing attractive enough that others want to be part of it. We have drawings for prizes at the end of all our regular meetings. The prizes are donated by people in the community. It might be a haircut, a ten-dollar gift certificate at the local pharmacy, or a case of soda from the convenience store. The prizes get people in the community to patronize each other, and it gives them something in common to talk about."

The coalitions mobilize the media to promote all the good things that are being done; people must know about their activities in order to get excited to help. Following are a few of the activities the neighborhood coalitions sponsored to bring a sense of community:

- Tree pruning of city-owned trees in one neighborhood got the residents out to work and talk together as they did a job that nobody "owned" but that benefited everybody. Members of the community were also invited so that they could learn how to prune trees, in hopes that they would teach others in all parts of town.
- One neighborhood had deteriorated so badly that the neighbors decided to hold a cleanup day. One Saturday, the town donated dumpsters and equipment, and everyone in the neighborhood was encouraged to clean up his or her own yard, as well as help others. People were all out talking with one another, helping carry objects together to the trash, and looking around to see what else they could do to make the neighborhood like nicer. The mayor and town council cooked hot dogs and hamburgers for the workers, while groceries donated chips and dessert, and a restaurant gave away drinks. A festive, carnivallike atmosphere resulted as children, teens, and adults worked together to make their neighborhood better. Afterwards, people were much less likely to allow the area to degenerate, and the community has been improving in appearance ever since.

- A walking group is being created. Walking is not just for fitness, but also for fun, and provides people who would not normally get out to meet each other a reason to do so. When walkers are out, they regularly knock on the doors of the elderly or shut-ins to offer them help. Walking allows regular checks at abandoned places and opportunities to say hello to kids, and increases the safety of the area.

"Incredible contacts" are made between people when they talk together, contacts that can help people to avoid homelessness. One woman was being forced out of her house when her husband was laid off. Yet the neighborhood knew they were good people who wanted to keep their kids going to school in the neighborhood. The informal network enabled them to find another place a block away.

It is entirely possible to build a network of caregiving that is all but invisible, costs little, preserves integrity, and restructures the entire community. Sometimes community change occurs by the actions of a single person whose generosity becomes contagious. Jerry Rainville of Rochester started a "no questions asked" food pantry out of his house. This quietly operated no-fanfare operation soon caught the attention of civic groups, who donated money, resources, and volunteers. Over time, the pantry became a part of the community service infrastructure, moving to a town-owned building where other services are provided. Jerry recently died, but he changed the world by his actions, and others now carry on his contrubution as their own.

While community change in Rochester was created by the actions of individuals such as Anne and Jerry, a different model of community development was used in Plymouth, New Hampshire. There, an ad hoc committee for youth at risk has been meeting for several years. This no-nonsense full-steam-ahead committee consisted of wise leaders who knew the importance of community action partnership with scholarly input, research, and grassroots fundraising efforts. It took the committee years to determine exactly what was needed and how to best fill those needs, but never ceasing, methodically planning, they are using funding from HUD in the form of community block grants to build a facility that will house and integrate all of the local human service agencies. In this way, they hope to avoid system fragmentation that has led to many families receiving inadequate care.

It *is* possible to re-create the best of the rural traditions for use in today's world. Rural areas can rebuild their traditional sense of community by the use of both caring, careful action and interaction.

The problems that confront local communities as they attempt to provide effective services for homeless children and families have developed over the course of many years. These problems have grown as the social and demographic changes affecting family functioning have outstripped communities' abilities to respond. In the last decade, when there has been recognized need to reform services, a typical solution has been bureaucratic reorganization. But bureaucratic reorganization has not yielded the intended results. All too often, such changes absorb most of an agency's energies, create a flurry of organizational and staff changes, but result in few tangible improvements for families.

Other reform efforts have engineered ineffective shifts of responsibility between state and local governments. In an effort to improve services, some agencies centralize their authority, others engage in rapid decentralization, and still others begin elaborate trades of fiscal and program responsibilities that often result in avoiding the largest dollar commitments. Block grant strategies constitute yet another way that the government has tried to simplify some of the mechanics of service funding and delivery. But these strategies do not necessarily translate into better services.

All of these attempts to streamline services miss the essential point—helping homeless children and families. In fact, many of these solutions move away from, rather than toward, a service system that is rooted more genuinely in local concerns, that is more responsive to individual needs and is more reflective of changing local priorities.

The process of local governance is one vehicle through which communities can shape services to achieve goals. While the federal and state governments can promote, encourage, and facilitate the development of this process, ultimately it is the responsibility of local community leaders to make it work. The effectiveness of children and family services in the years ahead may very well depend upon how well local leaders rise to this challenge. The strategy recommended here is one developed by the Center for the Study of Social Policy (1991).

To address the problem of rural housing distress, one must empower the rural community to develop local task forces that will plan, implement, and evaluate actions designed to address the causes and consequences of homelessness. The purpose of these local governing bodies is to facilitate community agreement on problems and to create more effective methods of achieving desired outcomes for families and children through improved and more comprehensive service strategies. The key is to work collaboratively toward agreement in problem solving that will work for the community. Every community must develop its own action plan. By bringing together a wide range of local agencies, institutions, and concerned citizens, communities can design and implement creative, cross-cutting, and cost-effective solutions to problems such as homelessness.

Rarely does one component in the rural community have the resources necessary to address any of the fundamental problems underlying child and family homelessness in rural areas. Even when an attempt is made, often planning activities stay in the process stage because implementation is too difficult and expensive for any unit to accomplish alone. Bringing together all of the agencies, institutions, and citizens who have resources and ideas to address the problem can produce remarkable results. Local governance of this nature seeks a broad definition of problems, reaching across agency and organizational boundaries to deliberately involve multiple systems of care. The new unit will be an entity whose responsibility is to ensure that action occurs. The governing entity's activities in the name of accountability should create a different culture of responsibility for children and families within a community. The aim should be to achieve an environment in which people become more aware of children's needs, grow concerned about their well-being, and act to improve their status. This means assuring the well-being of their parents, which is translated to increasing the stability of the schools, agencies, economic, and political institutions.

The four basic functions of this collaborative effort are (1) agenda-setting and strategy development around high-priority community problems; (2) developing new service capacities to meet needs more effectively; (3) coordinating fiscal strategies to support the community's service agenda; and (4) maintaining accountability for outcomes of the efforts. A communitywide action process of this nature must revolve around constant feedback on the state of the community's children and must reflect diverse perspectives relevant to local interests.

This approach is not easy to implement. The process of bringing together entities that have previously called their own shots under a different umbrella in which they must share ideas, resources, and responsibility is threatening to many people because it involves change. But if the change is carried out correctly and sensitively with true collaboration, the benefits of this type of local governance will emerge across time (Center for the Study of Social Policy 1991).

If such an approach is not adopted, it is likely that nothing will be done to improve the quality of life for the community and its residents who are in need or some other attempt to impose order on homeless children and families will be made. Too often, efforts emerge as expedient organizational and fiscal changes that ultimately do not make a difference. Faced with pressure to achieve something, political leaders may fall back on solutions that are ineffective or may actually add to the chaos surrounding local services. It is critical, then, that rural communities engage in some form of strategic problem solving to address the causes and consequences of homelessness.

As rural communities become aware that they have homeless people, there are a number of steps they can take in their planning process:

Step 1. Identify the problem. What is the problem of concern? Children who live in substandard housing? Teenagers who suddenly have nowhere to live? Families who live in campgrounds or different apartments every three months? Children who come to school hungry and improperly clothed? First, the problem that sparks the interest of the community must be clearly identified. There must be some consensus that this is a problem before communities can proceed with further action. The problem may be great or small but must be of sufficient interest to members of the community that they will want to do something about it.

Step 2. Document need. It is important to determine if the initial perception of the problem is accurate. Therefore, some data-gathering must occur to determine if the need is as great as—or greater than— initially identified. This need could be documented informally by interviews with key informants in the community who are "in the know." Need could also be much more formally calculated by the use of needs assessments. Newspaper stories, police reports, welfare statistics, hospital or public health reports can also be valuable sources of data that can help the community document need.

Step 3. Identify currently used interventions. Undoubtedly, the problem existed for some time before it was brought to the attention of community leaders. How has the problem been dealt with? What resources, both formal and informal, have been used by the individual or community to address the problem? How successful have these attempts been? Where are the gaps in service? Once these issues are determined, it will be possible to develop a more appropriate plan of action. For instance, a skeleton structure may already exist naturally that could be enhanced to address the problem. On the other hand, it may be that there is no vehicle currently available for addressing the homeless problem. Assessment of the currently used interventions will guide the planner about what to do and how to do it and will identify the costs of time, money, and human effort.

Step 4. Select ideal solutions. What is the ideal solution for the problem? It does not matter whether or not the ideal solution is within the reach of the community now. It can encompass the dream of constructing the community of the future, holding a vision of what the community would like for its children. The community governing task force is encouraged to reach toward truly ideal solutions, for as the adage goes, "if you only get halfway to lofty goals, you will have gone father than if you achieved a mediocre goal." The ideal solutions will shape the goals that need to be achieved to solve the problem.

Step 5. Determine objectives to achieve the goals. At this point, the community needs to develop three levels of objectives for achieving each of its goals. For each goal listed, there needs to be a short-term plan of action, an intermediate plan, and a long-range plan.

The long-term goal of a community may be to eradicate existing homelessness and prevent future homelessness. But this cannot be accomplished overnight. In order for a community to feel enthusiastic about undertaking an important new venture—especially one that is as controversial as programs for homeless children and families—the community and homeless people have to see early indications of success. Typically these short-term objectives should be easily attainable within a brief period of time at a modest cost. The short-term objectives should emotionally motivate others so that there is an increase in the number of people who can be enlisted for future efforts. Education programs are excellent first steps, because until the public understands the nature of the problem, they will not be motivated to do anything about it. Additionally, people whose consciousness is raised may want an outlet for the expression of their concern. Examples of short-term projects include a community food pantry; clothes closet; soup kitchen; speaker's series; newsletter; or library series. However, it will soon be clear that the short-term activities are not enough. As a member of a local women's club stated: "We learned about the problem of family homelessness and wanted to do something about it. So as a club, we decided to make curtains for the shelter so that it would be bright and cheery for the families. But now I am wondering if putting up curtains really did anything at all for the homeless families. I want to know now, what could I be doing that is more useful?"

Intermediate objectives are necessary within the community planning. These objectives typically take more coordination, more effort, more time, and more money. However, they are still concrete and doable projects. The intermediate objectives often concern tangible, long-lasting contributions to the homeless and at-risk populations. Such activities could include developing a shelter or host-home program for families or children; establishing a mentoring program in which a homeless person is linked with a stable community member who can model positive parenting or employment skills; creating a job bank; and instituting a breakfast or hot lunch program within the schools. It is hoped that once these programs are established, funding can be secured for them to be ongoing.

But these intermediate programs, while helpful, are just Band Aids. They do not solve the underlying problems that caused the homelessness. Since both structural and personal problems cause homelessness, the sources for each must be linked with specific types of interventions. If the economy is poor, how can new jobs be created? If there is a lack of affordable housing, what must be done? If substance abuse is a problem within the community, how can it be prevented? What kinds of family support programs need to be instituted—and where? What kinds of legislation needs to be introduced in the state and federal government that will enable the communities to construct the quality of life necessary for them to thrive? These are long-range objectives. It may take years for them to be realized. But if concrete steps are made to achieve them, then they *can* be obtained!

Step 6. Decide which objectives can be achieved in the short, intermediate, and long term. Identify short-term, intermediate, and long-term objectives. In doing so, the following questions must be addressed:

What resources are currently available?
What resources need to be acquired?
What are the barriers to achieving the objective?
What steps are to be taken?
Who will take those steps?
What is the timeline for achieving each step?

If a community or agency can go through these steps, there is a greater possibility that they will be able to achieve their goals of helping homeless children and families. In this way, they will be able to tailor their community resources and characteristics to meeting the problems.

Step 7. Evaluate! Is the selected course of action taking the community in the anticipated direction? Process and outcome evaluation are important parts of any programmatic effort. While community representatives will have good information about the strengths and weaknesses of efforts, it may also be useful to have outside evaluators assist in this process. People who have no vested interest in any particular outcomes may provide a more neutral set of data from which decisions can be made.

Agencies within a given community can exchange their comprehensive work plans so that they can network and plan activities in a partnership, rather than each organization acting independently. Ultimately, if a community wants to impact the problem of child and family homelessness, all of its components must work together. One unit—

such as the school or a church—cannot do it alone. It would be mutually beneficial if every community/agency would send its action plans to a central source that could consolidate all the programmatic information on homeless services in one location. This clearinghouse could (1) disseminate information about existing programs to other interested parties; (2) aggregate the information to determine what are commonly used strategies; (3) identify gaps in services within the region; (4) serve as a nucleus for networking among the divergent communities, groups, and professionals; and (5) provide information about funding or program opportunities so that the communities can expand or maintain their services to children.

Ironically, the entire community will ultimately benefit from the programs and structures put in place to address the needs of the homeless. By developing a safety net of human service programs, the entire community and its residents ultimately help themselves.

Throughout this book, I have alleged that homeless rural people are different than the urban homeless in demographic characteristics, reasons for homelessness, and response to services. I have also pointed out that rural areas are well apprised to develop their own solutions, using traditional rural strengths that will benefit not just the homeless but the entire community. But there are benefits to some urban models of service delivery that merit investigation for their use in rural areas. There are ways that local residents can utilize professionals in order to work successfully within rural areas with homeless people.

There are three models of service delivery that rural areas can implement.The first is an imported model in which outside agencies with professional expertise enter a rural community to offer services. This has advantages because it allows a rural community to bring in expertise from larger communities to help them solve problems. Such a model permits very rapid start-up and ensures that services are of high quality at the outset. For instance, a federal program may set up a regional office, or a private business may set up a satellite center in a rural area. The people who develop and administer the program are urban in orientation.

The second type of intervention consists of a local initiative model in which existing indigenous local resources are organized to offer services. This has advantages because the local agency personnel already know the community residents, their values, and their way of life. They also have relationships established with other agencies, providers, and community leaders, which makes it easier for them to expand into new service areas successfully. However, this local model has disadvantages when attempts are made to expand into needed areas in which the local staff has little expertise. Lead time for training is extensive—and expensive, and there is a period of development in which services may not be of as high quality as is desirable.

The third intervention is a partnership model in which organizational and professional resources can be imported from the outside but services and community organization are provided locally. This model combines the best of both worlds—bringing professional expertise from the outside, within the structure of a readily established organization in the community. Having local personnel there to interface between the outside professional and the local residents appears to be a better strategy for program success. It incorporates solutions for service delivery recommended for integrating basic health, mental health, and social service programs. This model is best when it recruits "natural helpers" in the community and volunteers among the townspeople. This has the virtue of using local individuals without incurring additional expense or building cultural barriers to care.

Homeless rural people do not like to ask professionals for help. When they do, help must be given in a way that is emotionally palatable if it is to be used. This means that in order to link people up with resources, special considerations must be given to the way help is provided and the manner of interaction by those who have the authority to award assistance.

It has been well established that there are significant differences in attitudes, values, and lifestyles between residents in rural areas and residents in urban areas (Butler 1992; Fitchen 1991; Flax et al. 1979; Flora et al. 1992). Urban areas and rural areas are different social worlds requiring different orientations in delivering vital social services. These differences directly influence the kinds of professional training required to meet successfully the needs of the homeless population.

Most professional training occurs in urban settings and is provided by faculty who are themselves urban in training and personal orientation. A few colleges and universities may specialize in rural delivery services, but most do not. Most schools of social work, nursing, counseling, and social policy are located in urban areas. Many teach students who are also from cities and small towns, students who plan to assume professional roles within the same civic environments. Even those that are not, remain captive to urban professional models: the training of practitioners to serve in rural areas is not a cost-effective program.

While this urban bias works satisfactorily for the homeless urban client, it may fail in serving those in rural areas (Martinez-Brawley 1990; Fitchen 1991; Vissing, Salloway, and Siress 1992). If we do not know how to train professionals to practice in rural settings, how are we attracting professionals to rural practice locations? "Not very well" must be the answer. There is a dearth of physicians, nurses, psychologists, and social workers in rural areas. When they are offered lower salaries with fewer resources, it is understandable that professionals may not choose to work in a rural area. Despite the lovely geographic environment, it is not easy for professionals to work with deprived populations in rural areas.

Rural residents, especially those who are vulnerable and ill-educated and have low self-esteem, organize their lives around issues of trust rather than issues of expertise. When problems eradicate housing, people ask family and friends for help first. They only go to professionals as a last resort.

This is in direct contrast to the implicit assumptions of professional culture. There is an opposition of trust versus expertise in the implicit norms of the professional and rural cultures. Professional culture relies upon expertise—especially that gained from academic training and practice. It also relies upon impersonal authority, in which "experts"—whom one does not know well—have the right to probe into one's personal life, asking questions about sensitive issues that will determine if help will be given. Professionals also diagnose, treat, and dictate one's behavior. The homeless resident, confronted by expertise, is not supposed to question the basis of authority but is expected to suspend disbelief and to comply with whatever he or she told to do. Professional culture focuses on conceptualization, training, systematic observations, results, application, replication, and generalization. It implies that the homeless should be self-motivated to get services and should openly report very personal situations to total strangers.

Professionalism requires that the rural homeless person delegate trust and authority. This model of professionalism is one of high-status authority. Rural culture, on the other hand, is founded on low-status authority, grounded in long-standing familiarity. It is based on trust between members of the community. Trust is not something that can be ascribed easily based on someone's professional status. To be a successful professional in a rural area, it is important to accept the rural setting on its own terms. It is critical to have the community accept the outsider, both as a member of the community (implying a multitude of roles) and as a professional (Flax et al. 1979). One cannot be a professional who goes to work and then leaves work behind at the end of the day. In a rural area, the professional will get coffee at the same restaurant as the person who has had no place to stay for the night. His or her child may go to school with previous—or potential—homeless children. In small towns, if the professional is approached by homeless clients while on "personal time," the professional can gain a reputation of being cold, uncaring, and disinterested if the homeless are not helped with whatever they may need at the moment.

Rural professionals who "live high" in fancy homes, who drive expensive cars, and whose lifestyle seems diametrically opposed to the reality of the homeless people whom they serve may find themselves targeted as unsympathetic and exploitative. One cannot separate personal from professional life in rural areas the way one can in cities. This means that one has to live out the commitment to the community. In rural areas, professionals are never "off duty."

Being a member of the community means that one talks the same language. Local residents, like Norm, can be transformed into paraprofessionals. The use of lesser-paid and lesser-trained people indigenous to an area might create a useful liaison, providing community information to the professional and helping the professional to modify his or her services or approach to gain greater acceptance. Norm is successful because of his low-status role and because he knows about what services are available and how to access them. If he doesn't have what he needs, he works to develop the necessary resources. He is willing to "do what it takes."

I found that a major problem experienced by the rural homeless was that once the informal network could no longer help them, they did not know where to go for help. Even those professionals who were "supposed" to know what services existed often did not. I contacted one shelter for a list of who they routinely contacted and was given only a one-page sheet with a dozen or so hand-scrawled phone numbers. There was no central depository of information where they could learn about what resources existed and how to access them.

A second problem experienced by the rural communities was that many times needed services simply did not exist. Sometimes rural areas have access to services that they may not know about. In many cases, the guidelines of existing agencies are in conflict with one another, making it difficult for providers and recipients alike to know what services are really available.

Small towns want to know about successful programs for homeless children and families that other small towns have instituted. But where do they get this information? In order to access a comprehensive, nonduplicating system of services for the rural homeless, the following types of networks could be developed.

Every region within every state has a set of organizations that are responsible for policies and programs that affect homeless children and families. Some of these players may include the state legislature, department of education, department of social services, employment office, department for protective services, department of mental health, welfare and financial assistance offices, housing authorities, shelter providers, lawyers, and health care providers. The purpose of this network is to make "bottom-line" decisions about which agency is responsible for what service. The network of professionals can review guidelines for service to determine if there is any category of people who will systematically fall through the cracks of the system. If so, the community agencies can work together to create safety net services.

Theoretically, if a service is available, one should be able to access it. While this may be the case, in rural areas the wheel moves much faster and smoother if local providers know one another. As I was told, "people help people" in small towns. Therefore, it is useful to have local providers meet with one another in order to share ideas and concerns and to build partnerships. Using the system approach, more can be done together than any single agency can do alone. For example, in one community, I found that four different agencies were planning on doing a community needs assessment. None had enough money to do a really good job. They would have been much better off pooling their money and ideas so that all of them could get a top-notch report, instead of a mediocre one.

Each community, or state, should develop its own "Resource Guide to Services." In New Hampshire there was no centralized source for this information. Director of the New Hampshire Coalition for the Homeless, Henrietta Charest was the individual that most people called upon when they did not know how to access a resource. If Henrietta did not know about a resource, she always knew where to go to find out. But when Henrietta died, the state was without a resource guide. Any time a system relies on a single gatekeeper for information, all service recipients are at risk. It is impossible to help if one does not know the "who, what, where, and how" of the helping systems.

Identifying providers by service and by geographic region in a resource guide will link these providers together to create a more systematic path of access for the homeless. It will help to identify both where services are duplicated and where they are unaddressed.

The proposed guide should:

1. Identify key public and private providers on federal, state, and local levels that every homeless person in the state may be able to access— such as AFDC, food stamps, and Section 8 housing.
2. Explain how to find and apply for these programs.

3. Identify major resources in different geographic regions so that the reader can quickly find resources that are available in specific areas.
4. Classify services by type, so that all resources of a particular type are located in the same section of the resource guide.
5. Include key services such as the following:
   A. Food—including food stamps, soup kitchens, food pantries, etc.
   B. Clothes—including free clothing locations and information on state, agency, or charity assistance.
   C. Housing—including lists of emergency shelters, short-term housing, and long-term housing.
   D. Social services—including mental health, substance abuse, and support services.
   E. Education—including requirements, where to go for help, information on vocational training programs
   F. Employment—including state employment centers, temporary employment centers, long-term employment resources.
   G. Legal issues for both providers and homeless people.
   H. Medical—including how to access Medicaid, physical and dental clinics that see low-income people, emergency prescriptions, eyeglasses, etc.
   I. Financial—including state and federal sources of income assistance.
   J. Transportation

As useful as a resource guide is, it cannot address all the questions that a person may have about homelessness or homeless services. It is desirable to have a physical location, staffed with trained personnel, that could serve as an information collector and disseminator about the types of resources that exist. Programs and personnel will change. In an emergency situation, it is helpful to have someone who knows all of the resources and people so that the best contacts are made in the most efficient ways. As one counselor pointed out, it took her three days to find emergency housing for a girl. If she had known where to call initially, the girl would not have been in limbo those extra days.

Information centers can also be the clearinghouse for materials that people can borrow or use for program development or research purposes. Videos, books, articles, curriculum materials, fund-raising information, and the like could all be compiled at a central location. Because of the access to information and resources, the information center can conduct workshops for local governance councils, schools, agencies, and public gatherings. The information center can also facilitate grant writing and disseminate information about funding opportunities. In this way, collaborative methods for working together and helping each other can result for rural towns.

This clearinghouse need not cost a great deal. While it may be logically located in the state capital city—near legislators and lobbyists—a clearinghouse could also be set up within a child or family service agency or within a homeless shelter or state coalition for the homeless. In fact, it may even be possible for a voluntary association—such as a civic organization—to take on the sponsorship of such a clearinghouse as a service to the state or regional community.

A homeless mother in a rural area may not know about the homeless resource guide or be able to get to the homeless information center. The greatest resource that she might have is the telephone. A toll-free number that could link the mother up with personnel trained in the area of homeless services could be life-saving for her.

There is another benefit of having a trained person answer the 1-800 telephone line. People call hotlines when they really need help. Homeless people may not be able to wait until tomorrow or next week for answers or help. Many are in immediate life and death situations. As a result, the professional talking with the distressed caller may be able to provide not just information but emotional support and care management.

A computer network could ideally work in a variety of ways. A teen in a given community may need immediate information about shelter for the night. A well-devised computer network could enter parameters such as age, sex, town, and need for shelter into the computer and be given information about all of the existing shelters that could serve his needs. In many rural communities, there may not be a shelter that could take him. What if the only shelter around is full? Where is the next closest place he could go? A computer system could be developed to provide this information immediately.

Computerized information could expand on the material contained in the homeless resource guide. It could also be programmed to allow for shelters to report availability, as well as to contain qualification information for receiving particular kinds of aid; where people are most likely to get the fastest help; and places that report helping, but don't do a good job of it.

Implementation of such a system is initially expensive. But prevention costs far less than treatment and crisis in the long run.

The Housing Assistance Council (1990a) acknowledges that rural communities are faced with many obstacles in addressing homeless;

lack of community awareness and scarce financial resources are prime among them. It has provided a guide to federal and state resources for rural homeless assistance providers, especially through community action programs. This guide also lists federal housing programs that are most accessible and useful to small communities and rural areas.

Rural areas that wish to engage in community development or establish programs for the homeless can benefit from the work done by those in other areas. There are agencies that specialize in helping the homeless and that work with people across the nation. They know about programs that work and those that don't, sources for funding, and legal concerns, and they have libraries of valuable information. Organizations that can provide ideas, materials, technical support, and consultation include:

> The National Coalition for the Homeless
> 1612 K St. NW, Suite 1004
> Washington, DC 20006
> 202-775-1322
>
> Interagency Council on the Homeless
> 451 Seventh St. SW, Suite 7274
> Washington, DC 20410
> 202-708-1480
>
> National Law Center on Homelessness and Poverty
> 918 F St. NW, Suite 412
> Washington, DC 20004
> 202-638-2535
>
> National Alliance to End Homelessness
> 1518 K St. NW
> Washington, DC 20005
> 202-638-1526
>
> Institute for Children and Poverty
> Homes for the Homeless
> 36 Cooper Square
> New York, NY
> 212-529-5252
>
> Health Care for the Homeless Resource Center
> 210 Lincoln St.
> Boston, MA 02111
> 617-482-9485

CASSP Technical Assistance Center
Georgetown University Child Development Center
Reservoir Rd. NW
Washington, DC 20007
202-687-8635

Housing Programs for Homeless in Rural Areas
Housing Assistance Council
1025 Vermont Ave. NW, Suite 606
Washington, DC 20006
202-842-8600

Children's Defense Fund
122 C St. NW
Washington, DC 20001
202-638-8787

Child Welfare League of America
440 First St. NW, Suite 310
Washington, DC 20001
202-638-2952

National Association of State Coordinators for the Education of
    Homeless Children and Youth
c/o Louisiana Department of Education
645 Main St., 3rd Floor
Baton Rouge, LA 70801
504-342-3431

These groups can save rural advocates hours of time and help communities develop more efficient and cost-effective programs.

Because schools may be the only refuge from a chaotic world for homeless children (U.S. Department of Education 1992), classrooms should be structured to support their diverse and comprehensive needs. In order partially to counteract adverse conditions of homelessness such as lack of control and instability, Klein et al. (1993) prescribe a predictable environment that offers choice within limits. Routines, materials and activities, adult-student groupings, space, comings and goings, parents, and staff support must all be considered in the development of programs that really work for homeless students. Guidelines for rural and small school settings that increase accessibility and services to homeless children are available (Stronge 1992). Small town schools can design many programs to meet homeless children's needs, and many documents exist that describe how to provide comprehensive and quality services to homeless rural children and their families through the schools (Vissing, Schroepfer and Bloise 1994; Children's Services Department 1990; Douglas 1992; Brands and DeBates 1992; Mann 1994; Taylor 1989; National Association of State Coordinators for the Education of Homeless Children and Youth 1993; National Law Center on Homelessness and Poverty 1990b; Bowen 1989; National Coalition for the Homeless 1994).

While most educational recommendations focus on elementary through high school students, colleges are also an important place to teach about homelessness and intervention programs. College curricula on hunger and homelessness are now provided at more than eighty universities across the nation in departments such as anthropology, biology, city planning, geography, hospitality, nutrition, philosophy, political science, religion, and sociology. The National Student Campaign Against Hunger and Homelessness (Nugent 1990) provides course syllabi, reading lists, and other curriculum materials. More than one hundred universities have sponsored National Teach-Ins about homelessness, and campus outreach opportunities leagues have been formed. The National Coalition for the Homeless and Student Homeless Action Campaign (Taylor 1988) can provide further information about such activities.

Another way that colleges could be useful in addressing the problem of rural homelessness is by incorporating training strategies that would better meet the needs of rural people. Traditional academic training encourages development of expertise and professional authority. Yet it is exactly these "trained incapacities" that hinder professionals from helping the rural communities they wish to serve. This is not to imply that professionals cannot be professional in rural areas. They can. But it is a different mode of professionalism. Put succinctly, skills of "staying low" are not taught to students. They can't be taught humility from behind a lectern or in front of a blackboard. Social workers, nurses, educators are all taught models of professional expertise and authority. But these are self-defeating for those who want to work with the destitute in rural areas. The model of education in the university is totally antithetical to instruction in staying low, in keeping down, in admitting ignorance in the face of what is important in the lives of others.

Successful professionals can be taught how to learn from the local residents; they can learn to say, "I don't know what your life is like. Please teach me." They must be taught to listen not just with ears but with hearts if they are to communicate effectively with rural homeless children and families. To speak the language, to understand the concerns of the residents of the area, and to be empathic to their needs as members of the community as well as family members—these are just as important as knowing the correct diagnosis in the American Psychological Association's Diagnostic and Statistical Manual or where to obtain emergency fuel and affordable housing.

There are a number of curricular innovations that any competent academic would conjure up in response to this challenge. The first obvious option is to offer on a recommended or required basis special classes in different aspects of rural life at the undergraduate or graduate level, such as Rural Sociology; Rural Poverty; Psychology of Rural Life; Rural Social Welfare; Health Care Delivery in Rural Areas; Organizational Systems in Rural Locations; and Program Development in Rural Areas. Such curriculum options would address issues that would prepare students for the challenges of a rural environment.

Obviously, specially designed internships that place trainees in rural settings are desirable. This would provide the student with a taste of being different and alienated, the experience that comes from trying to be an expert among those who distrust experts. If it is too much to ask students to spend an entire semester in a rural internship, it might be desirable for some students to live in the rural environment for a shorter period of time such as a winter break. During this time, they might have a specific job focus and be mentored by both professionals and community people. Other students might do well in an internship in which they work in a community two days a week and are located on campus going to school for the remainder of the week. They could keep this schedule over a year's time. A yearlong two-day-a-week internship creates a very different experience for a student than one that lasts a winter break.

Every state has a department of employment with regional offices. These offices are the link to work throughout the community and state. This agency can promote local, state, federal, public, and private jobs and training programs. Businesses may benefit by hiring homeless people. There must be both public and private avenues for matching businesses and homeless job seekers (Gilbert 1993). How well does the employment office in your rural area work? Some branches work much more effectively than others, and many need the partnership of people in their community to make them work better. Branch offices of federal or state programs do respond when local leaders "encourage" them to be more responsive.

Rural areas can have access to programs such as the Job Training Councils, Job Corps, Homes for the Homeless, Train and Gain program (Homes for the Homeless 1992), and AmeriCorps. Despite current limitations, the Job Opportunities and Basic Skills (JOBS) program established by the Family Support Act to help recipients of Aid to Families with Dependent Children can be accessed by rural communities to help families become self-sufficient (Foundation for Child Development 1992). Local communities may have vocational rehabilitation and vocational training programs. Schools are often good resources for the development of such programs, especially for students who are not college-bound.

Rural areas need access to a full range of health-care services, including dental, mental health, and physical health. Providing health-care services to youth and families needs to be holistic and comprehensive, as they may need not just housing but also medical care, mental health treatment, drug abuse services, education, job training, and legal services (Atchley 1991). Rural services must not only exist, they must be readily accessible. If people cannot get an appointment for eight weeks, if they have no insurance, or if doctors will not take Medicaid, the resources for all rights do not exist for the rural homeless. Such barriers must be overcome, and can be when the community agents work as partners together for the common goal of providing health care.

Rural areas may benefit from contacting the Division of Programs for Special Populations/Bureau of Primary Health Care, which supports grants to provide health-care services to homeless individuals and families. The Health Care for the Homeless Directory (National Association of Community Health Centers 1990) lists a variety of public and private agencies serving homeless people.

Helping homeless people to be healthier is just a small section of the Healthy People 2000 effort (Stoto et al. 1990), which is designed to make the United States a nation of healthy people, regardless of age, race, or socioeconomic status.

Rural areas have access to federal programs that can help feed homeless children. The federal Child Nutrition Program and the Child and Adult Care Food Program provide low-income children with free breakfast and lunch. This program is typically administered through the public schools. The Supplemental Food Program for Women, Infants, and Children (WIC) offers nutritious foods, nutrition education, breast-feeding support, and health care referrals. Food stamps should be available for eligible persons in every community. Organizations such as 4-H or the Cooperative Extension Service provide nutrition education to people in every state. Local areas may develop food pantries and soup kitchens.

Summertime is frequently a problem for children who rely on school as their source of not just social support but also food. A manual describing efforts to feed hungry children during the summer months and extended periods away from school can be obtained from the California Food Policy Advocates (1993). It details information about how to develop and administer such a program, as well as lists of offices, federal regulations, promotional materials, menus, and methods of reimbursement.

The best solution for homelessness is to create not emergency shelter but long-term shelter. The National Housing Law Project (1993b) asserts that the national goal should be permanent housing for homeless people, not emergency or transitional shelter. Section 8 housing, sponsored through the U.S. Department of Housing and Urban Development (HUD) allows for low-income people to lie in regular neighborhood housing. Rural communities can access or create a municipal housing authority to apply for this federal money. HUD also provides a variety of other grants, including community block grants, shelter grants, and the sale of foreclosed homes. Public housing is an option that a community may want to consider, although it is a less desirable homeless prevention program than Section 8 because public housing creates identifiable ghettos of indigent people.

The Farmer's Home Administration (FHA) leases single-family housing to public or nonprofit organizations for use as transitional housing for homeless people. It can also provide low-interest loans for home buyers. Most states have housing authorities that can help people in rural areas to identify special federal, state, and local programs. Low-interest mortgages are provided in some states to people who qualify.

Mulroy and Lane (1992) recommend reforming zoning regulations so that a wider array of communities include residents of mixed income levels, increasing AFDC benefits, ensuring comparable pay so that female heads of families can afford market rents, developing new assisted housing, and expanding Section 8 and housing voucher programs. In a study of housing programs for the homeless in rural areas, the Housing Assistance Council (1988) identified common elements that contribute to program effectiveness, including an understanding of the demographic characteristics of the area's homeless population; close ties of the project with the community in which housing is located; a supportive and involved board of directors; and an active social service network in the community. Habitat for Humanity provides tangible housing development in a community-spirited way. The Home Builders Institute (1993) has developed a Homeless Employment and Related Training (HEART) program, which rebuilds or builds affordable housing while training homeless people for jobs in the construction industry—thereby linking housing development with job training, employment, and social services. This program can be tailored to meet the needs of any size community. Other housing options available to communities are the HOME program, which gives federal money to each state and many communities for low-income housing. Through Community Housing Development Organizations, nearly $1.5 billion can be accessed (Gramlich 1992).

The religious community has found that it can make a difference by providing affordable housing to those with limited incomes. Housing programs depend upon cost, labor, expertise, financial and legal risk, personal ministry, and church mission (Monsma 1990). Practical guides for congregations that wish to establish a housing ministry outline the development process, from how a religious congregation can fit such a project into the church's missions and goals to developing a funding and financing plan, to designing the desired project, to proving support services to residents (Churches Conference on Shelter and Housing 1991). Also, churches can help rebuild community housing by sponsoring home improvement and weatherization efforts and support home ownership counseling and youth construction crews (Shabecoff 1992). For religious communities that want to develop a broader ministry in community development, the Lilly Endowment's Religious Institutions as Partners in Community Based Development Program (Scheie et al. 1991) may be of interest. This program aims to stimulate greater involvement of religious institutions in community revitalization, create new religious-community partnerships, strengthen community ministries, and attract new sources of funding for such initiatives.

Religious organizations, through organizations like the Children's Defense Fund (1992b), can set up special programs that emphasize the role of the church, temple, or mosque in helping children and those in need. There are specially developed materials to help incorporate social issues into religious programming.

Because many homeless youth have run away from home, a community may benefit by obtaining the 1994 North American Directory of Programs for Runaways, Homeless Youth and Missing Children (Wyman and Tranor 1993). This directory provides detailed profiles of more than 450 programs that can help children and those who serve them, as well as other useful information. Other useful materials can be found in the CASSP Technical Assistance Center's monograph that describes everything from how to create a board of directors and recruit staff to providing and evaluating services. It also describes service barriers and potential funding sources, training manuals, contracts, and data sheets (Pires and Silber 1991).

The police may be the first community agents to identify that a person or family is homeless. As a result, police agencies across the country are forced to respond to homelessness. In a national study, a third of the police departments had no policies specifically related to homelessness; the policies that did exist were related to making proper referrals or arrests (Plotkin and Narr 1993). What are the police policies regarding the homeless in your community? Homeless people are generally afraid of the police, because they do not know if the police will help them or arrest/incarcerate them because of their lack of housing. Their concern is often justified. Police are confronted with competing demands of political and business leaders, advocates for the homeless, the public, and the homeless persons themselves. In order to be effective, police officers need guidance in addressing individual needs, agency mandates, and community concerns (Plotkin and Narr 1993).

Local governments frequently harbor hostility towards homeless individuals and develop local ordinance that adversely affect them. Laws restricting zoning, where one can sleep, antiloitering and anti-begging ordinances, and unequal enforcement of the law are not uncommon (National Law Center on Homelessness and Poverty 1993). Does your local area have laws that make it difficult for the homeless to survive?

One resource that the rural homeless seldom have available is free legal representation. They may not know where to receive free legal counsel. Studies have found that lawsuits and bureaucratic obstacles create difficulties for attorneys who do represent homeless clients (Volz 1993; Coalition for the Homeless 1990). Where can homeless people in your community go for help in order to understand to what they are, and are not, legally entitled? The American Bar Association's Commission on Homelessness and Poverty (1991) has published a resource guide that lists bar, law school, and local nonprofit programs that provide direct legal assistance to homeless individuals and families. This guide can be valuable for providing basic information for those interesting in initiating similar programs in rural areas.

If media and community organization can champion homeless rural children and families, funders may be more receptive to providing the full range of prevention and treatment programs. In a study of foundation support, Roob and McCambridge (1991) found three patterns of giving. One funding approach places little emphasis on the systematic causes of poverty; a second approach relegates the problem of poverty to the pathologies of individuals; a third approach addresses economic factors such as housing affordability and income. Although 87 percent of private funders expressed a desire to fund programs to prevent homelessness, only 20 percent actually did so. Instead, when money is allocated, 80 percent of the foundations devote the majority of their grants to emergency services. Only 2 percent of the funders have a formal policy that expresses a commitment to eradicating homelessness.

Additionally, if advocates for the rural homeless can clearly state their needs, it may be possible to obtain support from funders that have historically funded urban homelessness endeavors. For instance, the Amoco Fund for Neighborhood Economies program (1991) was designed to revitalize community development, confront urban decay, and build grass-roots support for local businesses and residents. While they have focused on cities such as Atlanta, Denver, and Chicago, programs like this one may entertain projects for rural areas as well.

As Lisabeth Schorr points out in her book, *Within Our Reach* (1988), most of what we need to know about how to develop effective, efficient social services for families already exists. Social services have lessons from which we can guide the future by learning from the past—lessons that include the importance of modesty and humility, awareness that no single agency can solve all of the problems with the resources it has available, the need for diversity and collaboration, effects of complexity, and the need to build synergy among programs. Three models of social service delivery used in the past that may serve as guides to effective services for children and families in the future include multi-service centers and settlement houses, planning and resource allocation models, and place-specific models (Edelman and Radin 1991).

In this book, I have shown how personal and social chaos can lead to individual and community catastrophe. Rural homeless is complex in causation, but analyzable. In fact, the causes of it can be quite understandable and orderable. But if interventions do not address the complex causes, homelessness will become a normal part of the rural fabric.

Rural homelessness is caused primarily by systemic problems that are eroding the nature of the community and the lives of children and families within them. There are ways to address the root causes of rural homelessness. It is absolutely possible to prevent rural homelessness for children and families. But it will take a moral and financial commitment to do so.

My greatest concern is for the children who may grow up to believe that homelessness is a normal and acceptable way of life. A homeless lifestyle promotes risk for every aspect of a child's life—as well as for our nation's future. A century ago, the United States was regarded as a country in which all prizes were believed to be won by thought and labor. It was in conformity with the theory of equality to give every youth, as much as possible, an equal start in life. Advocates for children and the poor assert that this tradition has been utterly betrayed in recent years. In order to avoid the projected 29 percent child poverty rate and virtually eliminate child homelessness and poverty during the first decade of the next century, a set of economic and social policies could be crafted that will lead to sustained economic growth and effective social programs (Cook and Brown 1993). But will such policies be developed and implemented?

Healthy rural children, the rural tradition of caring, and democracy itself are at risk of being lost. It is not lack of knowledge (Schorr 1988) but economics that condemns poor rural children to their inheritance of a diminished destiny. While it is argued that there is not enough money to fund all worthy programs, the issue is not one of money. There is enough money to fund essential programs for children and families. There is always a way to do the things we really want to do.

If we would begin investing in rebuilding communities, in twenty years we would not see the kind of social and personal catastrophe that is now becoming inevitable even in rural areas. In 1988 the cost of eliminating poverty in families with children would have been only $26.1 billion, or 1.5 cents of every dollar that federal, state, and local governments spend. This $26.1 billion is less than half of the income actually redistributed in this nation from 1978 from 1988 when economic change and changes in social and tax policy shifted $61 billion from the poor and middle class to the rich. If the nation can afford to give an extra $61 billion to the richest one-fifth of the population; if bankers can get $164 billion to bail out deregulated, imprudent savings and loan associations; if we can afford to leave federal taxes on liquor, wine, beer and cigarettes at levels $11 billion a year less than they were in the early 1950s, then this nation can afford to lift its twelve million poor children out of poverty (Children's Defense Fund 1995).

Rural communities have the opportunity to use the crisis of child and family homelessness to rekindle the traditions that have been their strengths. Their future lies not in high-tech, professional, urban-based business solutions but in the common, everyday interactions that accumulate to create reality.

appendix a

My Wild Gypsy Life

by Yanali LaHaine

I went through a lot of things the last couple of years. I'm going to write about my big trip through the north and south. We lived in Michigan, and we were very miserable there. We lived there with my father. He used to terrify us. My moms name is Maria, My sister is Yamila, my brothers name is Sam, My name is Yanali. Michigan was a terrible place to live, and we couldn't stand living with our father any longer. So the first chance we got, we left him. My mom got a job in Marlin Texas. We sold most of our belongings to move. We travelled in a small Caravan car. The whole car was packed, and we took our cat Meso with us, which made the car smell. The states we had to go through to get to Texas—Indiana, Illinois, Missouri, and Oklahoma. Indiana was a boring state, Illinois had a lot of traffic, Missouri was an exciting state because a fugitive from the law was hiding out in the motel we stayed at over there. And Oklahoma was Okay. When we first got into Texas I was really worried about how school was going to be. We finally made it to Marlin Texas. It wasn't what we expected. My description of the place, copper tin roofs all over the town, and shacks that are still falling apart. But people still live in them anyway. We saw a school there, it was falling apart and didnt have any windows. We thought that was going to be our school. But later on we stayed in a in town motel. And the people that owned the motel told us that, that was the old black school. The town was segregated in the old days. Well Marlin scared us but we decided to stay. When my mom was registering us in school she found a trailer we could rent and live in. The land lord that owned it was very friendly and the whole time I lived there. He also gave us a calico cat. School was scary. There were more blacks, than there were whites and Mexicans. The school was terrible, and had roaches everywhere. The school was also dangerous and deserted. Teachers were in the newer parts of the school at lunch. I was in one of the bathrooms in one of the deserted buildings. All I'm going to say is that me and four Texas girls were almost raped in that bathroom by five or six black boys. I never went to that bathroom again. The school was scummy. We only lived in Marlin for six months. My mom got sick of the place and least a trailer in Riesel Texas *(population 354).* We moved to Riesel because we went to the fair there and it seemed nicer than Marlin. Well we got registered in school a week after the fair. The first few days of school was okay. But rumors started spreading about me and my sister. They said my sister drew demons in class. That wasn't true at all, my sister was writing a comic book. They thought I was a witch because I dressed like a punk. Texans are fifty years back in mind and fashion. Well half the school thought we were satanists, this got pretty serious. Kids started having riots in my sister's locker room. And at least fifty kids followed me to band. Even the principal thought we were witchs. My mom told him off though, and the principal made all the kids leave us alone. Anyway while I lived in Texas I saw, and been through alot of weird stuff. Like the time I saw fire balls in the sky, or the time I saw a Russian Satellite explode in the atmosphere. Or the time I met this really crazy drunk women in a bathroom and she tried to set me up with some guy named Bubba. Alot of strange things happened in Texas. And alot of bad things happened to. Like the time my sister was attacked by a dog. Well we lived in Riesel a couple of months. But my mom was losing her job. She got another one but that ment we were going to have to move to Miami Florida because thats were her new job was. Well we gave up our trailer, got rid of our Caravan mini van, and least a truck. We got a U-haul, and packed all of our stuff. And a few days later we left for Florida. The states we went through, Louisiana, Mississippi, Alabama, and then Florida. Louisiana was great, and Mississippi unfreindly and we lost our cat Meso there. Well to make this short on our way to Miami we spent a night in Orlando. It was beautiful there. And I saw wild aligators in a ditch next to the road. They were big. When we got to Miami we stayed in a motel and put our things in storage. We had to go back to Texas because the car dealer was trying to rip us off. So we went back to Texas. On our way there we used up our credit cards so we had to sleep in the car. It was tough. When we got back to Texas we gave back the truck and bought a yellow 1974 car for $500.00. After that we headed back to Florida. On they way there we had to sleep in rest areas. It was a scarey life. When we were almost in Florida our Calico cat had kittens. We each took a kitten for our very own. I named the kitten I got Telulah. When we got back to Miami we had to look for an apartment. All the apartments were expensive. Days later we ended up moving into a motel room for $500.00 every two weeks. The motel was called Beach motel. It was wicked slummy. The place was real bad.

After a few weeks of living there my mom makes friends with one of the maids there. The maid offered to get us registered in school for $50.00. My mom couldn't leave work to get us registered. She had to work to keep up with the rent. So the maid took us to the welfare dept. to get our shots. The maid brought three other kids with her. The welfare dept. was slummy. They gave physicals to convicts in this place. While we waited to get our shots. A guy with long hair and chackels on his legs started talking to me. He told me why he went to prison. After the whole run around in the welfare dept. We still couldnt get into school. Something about us being from out of state. So we ended up missing three months of school. The maid offered to take us back and get the whole mess straightened out. But my mom didn't want her to. Because our neighbor Tammy told us the maid had a pimp and was into white slavery. Tammy was our neighbor, she had three sons, and one baby girl. And she had a boyfriend living with her. Her baby was born hooked on cocaine, her three sons were uncontrolable, and her boyfriend was half crazy. Tammy is a prostitute, and she does cocaine and (ect.). She was always nice to me and my family. She gave me some pills because I had an ear ache for several months. She also gave my mom some address's of churches and emergency food places. Because we were so poor. We didn't have anything to eat. Tammy was a real nice person. When things got real bad, and we'd run out of food. We'd go to churches for food. All we got though was crackers, half rotten bananas, and flinstone fruit vitamin drink.

Well weeks went on, and my mom would go to work while me, Yamila, and Sammy would sleep all day. One morning I got up around 5:00 am in the morning to say good bye to my mom before she went to work. I heard yelling coming from outside. I went out to see what was going on. I saw a cop kick down a door like it was paper, and pull out a black guy. I was scared I thought it was a drug bust. I was scared because the landlord who owned the motel was a big drug dealer. Well I got a better look, and I saw two motel rooms go up in flames. It wasn't a drug bust, the place was on fire. I ran back to my motel room woke up my brother and sister. My mom got some of the kittens, and the rest of us got the rest of the kittens and some valuable belongings. We went to our car. The two motel rooms that were on fire blew up. It was scary, luckily our room wasnt touched.

The next few weeks were filled with fights and gunfights. Our room smelled like drugs. And life was depressing. Im going to mention a few more things that went on in the Beach motel, and then Ill get on with this story. One day I went to call my brother inside for dinner. He was out in the swimming pool with Tammy's kids. All of the sudden this big palm tree twisted backwards. And everyone were blown out of the swimming pool. My brother was holding on to a bar so he wouldnt fly away. I thought it was a hurricane. I got my brother inside. Tammy was outside against a wall with eight kids either side of her. And she was praying. A Cuban girl was flown up to the second floor. Meanwhile we got the kittens and ourselves in a closet. The lights kept flickering and the glass on the windows were ready to burst. I was leaning against the wall in the closet. Behind the wall was an alley. I was praying and saying all my sins. We lived on an island Miami Beach. I was scared there was going to be a flood. An hour later it was quiet. We went outside to see if it was over. Branches and trees were all over the place. We met up with Tammy and her boyfriend. Her boy friend said it was just a tornado. He said it went down the alley behind the Beach motel. That means that when I was leaning against the wall. The tornado was right behind me. I almost passed out when I heard that. The rest of the night we spend talking to Tammy and her boyfriend. We just talked about god and the devil. And when was god suppose to come back. And we talked about the Antichrist. Then we just talked about life.

The next few weeks, new faces began to show up at the motel. College kids and teenagers from the north and (ect.). They were pigs, we had all kinds of them there. My mom was doing laundry outside once. And one of them college brats with shoulder length hair. Urinated on a telephone pole in front of her. What an insulting pig!! When we were at the swimming pool gossiping with Tammy. They'ed be out there, drinking themselves silly. One guy wanted me to go up to a party at their room. He was so persistent to get me, and my sister, and Tammy to that stupid party. I didnt go, Im not that crazy. None of us went. Well we moved a little down the street from the beach motel. My mom couldnt stand those perverted college kids no more. We moved into a bigger motel room. It had on bedroom. The living room was quite creepy. And the kitchen was very small. In the time we lived in that motel. All we ever seem to do all the time there. Was sleep all day, catch lizards, cross the street to get junk food from the other motel, and stay up late at night talking to our Cuban neighbors. We loved catch lizards, in account they dont have teeth. And anytime they bit you it didnt hurt. So when we caught lizards we'd stick them on our ears and pretend they were new fashion earrings. I was really getting depressed there. I mean I couldnt help from sleeping all day. When I woke up sometimes, Id think Miami was a dream and I was in Texas. Relating to reality was hard when you sleep all day and sleep almost the whole night. It was almost like I was dead or something. Then I started to have nightmares. Horrible violent ones. I use to have nightmares about the trip from Texas to Miami. I used to wake up screaming. Sometimes it was a real struggle to wake up. The only other times we'd go outside. Was when we went to this new resteraunt. We'd have a lot of tropical drinks there. like Pina Colada, none of the drinks had alcohol. We usually talk about the Red Socks and Boston. We became good friends with the owners. They were two Greek boys, they were really friendly. Something we could never figure out, was when we got up one morning and found blood all over our living room. We could never figure out where the blood came from. I mean our doors were locked, and none of us did it. And our cats didnt do it. Theres alot of witch craft in Miami. So finding the blood there was really creepy. Theres alot of Haitians that practice black magic. Well, the weeks that passed seemed long and hot. One day my mom, me, my brother, and sister gathered around for an important decision. My mom knew she was going to lose her job. The qeustion was should we stay in Miami when she loses it, and tough it in Miami. Or go back New Hampshire. We decided that Miami was nothing but trouble. So we decided to leave. I wrote a letter to my father begging him to send money to help us get out Miami. Meanwhile we packed up. My mom told her boss she was quiting, and worked her last week. A few weeks later we got my fathers check. The last night in Miami, was spent talking to our Cuban neighbors. The next morning we started putting our things in a U-haul trailer we rented. It took us hours to get everything in. We tried to rush. Because this lady who lived in the Beach Motel wanted to come with us, and bring her son and daughter. She was trouble, and her son was into cocaine really bad. His mother brought him over to our place one night, and he was wasted really bad. It was terrible. You can see why we wanted to leave in a hurry. Mom said we were going to have to give the kittens and the cat away when we got to New Hampshire. Since we couldnt afford feeding them any more. Well we were on the road out of Miami, when we did something really weird. When we stopped at a stop light, we yelled over to the other car next to us. We asked him if he would like a kitten. He said yes, and we pulled over. He was rich you could tell by the car. He took my cat, Telulah. After that we got back on the road. I was crying because I was really going to miss that kitten. Well hours passed and we were in Vero Beach. We asked another guy if he would like a kitten. He said no. When we were about a mile out of Vero Beach. We heard this weird humming noise. We looked out the window at the telephone poles. And on them were hundreds and thousands of big black spiders. Ive seen them up close before, their almost as big as my hand. They were so creepy. About two hours later we got a flat tire. We got that fixed fast and we were on our way again. We finally came to a stop in Jacksonville. I remembered some of the buildings because in our last trip we went through there before. Any way we stayed at a motel there. We sort of had problems with the trailer, but it wasnt anything serious. That night I had a nightmare about Telulah. It was horrible, and depressing. I couldnt really go back to sleep.

Oh, I forgot to mention that we decorated our car a few days before we left Miami. We called our car The Gypsy Wagon. I had my nickname on my door (Generalee) and a confederate flag on the side of the door. My mom had (Zebra) on her door. My brother had (Dark shadow on) his door. And my sister had (Ace) on her door. We had two arrows on the front, and we had Gypsy Wagon on back. Any way back to my story. We entered Georgia the next morning, after Jacksonville. We made only one stop in Georgia. And that was to get something to eat at a resteraunt. I was very uncomfortable there. Georgia was a pretty state but soon we entered South Carolina. We started to see weird billboards on the side of the highway. It was some commercial to this tourist trap called South of the Border. We went into this really lonely country road. We went to this store at the end of it. It was a very small town, and very strange at that. There was these strange mexicans all over the place. We got some soda from this store. Then we got outside. Our cat got loose. So we went after it. There was this crazy black guy in a white van talking to himself. He gave us the creeps. We really wanted to get out of there real quick. And we did, we got our cat back to. When we got close to the end of South Carolina. We saw the place called South of the Border. We drove through it and took some pictures of it in account my brother had his camera out. We finally got into North Carolina. We stopped at a motel there. Part of the motel was having some construction still put on it. There was this drunk guy in the next motel room. He ask me if I could get some ice from an ice machine some where in the motel. I said sure why the hell not. And went through half the building looking for the ice machine. Meanwhile my brother and sister went looking for a candy machine. About thirty minutes later I met my sister and brother in the hallway. I had my ice and they had their candy. We were on the part of the motel that was still going under construction. We ended up running back to our room because there was hundreds of jumping spiders roaming around. When I got back to my room the drunk guy paid me a dollar for the ice, and then he went back to his room. The next morning we got up and watched some TV while we got ready to leave. We got a real scared when we found out the Klu Klux Klan were having their stupid march through a near by town. The reason why we worried a little about the march is because my mother is Puerto Rican. Anyway we got back on the road, avoided the march. We finally made it to Virginia. We stopped at a rest area to use the bathroom. In the bathroom was a note saying. *Our car is running out of gasoline and we have no money. We are trying to get to Corpus Christi Texas.* The letter had alot of spelling mistakes. When we came out of the bathrooms we saw the only other car in the rest area. They were the people who wrote the note. We knew that because they had a Texas license plate. My mom walked over to them and asked them if they wrote the note. It was a man and a woman with two boys and a baby girl. They looked like they lived in their car. They were trying to get to Corpus Christi Texas for a job. My mom gave them ten dollars and told them good luck. That was very depressing because they were going through what we were going through. Well the poor help the poor. Hours later we made it to an amazing sight. We were in Washington D.C. Virginia. We took so many pictures. When we left Washington D.C. we ended up going back. In account that we got a little lost.

We went through Richmond Virginia and it smelled like one big cigarette. Night time came, and we got lost again. We ended up in West Virginia. We stopped at rest area, and tried to figure out the map. When we got the map figured out, we headed to Pennsylvania. When we made to Pennsylvania that night. We spent the night in a motel. The next morning, when we walking out of the motel. Some dumb tourist asked us if we had accents. They asked that because they saw our Texas license plates. Talk about idiots. Any way we got back on the road. Ill tell you this we crossed New Jersey, and went in to Connecticut. Here comes the hard part. Night time came, and we spent the night in our car. It was freezing, and the kittens were climbing all the place. We parked next to the rigs for protection. In case someone tried to break into our car. All we had to do was yell and get some truckers attention. The next morning we started to drive. I know we stopped at a rest area and got a bumper sticker and free doughnuts, and drinks. A few hours later we entered New York. Not New York City, the state but the traffic was just as bad. Some kids on a bridge Yelled out Texas when they saw our license plates. Before that, I thought they were going to throw something at our car. Well you can't judge a book by its cover. Any way while we went through the traffic. I think we went through Massachusetts, I cant really remember that part. Any way the big moment arrived we entered New Hampshire. I haven't been in this state in nine years. We stopped at a rest area. We had a problem, our car was breaking down. We started on the road, and came to a town looking for a garage. When we found a garage, we didnt really have

very much money to get into a motel. We were going to have to sleep
in the parking lot of the garage until they fixed our car the next morning. How humiliatng. Then my mom decided to call an old friend. She
called Chris Edmond a real old friend we havent seen since we left
New Hampshire back in 1980. Any way Chris and his wife owned a
christian camp. They have eight kids they teach at home instead of
sending them to school. They're heavilly into Christianity. Well she
called him up, and he said he had a friend who live near the town we
were at. Well we stayed with Chris' friends that night instead of sleeping in a cold parking lot. We slept on their floor, it was cold but it was
better than sleeping in the car. Thank God for Chris' friends!! Any way
this guy was a pastor and he had three duaghters and one son, and his
wife taught them at home. The next morning I went exploring the
wilderness next to their house. Meanwhile, the pastor was fixing our
car. He got it back from the garage. That was awfully nice of him. *By
the way the year is 1988 and Im 15 right now.* When we got back on the
road. We headed towards New Durham. Our car was starting to break
down on us. But we tried so hard to get to our destination. We went
through Rochester. And then we went through Farmington. I haven't
seen that town for nine years. I use to live in that town in the 70's. We
saw our old neighbor she couldnt believe we came back. Her husband
died and the old ladys I knew when I was eight. My old house and
swing set were still there. All these old memorys came back. That night
we got to New Durham and went to Chris' camp. *Camp Maranatha.* His
house never really changed. And his wife had a new baby. And all
his kids I new when I was a child were my age. It was so weird. He
let us stay at one of his cabins until we found an apartment. As days
passed we looked hard for an apartment. Then we found one in the
newspaper. *APARTMENT FOR RENT 24A LAFEYETTE STREET ROCH-
ESTER.* (That street really destroyed me). Any way we went over
there to meet the land lord. It was terrible. Bikers all over the place,
boys playing electric guitars out on their lawns. The atmosphere of the
place was getting to me. We couldn't find any other good apartment to
try and get. Plus what was causing the excitement in Lafeyette street,
was the Rochester fair. I havent been to that fair in nine years. We
dared to ask some bikers where 24A was. They were pretty freindly,
They told us where it was. The apartment building was terrible, the
hallways were a mess, and one door had a hole in it. But when we met
the landlord, we took the apartment anyway. That day we went to the
welfare department and tried to get some help. After that my sister
and my brother wanted to go to the fair. I really didnt want to go. But
we went any way. *The fair was on the street I was moving on. (Lafeyette*

Street). It was a big fair, and there were so many carnies. It was unbelievable. The atmosphere of this fair was so slummy. I went on the first ride. It was called the Gravitron or something. It spins around, and you stick to the wall while it plays loud music. Then I went on these other rides during the fair. The lightening Bolt, the Casino, Cicuit Rouge, Scrambler, and some others. I went into the haunted house. It was scary, there was strobe lights and it was dark. Some girl in there grab my hand thinking I was somebody else. Its was funny because when she found out I wasn't her freind. She still wanted to hold my hand. I have to admit it was pretty scary. Then some one in a costume jumped out of the wall, and we all ran out of the haunted house screaming. One ride I didn't go on was the Ferris wheel. Because of superstition, my mom didnt want me to go on it because she just had bad vibes about it. My favorite ride was the circuit Rouge. It goes really fast and backwards sometimes. It plays loud music and has a D.J. The fair was lots of fun. But I started to notice the kids that were around. They really looked tough. Boys with long hair, and cheap looking girls. Are these the kids Im going to go to school with? They were all heavymetal looking. Which scared me to death. After the fair we went back to the cold cabin back New Durham.

The next night we got our U-haul and started to move our things into our new apartment. Chris and his family brought a truck with some old beds and furniture. He gave them to us so we didnt have to sleep on the floor. It was a real mess on Lafeyette street that night, with the fair going on. While we drove up the street. Some lady yelled some words at us, but some bikers told her to f-off. After we got everything moved in. We got as much unpacked as possible. Our apartment was a two bedroom one. My brother slept in one room, My mom slept in the living room, and me and my sister shared one bedroom. That night you could here the fair, and you could hear everybody walking by and talking. Which was very nerve wreckoning. The next day we had to give our kittens to a pound since we were going into an apartment. That was so depressing. A week passed, and during that week we got regisitered in school. And my mom got a job as dishwasher at Nicholas, but she quit that job sooner or later and got a job at Encore. Spaulding let me into tenth grade even though I missed the last three months of ninth grade. They let my sister and brother into school without any problems. The day before we started school I went back to the fair with my brother and sister. While we were there I bought a Def Leppard shirt so I could try to fit in. The next day we started school. We were a couple of weeks late for school. So that meant we were the new kids in school. I was so nervous. The first few days I made alot of friends. The really low slummy, and bad attitude kids. I hated my first period class though. The kids were nasty. I had three friends in that class. Thats probably what made me put up with that class. I made a real good friend named Melissa Cedar. She was really nice. She was the one who got me hooked to heavy metal music. Because she loaned me her Guns N Roses tape. And ever since then Ive been buying more and more different heavy-metal tapes. I made lots of friends. A few weeks passed and I started to go a little crazy. Like I got into smalltime trouble with teachers. And I did what my gang of friends did. I started smoking. Id smoke right in front of the school. My mom didnt know and I wasnt about to let her. I went out with this guy in first period. Im not even going to describe this character. What an idiot. I cant believe I went out with this guy. My friend Melissa knew him too. I only went out with him for a week and a few days. I only went out with him because he could get me pot, beer, or anything else I wanted. I was really going wild in Rochester. My friend Melissa brought in a joint to one day. And I use pass and pick up in the hallways if you know what I mean. By now I was completely into the heavymetal look. I had a jean jacket with skull pins and patches all over it. Any way my life was going down hill. Well anyway we got to know Rochester. One day my sister got into a fight. *This was a couple of months after we moved to Layefette street.* It was a big fight with some sluts down the street. Well I got warnings from their friends at school and we tried to avoid a certain part of Lafeyette. If I was my sister I would of been able to avoid the fight. A week after that, something scary happens. My family wanted to go to a comic book store and pick up a pizza and bring it home. It was Friday and I was tired from school. And all I wanted to do was go to sleep, and any way I was kind of depressed. But my mom talked me into going with them. After we got the pizza and picked up a few comic books. We drove home. When we got to the entrance of Lafeyette was blocked up by police cars. So we couldn't get in from the first part of the street. From the distance I could see a fire truck. We made some jokes about some idiots house was burning down. Then we came from the other side of Lafeyette street. When our car was getting close enough. I noticed it was our apartment building. I jumped out of our car, And I started running down the street. The fire engine had its light on my bedroom window. While I was running down the street, some biker guy told me my room was totaled. When I got there. Smoke was everywhere. I started to hyperventilate, and some fire men locked me up in an ambulance to ask me some questions. They thought I was a mother who lived there. I tried to explain who I was, but they werent really paying attention. I tried to get out of the ambulance, but it was locked. Then that one biker got me out of the ambulance. I guessed he felt sorry for me or something. Then he told me he knew how it was to be locked up. An hour later the fire men let us go in to our apartment three at a time. They let me go first, in account I put a big fit when they tried to put me in the abulance. Everything was smoke damaged. But the apartment downstairs was totalled. One of the firemen told us if there had been somebody sleeping here. They would of suffocated to death from all the smoke. To think, I was going to sleep that night instead of go for pizza. Boy did that really make me think of my life. That night we called Chris and he let us stay in one of his cabins. The next few days the land lord had a cleaning company come and fix up our apartment. I stayed home from school for four days. Smoking cigarettes and pot. Id talk to the cleaning people while they cleaned to. It was almost Christmas. The Salvation Army bought us new beds and stuff, because everything was smoked damaged. They brought us Christmas presents, since it was almost Christmas. While they were moving the stuff into our apartment. I tried to kill myself by taking 15 tylenols. Then I went to sleep right after that. The next morning I got up. I was really mad I survived. Nothing happened to me, I didnt even throw up. Well Christmas came and went. And I still got my joints and stuff from my boyfriend. I broke up with him a week later, When I found out he was talking about me and Melissa. We were out in front of Spaulding one morning. When some kid came up to me and my group of friends. And exactly what he was spreading around school. Everyone was shocked. No one said anything, Melissa was so angry. My bodyguard Jason even asked if he could punch him a couple of times. I was so insulted I went right into the school. Well two months later we had another fire. We were watching Friday The Thirteenth the Final Chapter or something. I heard some screaming outside. So I looked out the window, across the street. The house across the street, had this big fire ball come straight through its roof. It was a scary sight. My mom called the fire department, because no one seemed to have called. I went outside, the smoke was so bad. You couldnt see the fire engines any more. Soon my sister and mike came through the door. *Mike is a friend of ours my sister was babysitting for.* Mike told us we could stay over a night at his house. The next morning, when we came back. Everything was smoked damaged again. I was so depressed and I kept going through some mood swings. Summer was coming, you could really tell. A few of the neighbors playing their electric guitars on their porches. And people started thier big drug partys. Like the one going on downstairs. They played their rock music so loud it sounded like Axl Rose was singing in my bedroom. The windows in our apartment were rattling. We called the cops a couple of times, on them. But they still went on.

There were so many partys going on. It was hard to get any sleep at night. There were so many fights taking place on Lafeyette street. Fights over kids, girls, drugs, and reputations. My mom finally got sick of it all. And started looking for a new apartment. We found one a couple of weeks later. Chris brought his truck and helped us move into the new apartment. He had a few of his kids help move the furniture with us. My description of the new street we move on. Qiuet at first, but later on it got as bad as Lafeyette street. It was hard to park our car, the landlord was crooked. The place was crawling with little welfare kids. The street was named Woodman street. My description of the apartment. Creepy, large, cob webs, holes in the walls, dirt everywhere. It was a messy dump. But it was the only other place we could find in Rochester. The place sickening. School was almost out. My sisters enemies found her. From one of our neighbors. My sister lost all her friends in school. Her school year was a nightmare. Well I spent that summer working in job training. Well After that beg trip across the south and north. Ive become street wise. I know who to stay away from, even if I dont know who the person is. Im usually right. Any way I got up every day at 5:00 am and walked to job training. I walked that early to job training to avoid family enemies. One day about 6:20. I was walking on a deserted street near a bar. The street was totally empty. Not a soul in sight. I kept walking down the street. Suddenly, about twenty feet behind me. A guy comes from out of no where. I walk faster because I dont like strange men walking behind me. He starts walking faster. That really surprised me. I started to walk really fast, I was almost running. Then he started running super fast. Then I took off down that deserted street praying for a cop to come down the street and help me. Suddenly this police car comes the street. I couldnt believe this. Thank God!!! Well they pulled over and started talking to this strange guy. Then all of a sudden the strange guy takes off up the street. And the police car drove full speed after him. Talk about an exciting morning. I met up with a freind and walked the rest of the way to school with him. Everyday Id walk to job training. One day I decided to hitch hike. Ive never hitch hiked before, I guess that summer I was very daring. Now that I look back at that strange summer, I think I was pretty crazy. Well I got picked up by this southern guy. He started driving me to my school. We had a very interesting conversation. He bought me a pack of cigarettes. During that summer he'd see me and give me rides. He asked me out. But I said no because he was twenty five. The summer was going by slow. And the neighborhood was pretty rowdy. So my mom went looking for another apartment. Well a few weeks my mom found an apartment in Dover. It was some kind of projects. And we had Chris help us move. It took two days to move everything. Summer was oming to an end. The new apartment had three bedrooms and it was nice. I very depressed and I was going through some of the worst mood swings. First I was okay, then I was violent, and then I was very depressed. My mom was very worried about me, because I took a knife and carved the word Ozzy in my arm. Blood on my arm, And I was spitting on my posters and tore apart my radio. My mom was really upset I carved Ozzy in arm. Id take the knife and stab my arms until I saw blood. This my way of taking out the anger and violence on myself. Instead of doing it to one of my family members. My mom had a meeting with my therapist. My mom was worried that I might kill myself. The therapist took me to a shrink. I talked to the shrink. He said that I shouldnt be put on medication. He said That I had a lot of anger kept inside, and that one day Im going to let it all out. A lot of my anger was about my father. He use to beat me, and tried to kill me when I was two. My father did horrible things to me. Another part of my mood swings, was because I was having a lot of flash backs of the trip. And I still kept having nightmares about it. And the fires in Miami Beach and Lafeyette street really got me. When I started school in Dover High I had no friends. The classes were hard, and there were so many preppy kids. I couldnt fit in. Everyday after school Id go home and be really depressed. Id cry until my throat hurt and Id start choking. Well my sister maded friends and she introduced me to them. We started meeting alot of our friends at the mall. I guess we became mall rats. I met Two old friends from Rochester at school. And I started eating lunch with them at the cafeteria. I started to make alot of friends. I got my schedule straighten out. And I got good classes after that. Well This year and the next year worked out good. I have'nt had any real bad mood swings. I think alot of things worked out. I made honor roll for the first time, and I finally got a electric guitar. And me and my sister got a job at a greenhouse. This year has been great compared to the others. Well Im done with this story of my pathetic life.

The end

By General Lee

Note: Five years after General Lee wrote this story, I had the opportunity to re-establish contact with the family. The mother had been employed full time as a medical records clerk for a major medical institution for five years. The sister was a student at a local college, and the brother was attending a vocational college. General Lee was employed full-time and planned to attend college the following fall. Each member of the family seemed emotionally, financially, and socially secure, because of their own determination and because they had found help when they needed it. Their story represents the stories told by hundreds of others I interviewed who demonstrated that they were able to overcome homelessness and economic distress when appropriate services were provided at the right time.

a p p e n d i x   b

Summary of Causes of Rural Child-Family Homelessness

I. Infrastructure Causes
    1. Economic
        1.1 National economic condition
        1.2 State economic condition
        1.3 Local community economic condition
        1.4 Taxes: who pays them, how much, and who gets the benefit
            of them
        1.5 Job availability
        1.6 Income levels for those who work
        1.7 Benefits for those who work
        1.8 Aid for those unable to find work
    2. Governmental
        2.1 Laws
        2.2 Policies (ie-toward children, families, women, rural areas)
        2.3 Programs (ie-housing, social service, economic, health,
            education, training)
        2.4 Funding Allocations
        2.5 Special interest group influence
    3. Housing
        3.1 Policies
        3.2 Programs
        3.3 Requirements
        3.4 Allocations for low income housing
        3.5 Availability
        3.6 Cost of renting
        3.7 Cost of buying
        3.8 Maintenance assistance
    4. Education
        4.1 Policies
        4.2 Curriculum
        4.3 Programs
        4.4 Job Training
        4.4 Post-high school educational opportunities
        4.5 Training for self sufficiency

5. Human Services
     5.1 Policies
     5.2 Programs
     5.3 Requirements
     5.4 Funding
     5.5 Network of agencies re: information and resource
     5.6 Staff sensitivity and resourcefulness
     5.7 Geographic barriers to seeking assistance
     5.8 Publicity, information, and referral
     5.9 Operation factors (ie-hours, cost, staff-client ratio)

II. Demographic Dimensions of Homelessness, by Community
     6.1 Age distribution
     6.2 Sex of the residents
     6.3 Size of community
     6.4 Race/ethnic breakdown
     6.5 Economic status of the community
     6.6 Social class distribution of people within the community
     6.7 Resources available within a community, type and number
     6.8 Number of people in economic distress
     6.9 Standard of living, actual and projected

III. Personal Contributors to Homelessness
     7. Employment
        7.1 Does the person have a job?
        7.2 Is the person employable?
        7.3 Job history
        7.4 Future security at work
        7.5 Wages
        7.6 Hours
        7.7 Working conditions
        7.8 Performance
        7.9 Quality of relationships with c-workers
     8. Financial Resources
        8.1 Savings
        8.2 Other monetary assets
        8.3 Non-monetary assets (ie-house, car, jewelry, boat)
        8.4 Insurance, benefits
        8.5 Assistance programs
     9. Support Network
        9.1 Family (ie-who, #, relationship)
        9.2 Friends (ie-who, #, relationship)
        9.3 How emotionally close or distant
        9.4 How geographically close or distant
        9.5 History of support

10. Character Resources
  10.1 Self esteem
  10.2 Attitude (ie-challenged, defeated, depressed, optimistic)
  10.3 Resourcefulness
  10.4 History of dealing with problems
11. Substance Abuse
  11.1 Type of substances used
  11.2 Amount typically consumed
  11.3 How frequently used
  11.4 Effect of substance on psyche
  11.5 Effect of substance on performance
12. Mental-Emotional factors
  12.1 Mental problems
  12.2 Severity of problems
  12.2 Mental strengths
  12.3 Ability/Barriers to obtaining mental health
13. Physical factors
  13.1 Physical health
  13.2 Physical problems
  13.3 Severity of problems
  13.4 Ability/barriers to address problems
14. Geographic mobility
  14.1 How long hove lived at current residence
  14.2 How frequently moved
  14.3 How long stay at other residences
  14.4 How close or far apart were the residences (ie-within same community, jumping from state to state)

IV. Ideological Cause of Homelessness
15. Media Portrayal of Homelessness
  15.1 Television
  15.2 Radio
  15.3 Newspapers
  15.4 Magazines
  15.5 Books
  15.6 Journals and scholarly writings
16. Personal Experience with the Homeless
  16.1 Personal observation
  16.2 Experiences of family, friends, $ acquaintances
  16.3 "Hear-say" experiences of strangers
17. Opinions of Significant Others
  17.1 Political leaders
  17.2 Religious leaders
  17.3 Media leaders
  17.4 Scholarly leaders
  17.5 Others

18. Philosophy About Helping Others
    18.1 Personal
    18.2 Religious/spiritual
    18.3 Organizational
    18.4 Community
    18.5 National

Bibliography

Abdella, Faye, Jeanette Chamberlain, and Irene S. Levine. 1986. "Role of Nurses in Meeting Needs of the Homeless: Summary of a Workshop for Providers, Researchers, and Educators." *Public Health Reports* 101, no. 5:494–98.

Abramovitz, Mimi. 1986. "The Privatization of the Welfare State." *Social Work* (July–Aug.): 257–64.

Acker, P., A. Fierman, B. Dreyer. 1987. An Assessment of parameters of health care and nutrition in homeless children. *American Journal of Disabled Children* 2: 141, 388.

Adler, Jerry. 1995. "Bye-Bye Surburban Dream." *Newsweek*, May 15.

Adler, Patricia A., and Peter Adler. 1986. *Sociological Studies of Child Development.* Greenwich, Conn.: JAI Press.

Agee, James, and Walker Evans. 1960. *Let Us Now Praise Famous Men.* Boston: Houghton-Mifflin.

Aiken, W., and H. LaFollette. 1980. *Whose Child? Children's Rights, Parental Authority, and State Power.* Totowa, N.H.: Rowman and Littlefield.

Ainsworth, Mary D. Salter. 1989. "Attachments Beyond Infancy." *American Psychologist* 44, no. 4:709–16.

Alker, Joan, and Cheryl Derricoutte. 1989. "Unfinished Business: The Stewart B. McKinney Homeless Assistance Act after Two Years." Washington, D.C.: National Coalition for Homeless.

Alperstein, G., and E. Arnstein. 1988. "Homeless Children—A Challenge for Pediatricians." *Pediatric Clinics of North America* 35, no. 6:1413–25.

Alperstein, Garth, Claire Rappaport, and Joan M. Flanigan. 1988. "Health Problems of Homeless Children in New York City." *American Journal of Public Health* 78, no. 9:1232–33.

Amato, Paul, and Jiping Zuo. 1992. "Rural Poverty, Urban Poverty, and Psychological Well-Being." *Sociological Quarterly* 33, no 1:229–40.

American Bar Association. 1991. "State and Local Bar Association Homelessness Programs." Washington, D.C.: American Bar Association.

American Psychologist. 1991. Special issue on Homelessness. Vol. 46, no. 11.

Amoco Foundation. 1991. "Rebuilding Economies through Neighborhood Job Creation." Chicago, Ill.

Anderson, Dick. 1987. "When the Bough Breaks: Homeless Families Are Everywhere Across the Country." *Networker* (Nov.–Dec.): 18–30.

———. 1987. "When the Bough Breaks: Homeless Families Are Everywhere Across the Country." *Networker* (Nov.–Dec.): 18–30.

Anderson, Peter. 1990. "The Rural Poor: Misery on the Back Roads of New England." *Boston Globe Magazine,* 16 Sept., 20–41.

———. 1990. "The Rural Poor: Misery on the Back Roads of New England." *Boston Globe Magazine* (16 Sept.): 20–41.

Ansely, Leslie. 1992. "Up from the Streets." *Parade Magazine,* 7 Mar. 4–6.

Apgar, John C., and H. James Brown. 1988. *The State of the Nation's Housing.* Cambridge, Mass.: Joint Center for Housing Studies of Harvard University.

Appleby, Lawrence, and Prakashi Desai. 1985. "Documenting the Relationship between Homelessness and Psychiatric Hospitalization." *Hospital and Community Psychiatry* 36, no. 7:732–37.

Appleby, Lawrence, Nancy Slagg, and Prakash Desai. 1982. "The Urban Nomad: A Psychiatric Problem?" In *Current Psychiatric Therapies,* ed. J.H. Masserman. New York: Grune and Stratton.

Arce, Anthony, et al. 1983. "A Psychiatric Profile of Street People Admitted to an Emergency Shelter." *Hospital and Community Psychiatry* 34, no. 9:812–21.

Armstrong, Scott. 1989. "How to School Homeless Children." *Christian Science Monitor,* 28 Nov.

Athey, Jean. 1991. "HIV Infection and Homeless Adolescents." *Child Welfare* 70, no. 5:517–28.

Atlanta Task Force for the Homeless. 1991. "Misplaced Priorities: Atlanta, the '96 Olympics, and the Politics of Urban Renewal." Atlanta, Ga.

Auletta, Ken. 1983. *The Underclass.* New York: Random.

Azeni, Hocine. 1988. *Halfway House Versus Apartment Programs: The Case of Quality of Life; A Comparative Evaluation.* Boston: University of Massachusetts.

Bahr, Howard. 1970. *Disaffiliated Man.* Toronto: University of Toronto Press.

Baily, Susan. 1992. *How Schools Shortchange Girls.* Final report commissioned by the American Association of University Women Educational Foundation and researched by the Wellesley College Center for Research on Women. Wellesley, Mass.: American Association of University Women.

Bandura, A. 1965. "Vicarious Processes: A Case of No-Trial Learning." In *Advances in Experimental Social Psychology,* vol. 2, ed. L. Berkowitz. New York: New York Academic Press.

Barak, Gregg. 1991. *Gimmie Shelter: A Social History of Homelessness in Contemporary America.* New York: Praeger.

Baranick, Scott. 1990. "The Rural Disadvantage: Growing Income Disparities Between Rural and Urban Areas." Washington, D.C.: Center on Budget and Policy Priorities.

Barber, Benjamin. 1992. *An Aristocracy of Everyone: The Politics of Education and the Future of America.* New York: Ballentine.

Bassuk, Ellen. 1986. "Homeless Families: Single Mothers and Their Children in Boston Shelters." In *The Mental Health Needs of Homeless Persons*, ed. E.L. Bassuk. New Directions for Mental Health Services, no. 30. San Francisco: Jossey-Bass, June.

Bassuk, Ellen. 1990. "Community Care for Homeless Families: A Program Design Manual." Washington, D.C.: Interagency Council for the Homeless.

Bassuk, Ellen L., and Lynn Rosenberg. 1988. "Why Does Family Homelessness Occur? A Case-Control Study." *American Journal of Public Health* 78, no. 7:783–87.

Bassuk, Ellen, and Alison Lauriat. 1986. "Are Emergency Shelters the Solution?" *International Journal of Mental Health* 14, no. 4:125–36.

Bassuk, Ellen, and Ellen Gallagher. 1990. "The Impact of Homelessness on Children." *Children and Youth Serivces.* 14L 19–33.

Bassuk, Ellen, and L. Rubin. 1987. "Homeless Children: A Neglected Population." *American Journal of Orthopsychiatry* 57, no. 2:279–86.

Bassuk, Ellen, et al. 1990. *Community Care for Homeless Families.* Newton Center, Mass.: Better Homes Foundation.

Bassuk, Ellen, Leonore Rubin, and Alison Lauriat. 1984. "Is Homelessness a Mental Health Problem?" *American Journal of Psychiatry* 141, no. 12:1546–50.

Battle, Stanley F. 1990. "Homeless Women and Children: The Question of Poverty." In *Homeless Children: The Watchers and the Waiters*, ed. Nancy A. Boxill. New York: Haworth.

Baum, Alice, and Donald Burnes. 1993. *A Nation in Denial: The Truth about Homelessness.* Boulder, Colo.: Westview.

Bean, Gerald, Mary Stefl, and Steven Howe. 1987. "Mental Health and Homelessness: Issues and Findings." *Social Work* (Sept.–Oct.): 411–16.

Becker, Howard. 1963. *Outsiders: Studies in the Sociology of Deviance.* New York: Free Press.

Bedard, M. 1992. *Breaking with Tradition: Diversity, Conflict, and Change in Contemporary American Families.* Dix Hills, N.Y.: General Hall.

Bekin, Lisa. 1985. "Parents Weigh Costs of Children." *New York Times,* 23 May.

Belcher, John, and Glenn McCleese. 1988. "The Process of Homelessness among the Mentally Ill: Rural and Urban Perspectives." *Human Services in the Rural Environment* 12, no. 2:20–25.

Bellah, Robert, Richard Madsen, William Sullivan, Ann Sindler, and Steven Tipton. 1991. *The Good Society.* New York: Random.

Bennett, Philip. 1992. "Growing Up Skewed with Violence." *Boston Globe,* 4 June.

Berck, Judith. 1992. *No Place To Be: Voices of Homeless Children.* Boston: Houghton Mifflin.

Berger, Deborah. 1990. "When School Is a Haven." *Parade Magazine,* 7 Jan., 4–5.

Best, Joel. 1994. *Troubling Children: Studies of Children and Social Problems.* Hawthorn, N.Y.: Aldine.

Better Homes Foundation. 1991. *Helping Homeless Families.* Boston: Better Homes Foundation.

Bettmann, Otto L. 1974. *The Good Old Days—They Were Terrible!* New York: Random.

Bingham, Richard, Roy Green, and Sammis White. 1987. *The Homeless in Contemporary Society.* Newbury Park, Calif.: Sage.

Black, Lascelles W. 1987. "The Shelter: Every Day Is a Struggle to Keep the Faith." *Networker* (Nov./Dec.): 30–38.

Blau, Joel. 1988. "On the Uses of Homelessness." *Catalyst* 6, no. 2:5–25.

———. 1992. *The Visible Poor: Homelessness in the United States.* Oxford, England: Oxford University Press.

Block, Fred, et al. 1987. *The Mean Season: The Attack on the Welfare State.* New York: Random.

Bobo, Kim, et al. 1991. *Organizing for Social Change: A Manual for Activists in the 1990s.* Cabin John, Md.: Seven Locks.

Border, David. 1991. "Now to Rescue Our Children." *Washington Post National Week Edition,* 11–17 Mar., 4.

Bowen, Jeffrey, et al. 1989. "Educating Homeless Children and Youth: A Policy Analysis." Paper presented at symposium, American Educational Research Association Annual Conference, 27 Mar.

Boxill, Nancy A. 1990. *Homeless Children: The Watchers and the Waiters.* New York: Haworth.

Boxill, Nancy A., and Anita L. Beaty. 1990. "Mother/Child Interaction among Homeless Women and Their Children in a Public Night Shelter in Atlanta, Georgia." In *Homeless Children: The Watchers and the Waiters,* ed. Nancy A. Boxill. New York: Haworth.

Boyce, W. 1985. "Social Support, Family Relations, and Children." *Social Support and Health,* ed. S. Cohen and S. Syme. Orlando: Academic Press.

Bradley, Robert, et al. 1994. "Early Indication of Reslience and Their Relation to Experiences in the Home Environments in Low Birthweight, Premature Children Living in Poverty." *Child Development* 65, no. 2.

Brands, Marlene, and Debra DeBates. 1992. Homelessness: Teacher Resource Packet I. Brookings: South Dakota State University.

Brazelton, T. Berry. 1994. *Touchpoints.* Reding, Mass.: Addison Wesley.

Brickner, P.W. 1987. "Health Care for the Homeless." In *Homelessness: Critical Issues for Policy and Practice,* ed. Russell Schutt. Boston: Boston Foundation.

Brim, Orville. 1958. "Family Structure and Sex Role Learning by Children." *Sociometry* 21:1–15.

Broder, David S. 1991. "Now to Rescue Our Children." *Washington Post National Weekly Edition,* 11–17 Mar., 4.

Browne, Angela. 1987. *When Battered Women Kill.* New York: Free Press.

Bruce, Heather. 1994. "U.S. Report Finds a Growing Gap between High and Low Pay Earners." *Boston Globe,* 3 June. A–1.

Buck, Cindi, and Peg Dunlap. 1991. There's No Place Like Home: Homelessness in Kansas. Topeka, Kans.: Junior League.

Bucy, June, and Nexus Nichols. 1991. "Homeless Youth: Statement of Problem and Suggested Policies." *Journal of Health and Social Policy Special Issue: Homeless and Runaway Youth* 2, no. 4:65–71.

Bumpass, Larry L. 1990. "What's Happening to the Family? Interactions between Demographic and Institutional Change." *Demography* 27, no 4: 47–63.

Burt, Martha. 1991. *Alternative Methods to Estimate the Number of Homeless Chidlren and Youth.* Washington D.C.: Urban Institute Press.

———. 1992. *Over the Edge: The Growth of Homelessness in the 1980s.* New York: Russell Sage Foundation.

Burt, Martha, and Barbara Cohen. 1989. *America's Homeless: Numbers, Characteristics, and the Programs that Serve Them.* Washington, D.C.: Urban Institute Press.

Burt, Martha, and Karen Pittman. 1985. *Testing the Social Safety Net.* Washington, D.C.: Urban Institute Press.

Bush, Paul. 1987. "Vermont's Invisible People." *Southern Vermont* (Feb./Mar.): 5–7, 36–37.

Butler, Jeffrey. 1992. "Poor Families in New Hampshire." Concord, N.H.: Action for Decent Care Coalition.

California Food Policy Advocates. 1993. "School's Out . . . Let's Eat: An Organizing Guide for the Summer Food Serivce Program." San Francisco, Calif.

Canellos, Peter. 1991. "Lawsuits Say State Adding to Homeless." *Boston Globe,* 15 Aug., 23.

Caton, Carol L. 1986. "The Homeless Experience in Adolescent Years." In *The Mental Health Needs of Homeless Persons,* ed. E.L. Bassuk. San Francisco: Jossey-Bass.

———. 1990. *Homeless in America.* New York: Oxford Univ. Press.

Center for Community Change. 1990. "America's Third Deficit." Washington, D.C.: Center for Community Change.

———. 1993. "The Low Income Housing Crisis: It Keeps Getting Worse." Washington, D.C.: Center for Community Change

Center for Law and Education. 1987. Homelessness: A Barrier to Education for Thousands of Children. *Newsnotes* 38. Cambridge, Mass.: Center for Law and Education.

Center for the Study of Social Policy. 1991. *Building a Community Agenda: Developing Local Governance Entities.* Washington, D.C.: Center for the Study of Serial Policy.

Center on Budget and Policy Priorities. 1990. "Rich-Poor Income Gap Hits 40–Year High as Poverty Rate Stalls." Washington, D.C.

Center on Social Welfare Policy and Law. 1993. "Living at the Bottom: An Analysis of AFDC Benefit Levels." Washington, D.C.: Center on Social Welfare Policy and Law.

Chadwick, Bruce A., and Howard M. Bahr. 1978. "Rural Poverty." In *Rural U.S.A.: Persistence and Change,* ed. Thomas R. Ford. Ames: Iowa State Univ. Press.

Chan, Vera, and Michele Momparler. 1991. "What's He Got against Kids? George Bush's Report Card." *Mother Jones,* May/June, np.

Chavkin, Wendy, A. Kristal, C. Seabron, and P. Guigli. 1987. "Reproductive Experience of Women Living in Hotels for the Homeless in New York City." *New York State Journal of Medicine* 87:10–13.

Chicago Coalition for the Homeless. 1993. "Alone after Dark: A Survey of Homeless Youth in Chicago." Chicago: Coalition for the Homeless.

Children's Action Alliance. 1989. "Arizona's Forgotten Children: Promises to Keep." Sponsored by Margaret T. Morris Foundation, Prescott, Arizona.

Children's Defense Fund. 1987. "A Growing Number of Families Face the Crisis of Homelessness." *CDF Reports* (May): 1, 7.

————. 1988. *A Children's Defense Budget (FY 1989)*. Washington, D.C.

————. 1989. *A Vision for America's Future: An Agenda for the 1990s; A Children's Defense Budget.* Washington, D.C.: Children_s Defense Fund.

————. 1992a. An Opinion Makers Guide to Children in the Election Year 1992: Leave No Child Behind. Washington, D.C.: Children_s Defense Fund.

————. 1992b. *Welcome The Child.* Washington, D.C.: Children_s Defense Fund.

————. 1995. *The State of America's Children Yearbook.* Washington, D.C.: Children's Defense Fund.

Children's Services Department. 1990. "A Guide to Provide Comprehensive and Quality Services to Homeless Children and Their Families." San Jose, Calif.: Santa Clara County Office of Education.

Church, George. 1993. "Jobs in an Age of Insecurity." *Time*, 22 Nov.

Churches Conference on Shelter and Housing. 1991. "Making Room at the Inn: Congregational Investment in Affordable Housing." Silver Spring, Md.: McAuley Institute.

Clements, Mark. 1994. "What Americans Say about the Homeless." *Parade Magazine*, 9 Jan.

Coakley, Tom. 1992. "Out of Work, Out of Hope: Unemployed See Their Lifeline Cut with Benefits' End." *Boston Globe*, 24 Sept, A–1.

Coalition for the Homeless. 1983. "A Crying Shame: Official Abuse and Neglect of Homeless Infants." New York: Coalition for the Homeless.

————. 1987. "Rural Homelessness in America: Appalachia and the South." New York: Coalition for the Homeless.

————. 1990. "Lawsuits Involving the Coalition for the Homeless." Washington, D.C.: Coaltion for the Homeless.

————. 1993. "Homelessness: An Outcome Not a Condition." Washington, D.C.: Coaltion for the Homeless.

Coates, Robert. 1990. *A Street Is Not a Home.* Buffalo, N.Y.: Prometheus.

Cohen, Barbara, and Martha Burt. 1990. "Food Sources and Intake of Homeless Persons." In *Data and Issues*, vol. 2 of *Homelessness in the United States*, by Jamshid A. Momeni. New York: Greenwood.

Cohen, F. 1984. "Coping." In *Behavioral Health: A Handbook of health enhancement and disease prevention*, ed. J. Matarazzo. New York: Wiley.

Cohen, Jack, and Ian Stewart. 1994. *The Collapse of Chaos.* New York: Viking.

Cohen, Marc J. 1992. Hunger 1993: Uprooted People. Silver Springs, Md.: Bread for the World Institute.

————. 1993. "Hunger in Uprooted People." Silver Springs, Md.: Bread for the World Institute.

Colby, Ira C. 1990. "The Throw-Away Teen." *Journal of Applied Social Sciences* 14, no. 2:277–94.

Coles, Robert. 1967. *Children of Crisis: A Study of Courage and Fear* Boston: Little-Brown.

Comer, James P. 1984. "Home-School Relationships as They Affect the Academic Success of Children." *Education and Urban Society* 16, no. 3:323–37.

Committee for Economic Development. 1987. "Children in Need: Investment Strategies for the Educationally Disadvantaged." New York: Committee for Economic Development.

———. 1991. "The Unfinished Agenda: A New Vision for Child Development and Education." New York: Research and Policy Committee.

Conger, John J. 1988. "Hostages to Fortune: Youth, Values, and the Public Interest." *American Psychologist* (Apr.): 291–300.

Conger, Rand, and Glen Elder. 1994. *Families in Troubled Times: Adapting to Change in Rural America*. Hawthorne, N.Y.: Aldine de Gruyter.

Congressional Research Service. 1993. "Homeless in America" (IP 314H). March.

Conrad, Peter. 1992. *Deviance and Medicalization*. Philadelphia: Temple Univ. Press.

Cook, John, and Larry Brown. 1993. Two Americas: Alterative Futures for Child Poverty in the U.S. Medford, Mass.: Tufts University.

Cook, Ronna. 1988. "Trends and Needs in Programming for Independent Living." *Child Welfare* 67, no. 6:497–514.

Cooley, Charles Horton. 1932. *Human Nature and the Social Order*. New York: Scribners.

Coontz, Stephanie. 1992. *The Way We Never Were: American Families and the Nostalgia Trap*. New York: Basic Books.

Cooper, Edith Fairman. 1991. "Homeless: Medical Conditions." *CRS Report for Congress*, 26 Feb., 91–201.

Coughenour, C. Milton, and Lawrence Busch. 1978. "Alternative Futures for Rural America: The Cloudy Crystal Ball." In *Rural U.S.A.: Persistence and Change*, ed. Thomas R. Ford. Ames: Iowa State University Press.

Coughlin, Ellen. 1988. "Studying Homelessness: The Difficulty of Tracking a Transient Population." *Chronicle of Higher Education* (Oct. 19): A12.

Couto, Richard. 1992. "Beyond Distress: New Measure of Economic Need in Appalachia." Knoxville, Tenn.: Commission on Religion in Appalacia.

Craig, Susan E. 1992. "The Educational Needs of Children Living with Violence." *Phi Delta Kappan* 74 (Sept.):67–71.

Dail, Paula. 1990. "The Psychosocial Context of Homeless Mothers with Young Children." *Child Welfare* 69, no. 4:291–308.

Danzinger, K., ed. 1970. *Readings in Child Socialization*. New York: Pergamon.

Danzinger, Sheldon. 1985. "Effects of Unemployment and Policy Changes on America's Poor." *Journal of Social Policy* 14, no. 3:313–31.

———. 1986. "Poverty and Policy: Lessons of the Last Two Decades." *Social Service Review* 60, no. 1:34–51.

Darnton, Nina. nd. "A Mother's Touch." *Newsweek Special Issue*, 60–61.

Daro, Deborah. 1991. "Child Sexual Abuse Prevention: Separating Fact from Fiction." *Child Abuse and Neglect* 15:1–4.

Davidson, Barbara Parmer, and Pamela Jenkins. 1989. "Class Diversity in Shelter Life." *Social Work*, Nov., 491–94.

Davis, William E., and Edward J. McCaul. 1991. "The Emerging Crisis: Current and Projected Status of Children in the United States." Augusta: University of Maine, Institute for the Study of At-Risk Students, sponsored by Maine State Department of Education.

Dawida, Michael, 1988. *Final Report on Homelessness in Pennsylvania*. Philadelphia: Subcommittee on Welfare of the House Committe of Health and Welfare. January.

Dear, Michael. 1991. "Gaining Community Acceptance." Princeton, N.J.: Robert Wood Johnson Foundation.Deepening Poverty in America." 1992. *Boston Globe*, 7 Sept.

Denman, Jackie. 1980. "Problems of Rural Areas." In *Rural Human Services: A Book of Readings*, ed. H. Wayne Johnson. Itasca, Ill.: F.E. Peacock.

Denzin, Norman K. 1970. *The Research Act*. Chicago: Aldine.

DeParle, Jason. 1991. "Poverty Rate Rose Sharply Last Year as Incomes Slipped." *New York Times*, 27 Sept.

DiIulio, John. 1991. "The Homeless: Who They Are and How to Help Them—There but for Fortune." *New Republic* 204, no. 25:27–36.

Dolbeare, Cushing. 1991. "Economic Causes of Homelessness." Washington, D.C.: National Coalition for the Homeless.

Donnelly, Anne H. Cohn. 1991. "What We Have Learned about Prevention: What We Should Do about It." *Child Abuse and Neglect* 15, sup. 1:99–106.

Dorobeck, Christopher J., and Ann M. Stifter. 1992. "Foreclosures Hit 60-Year High Here." *Foster's Daily Democrat* 17 Jan., 1A.

Douglas, Ann. 1992. *Homeless Children and Their Families: A Resource Booklet for School Personnel*. Malden: Massachusetts Department of Education.

Douglass, Richard. 1995. "The State of Homelessness in Michigan." Lansing: Michigan State Housing Development Authority.

Duncan, Cynthia M., Nita Lamborghini, and Esther Pank. 1993. "Young Families and Youth in the North Country." A report to the Northern New Hampshire Foundation, Jan.

Duncan, Greg, Jeanne Brooks-Gunn, and Palema Kato Klebanov. 1994. "Economic Deprivation and Early Childhood Development." *Child Development* 65, no. 2:296–318.

Durkheim, Emile. 1966; originally 1897. *Suicide*. New York: Free Press.

Dustin, Sara. nd. "Act for the Relief of Childhood Poverty." Draft statement by Parents for Justice, Concord, N.H.

Easterlin, Richard. 1987. *Birth and Fortune: The Impact of Numbers on Personal Welfare*. Chicago: University of Chicago Press.

Eddowes, E. Anne, and John R. Hranitz. 1989. "Educating Children of the Homeless." *Childhood Education* 54, no. 4:197–200.

Edleman, Marian Wright. 1991. "Kids First." *Mother Jones* 166, no. 3 (May/June):40–45.

Edleman, Peter, and Beryl Radin. 1991. "Serving Children and Families Effectively: How the Past Can Help Chart the Future." Washington, D.C.: Institute for Educational Leadership.

Edleman, Peter, and Joyce Ladner. 1991. *Adolescence and Poverty: Challenge for the 1990s.* Lanham, Md.: University Press of America.

Edsall, Thomas Byrne. 1988. "The Return of Inequality." *Atlantic Monthly* 4, no.2, 86–94.

Ehrenreich, Barbara. 1990. *Fear of Falling.* New York: Harper.

Elias, M.J., Gara, M., and Ubriaco, M. 1985. "Sources of Stress and Support in Children's Transition to Middle School: An Empirical Analysis." *Journal of Clinical Child Psychology* 13, no. 2:171–85.

Elison, Gar. nd. "Frontier Areas: Problem for Delivery of Health Care Services." *Rural Health Care: The Newsletter of the National Rural Health Association* 8, no. 5.

Ellis, David. 1991. "Cutting the Costs." *Time,* 23 Dec., 40.

Ellwood, David. 1988. "Divide and Conquer: Responsible Security for America's Poor." Paper no. 1, Ford Foundation Project on Social Welfare and the American Family, New York, 1988.

———. 1988. *Poor Support.* New York: Basic Books.

Ely, Lydia. 1987. "Broken Lives: Denial of Education to Homeless Children." Washington, D.C.: National Coalition for the Homeless.

Employment and Training Administration. 1994. "Employment and Training for America's Homeless: Report on the Job Training for the Homeless Demonstration Program." Washington, D.C.: Employment and Training Administration.

Erickson, Jon, and Charles Wilhelm. 1986. *Housing the Homeless.* New Brunswick, N.J.: Rutgers Univ. Press.

Erikson, Erik. 1963. *Childhood and Society.* New York: W.W. Norton.

Escalona, S.K. 1974. "Intervention Programs for Children at Psychiatric Risk." In *The Child in His Family,* vol. 3, ed. E.J. Anthony and C. Koupernick. New York: Wiley and Sons.

Etizoni, Amiti. 1993. *The Spirit of Community.* New York: Crown.

Fagan, Tricia. 1990. "Small Hope: America's Homeless Children." *State Government News* (June): 14–17.

Faludi, Susan. 1991. *Backlash: The Undeclared War against American Women.* New York: Crown.

Farrell, John A. 1992. "Welfare Battlefield." *Boston Globe,* 19 Apr., 1.

Fenby, Barbara Lou. 1980. "Social Work in a Rural Setting." In *Rural Human Services: A Book of Readings,* ed. H. Wayne Johnson. Itasca, Ill.: F.E. Peacock.

Ferguson, Sarah. 1990. "Us vs. Them: America's Growing Frustration with the Homeless." *Utne Reader,* Sept./Oct.

Fink, Arlene, and Lois McCloskey. 1990. "Moving Child Abuse and Neglect Prevention Programs Forward: Improving Program Evaluations." *Child Abuse and Neglect* 14:187–206.

Finkelhor, David, Gerry Hotaling, and Angela Sedlack. 1990. "Report of Missing and Runaway Children." Durham, N.H.: University of New Hampshire Family Research Laboratory.: Prepared for the U.S. Department of Justice.

First, R., J. Rife, and B. Toomey. 1994. "Homelessness in Rural Areas: Causes, Patterns, and Trends." *Social Work* 39, no. 1:97–108.

First, Richard J., Dee Roth, and Bobbie Darden Arewa. 1988. "Homelessness: Understanding the Dimensions of the Problem for Minorities." *Social Work* 33, no. 2:120–24.

First, Richard, Beverly Toomey, and John Rife. 1990. "Preliminary Findings on Rural Homelessness." Columbus: Ohio State University.

Fisher, Gene, Peter Rossi, Georgiana Willis, and James Wright. 1987. "The Urban Homeless: Estimating Composition and Size." *Science* (Mar.): 1336–41.

Fisher, Pamela. 1991. *Alcohol, Drug Abuse, and Mental Health Problems among Homeless Persons: A Review of the Literature, 1980–1990.* Rockville, Md.: U.S. Public Health Service, #91-M-1763.

Fisher, Pamela, and William Breakey. "The Epidemiology of Alcohol, Drugs, and Mental Disorders among Homeless Persons." *American Psychologist* 46, no. 11: 1115-28.

Fitchen, Janet M. 1991. "Homelessness in Rural Places: Perspectives from Upstate New York." *Urban Anthropology* 20, no. 2:177–210.

Flax, James, and Morton Wagenfeld, Ruby Ivens, and James Weiss. 1979. *Mental Health and Rural American: An Overview and Annotated Bibliography.* Washington, D.C.: National Institute on Mental Health.

Flora, C., and J. Flora. 1989. "Rural Area Development: The Impact of Change." *Forum for Applied Research and Public Policy* 4, no. 3:50–52.

Flora, C.B., J.L. Flora, J.D. Spears, and L.E. Swanson. 1992. *Rural Communities: Legacy and Change.* Boulder: Westview.

Flora, Cornelia Butler, et al. 1992. *Rural Communities: Legacy and Change.* Boulder: Westview.

Ford, Royal. 1994. "The Other Vermont." *Boston Globe Magazine,* 4 Dec.

Ford, Thomas R. 1978. "Contemporary Rural America: Persistence and Change." In *Rural U.S.A.: Persistence and Change,* ed. Thomas R. Ford. Ames: Iowa State University Press.

Fordham Institute for Innovation in Social Policy. 1989. *Measuring the Social Well-Being of the Nation: The Social Health of Children and Youth.* New York: Fordham University Graduate Center.

Foundation for Child Development. 1992. "Pathways to Self Sufficiency for Two Generations: Designing Welfare to Work Programs that Strengthen Families and Benefit Children." New York: Foundation for Child Development.

Fox, Mary Frank, and Sharlene Hesse-Beiber. 1984. *Women at Work.* Mountain View, Calif.: Mayfield.

Frank, Robert, and Calvin Streeter. 1987. "Bitter Harvest: The Question of Homelessness in Rural America." In *Social Work in Rural Areas,* ed. Anne Summers, et al. Batesville: Arkansas College Social Work Program.

Frisby, Michael. 1991. "Bush's Veto of Jobless Bill Is Sustained." *Boston Globe,* 17 Oct. A-1.

Gaines, Judith. 1990. "Outside: New Hampshire's New Homeless Belie the Stereotypes." *Boston Globe,* 2 Dec., 85–86.

Gallagher, E. 1986. "No Place Like Home: A Report on the Tragedy of Homeless Children and Their Families in Massachusetts." Boston: Massachusetts Committee for Children and Youth.

Garbarino, James, and Gwen Gilliam. 1980. *Understanding Abusive Families.* Lexington, Mass.: Lexington Books.

Garmezy, N. 1983. "Stressors of Childhood." In *Stress, Coping, and Development in Children,* ed. N. Garmezy and M. Rutter. New York: McGraw-Hill.

Garmezy, N., and A. Tellegren. 1984. "Studies of Stress Resistant Children." In *Advances in Applied Developmental Psychology,* ed. F. Morrison. New York: Academic Press.

Garrett, Patricia, Nicholas Ng'andu, and John Ferron. 1994. "Poverty Experiences of Young Children and the Quality of Their Home Environments." *Child Development* 65, no. 2: 18–31.

Gaventa, John, and Helen Lewis. 1991. "Participatory Education and Grassroots Development: The Case of Rural Appalachia." London: International Institute for Environment and Development.

Geisler, C. 1988. "Homelessness and Landlessness." *Earth Matters* 37, no. 4:12–16.

Gelbert, Lilian, and Lawrence Linn. 1988. "Social and Physical Health of Homeless Adults Previously Treated for Mental Health Problems." *Hospital and Community Psychiatry* 39, no. 5:510–16.

Gewirtzman, R., and I. Fodor. 1987. "The Homeless Child at School: From Welfare Hotel to Classroom." *Child Welfare* 66, no. 3:237–45.

Giamo, Benedict, and Jeffrey Grunbert. 1992. *Beyond Homelessness.* Ames: University of Iowa Press.

Gil, David. 1973. *Violence Against Children.* Cambridge, Mass.: Harvard Univ. Press.

Gleick, James. 1987. *Chaos: Making a New Science.* New York: Penguin.

Goodman, Ellen. 1991. "The Working Poor or the Welfare Poor." *Boston Globe,* 29 Dec. A-1.

Goodman, Lisa, Leonard Saxe, and Mary Harvey. 1991. "Homelessness as Psychological Trauma." *American Psychologist* 46, no. 11:1219–25.

Gornstein, Aaron. 1990. "Living on the Edge: The Housing Crisis Facing Teen Parents and Their Children." Boston: John Hancock Financial Services.

Gosselin, Peter. 1992a. "Across U.S., Families Face More of Less." *Boston Globe,* 19 Jan., A-1.

———. 1992b. "The Downsized American Dream." *Boston Globe,* 19 Jan., 1–2.

———. 1992c. "Poverty Rate in U.S. Hits 8-Year High." *Boston Globe,* 4 Sept. A-1.

———. 1992d. "Poverty Traps More Workers." *Boston Globe,* 12 May, A-1.

"Governor vetos Education Funding." 1995. *New Hampshire Union Leader,* 23 June. A:1.

Graber, C. Scott. 1980. "Where There's No Will, There's No Way." In *Rural Human Services: A Book of Readings,* ed. H. Wayne Johnson. Itasca, Ill.: F.E. Peacock.

Graham, Renee. 1990. "The New Face of Hunger." *Boston Globe,* 15 Nov., 1.

Gramlich, Ed. 1992. "The Home Program: A Brief Guide for Community Organizations." Washington D.C.: Center for Community Change.

Gray, Mary McPhail. 1989. "Census of Missouri Homeless Children." Columbia: University of Missouri.

Greenblatt, M., and M. Robertson. 1993. "Lifestyles, Adaptive Strategies, and Sexual Behaviors of Homeless Adolescents." *Hospital and Community Psychiatry* 44, no. 12:1177–80.

Greenstein, Robert. 1992. "Attempts to Dismiss the Census Poverty Data." Center on Budget and Policy Priorities. Washington, D.C.

Greenstein, Robert, and Art Jaeger. 1992. Number in Poverty Hits 20 Year High as Recession Adds 2 Million More People Poor. Washington, D.C.: Center on Budget and Policy Priorities.

Greenstein, Robert, and Scott Baranick. 1990. "Drifting Apart: New Findings on Growing Income Disparities between the Rich, Poor and Middle Class." Washington, D.C.: Center on Budget and Policy Priorities.

Greer, Nora Richter. 1988. *The Creation of Shelter.* Washington, D.C.: American Institute of Architects Press.

Grigsby, Charles, et al. 1990. "Disaffiliation to Entrenchment: A Model for Understanding Homelessness." *Journal of Social Issues* 46, no. 4:141–74.

Gulati, Padmini. 1992. *Homelessness.* Western Michigan University. Kalamazoo, Mich.

Hacker, Andrew. *Two Nations: Black and White, Separate, Hostile, and Unequal.* New York: Scribner.

Hall, Judy A., and Penelope L. Maza. 1990. "No Fixed Address: The Effects of Homelessness on Families and Children." In *Homeless Children: The Watchers and the Waiters,* ed. Nancy A. Boxill. New York: Haworth.

Hall, Mimi. 1990. "Mayors: More Hungry, Homeless." *USA Today,* 20 Dec., 3A.

Hamilton, Lee M. 1988. "Report on Survey of Homelessness on Families on Cape Cod." Hyannis, Mass.: Community Action Committee of Cape Cod and the Islands.

Harmon, Natasha. 1992. "Affordable Housing: The Vermont Model." Amerherst: University of Massachusetts Center for Rural Massachusetts.

Harrington, Michael. 1984. *The Other America.* New York: MacMillian.

Harrington-Lueker, Donna. 1989. "What Kind of School Board Member Would Help Homeless Children?" *American School Board Journal* (July): 12–19.

Hart, Jordana. 1991. "Homeless Populations Up, City Census Data Indicate." *Boston Globe,* 26 Dec., 27–28.

Hassinger, E. 1982. *Rural Health Organization.* Ames: Iowa State Univ. Press.

Hawkins, J., D. Lishner, R. Catalano, and M. Howard. 1985. "Childhood Predictors of Adolescent Substance Abuse: Toward an Empirically Grounded Theory." *Journal of Children in Contemporary Society* 5, no. 18:11–48.

Hawkins, J., P. Pastor, M. Bell, and S. Morrison. 1980. "A Typology of Cause Focused Strategies of Delinquency Prevention." *Reports of the National Juvenile Justice Assessment Centers.* Washington, D.C.: Office of Juvenile Justice and Delinquency Prevention, U.S. Department of Justice.

Health Care for the Homeless Information Resouce Center. 1992c. "Annotated Bibliography: Working with Homeless Children at Risk for Severe Emotional Disturbance." Boston: Health Care for the Homeless Information Resource Center.

———. 1992a. Annotated Bibliography: Child Development and Developmental Delays among Homeless Children. Boston: Health Care for the Homeless Information Resource Center.

———. 1992b. "Annotated Bibliography: Immunization Status of Homeless and Low-Income Children." Boston: Health Care for the Homeless Information Resouce Center.

Heffernan, Judith, and William Heffernan. 1986. "Impact of the Farm Crisis on Rural Families and Communities." *Rural Sociologist* 6(3):160–70.

Helfer, Ray E. 1984. *Childhood Comes First.* East Lansing, Mich.: Ray E. Helfer.

Helge, Doris. 1990. "A National Study Regarding At-Risk Students." National Rural Development Institute, Western Washington University, Bellingham.

Hennepin County Board of Commissioners. 1991. "A Community Response to the Needs of Homeless Families." Minneapolis: Hennepin County Board of Commissioners.

Hewelett, Sylvia Ann. 1986. *A Lesser Life: The Myth of Women's LIberation in America.* New York: Morrow.

———. 1991. *When the Bough Breaks: The Cost of Neglecting our Children.* New York: Basic Books.

Hier, Sally J., Paula J. Korboot, and Robert D. Schwietzer. 1990. "Social Adjustment and Symptomatology in Two Types of Homeless Adolescents: Runaways and Throwaways." *Adolescence* 25, no. 100:761–71.

Hillfiker, David. 1994. *Not All Of Us Are Saints.* New York: Hill and Wang.

Hilyard, Scott. 1991. "Not Kids Anymore: Seniors Are Married, Homeless, Expecting." *Concord Monitor,* 12 June, A-1.

Hoch, Charles, and Robert Slayton. 1989. *New Homeless and Old.* Philadelphia: Temple University Press.

Hochschild, Arlie. 1989. *The Second Shift: Working Parents and the Revolution at Home.* New York: Viking-Penguin.

Hohler, Bob. 1992. "Missing Medicine: Basic Health Care Grows Dangerously Elusive in Rural New England." *Boston Globe,* 22 Mar., A-1.

Hombs, Mary Ellen. 1992. "Reversals of Fortune: America's Homeless Poor and Their Advocates in the 1990s." In *The Question of Home* 17 (summer).

Hombs, Mary Ellen, and Mitch Snyder. 1982. "Homelessness in America: A Forced March to Nowhere." Washington, D.C.: Community for Creative Non-Violence.

Home Builders Institute. 1993. "Heart to Heart: Creating a Solution to Homelessness." Washington, D.C.: Home Builders Institute.

"The Homeless: Who? How Many? A State Task Force Seeks Answers." 1987. *Manchester Union Leader,* 31 Oct.

Homeless Information Exchange. 1989. "Family and Child Homelessness." Distributed by the National Coalition for the Homeless.

Homelessness and Cognitive Performance in Children: A Possible Link." 1990. *Social Work* 35, no. 6 (Nov.): 516–19.

Homes for the Homeless. 1992a. "The New Poverty: A Generation of Homeless Families." *Newsletter* 1, no. 2 (June): 1.

------. 1992b. "Train and Gain: An Apprentice and Employment Program at Homes for the Homeless." New York: Homes for the Homeless.

------. 1994. "Hopes, Dreams, and Promises: The Future of Homeless Children in America." New York: Homes for the Homeless.

Hope, Marjorie, and James Young. 1986. "From Backwards to Back Alleys: Deinstitutionalization." *Urban and Social Change Review* 17, no. 2:7–11.

Hopper, Kim, and Jill Hamberg. 1985. *The Making of America's Homeless: From Skid Row to the New Poor.* New York Community Service Society.

Housing Assistance Council. 1988. "Housing Programs for the Homeless in Rural Areas." Washington, D.C.: Housing Assistance Council.

------. 1990. "Shelter and Housing Resources for Homeless Assistance: A Guide for Small Towns and Rural Communities." Washington, D.C.: Housing Assistance Council.

------. 1992. "Assessing Local Housing Needs: A Guide for Rural Communities." Washington, D.C.: Housing Assistance Council.

Hudson, Christopher. 1994. "A Causal Model of Distribution of Homeless Persons in the United States." Paper presented at the 40th annual program meeting of the Council of Social Work Education. Atlanta, Ga. Feb. 9.

Hudson, C., J. Salloway, and Y. Vissing. 1992. "The Impact of State Administrative Practices on Community Mental Health." *Journal of Mental Health Administration* 19, no. 6, 417–36.

Hurrelmann, Klaus. 1988. *Social Structure and Personality Development: The Individual as a Productive Processor of Reality.* New York: Cambridge Univ. Press.

Hurst, Charles. 1995. *Social Inequality.* Boston: Allyn and Bacon.

Hyde, Margaret O. 1989. *The Homeless: Profiling the Problem.* Hillside, N.J.: Enslow.

Illinois Coalition for the Homeless. 1991. "Heartbreak in the Heartland." Chicago: Illinois Coaliton for the Homeless.

Institute for Children and Poverty. 1993. "Homelessness: The Foster Care Connection." *Newsletter* 2, no. 1 (Aug.): 1.

------. 1994. Job Readiness: Crossing the Threshold from Homelessness to Employment. New York.

Institute of Medicine. 1988. *Homelessness, Health, and Human Needs.* Washington, D.C.: National Academy Press.

Interagency Council on the Homeless. 1991. "The McKinney Act: A Program Guide." Washington, D.C.: Interagency Council on the Homeless.

------. 1992. "Implementation Action for the Federal Plan to Help End Homelessness." Washington, D.C.: Interagency Council on the Homeless.

Jackson, Shelly. 1990. "Education Rights of Homeless Children." Cambridge, Mass.: Center for Law and Education.

Jacobo, April. 1992. Welfare up 100 Percent as New Hampshire Economy Sage." *Portsmouth Herald,* 19 June, 1.

James, Franklin. 1992. "Homelessness among Youth on Their Own Is a Serious Problem for Colorado." Denver: University of Colorado.

Jenecks, Christopher. 1994. *The Homeless.* Cambridge, Mass.: Harvard Univ. Press.

Jennings, Lisa. 1988. "Panel Says Children Fastest-Growing Portion of Home-
less." *Education Week,* 28 Sept. 5.
————. 1989. "Sixty Eight Thousand Children Are Homeless, GAO Report."
Education Week, 13 Sept.
Johnson, Clifford, et al. 1991. *Child Poverty in America.* Children's Defense
Fund, Washington D.C.
Johnson, Joan. 1991. *Kids Without Homes.* New York: Franklin Watts.
Johnson, Joseph, and Barbara Wand. 1991. "Homeless, Not Hopeless: Ensuring
Educational Opportunity for America's Homeless Children and Youth."
National Association of State Coordinators for the Education of Homeless
Children and Youth. Maryland Department of Education. Baltimore, Md.
Johnson, Louise C. 1980. "Human Service Delivery Patterns in Nonmetropolitan
Communities." In *Rural Human Services: A Book of Readings,* ed. H. Wayne
Johnson. Itasca, Ill.: F.E. Peacock.
Jonas, S. 1986. "On Homelessness and the American Way." *American Journal of
Public Health* 76: 1084–86.
Jones, James, Irene Levine, and Allison Rosenberg. 1991. "Introduction." *Amer-
ican Psychologist* 46, no, 11 (Nov.): 1108.
Jones, Loring P. 1988. "A Typology of Adolescent Runaways." *Child and
Adolescent Social Work Journal* 5, no. 1:15–29.
Jordan, Robert. 1991. "Threadbare Compassion." *Boston Globe,* 10 Aug., 21.
Kalob, Dennis, and Catherine Foley. 1992. "A Community Effort to End Home-
lessness: Is Unity Possible?" New Orleans: Unity.
Kane, Thomas. 1987. "Giving Back Control: Long Term Poverty and Motiva-
tion." *Social Service Review* 61, no. 3 (Sept.): 406–19.
Katz, Michael. 1989. *The Undeserving Poor: From the War on Poverty to the War on
Welfare.* New York: Pantheon.
Kaufman, Nancy. 1986. "Homelessness: A Comprehensive Policy Approach."
In *Housing the Homeless,* ed. Jon Erickson and Charles Wilhelm. New
Brunswick, N.J.: Rutgers University Press.
Kayne, Andrea. 1989. *Annotated Bibliography of Social Science Literature Concern-
ing the Education of Homeless Children.* Center for Law and Education.
Cambridge, Mass. Sept.
Kelly, Patricia, and Verne Kelly. 1980. "Training Natural Helpers in Rural Com-
munities" In *Rural Human Services: A Book of Readings,* ed. H. Wayne
Johnson. Itasca, Ill.: F.E. Peacock.
Kessler, Brad. 1989. "Down and Out in Suburbia" *The Nation,* 25 Sept.
Kilman, Scott, and Robert Johnson. 1991. "Homelessness Spreads to the
Countryside, Straining Resources." *Wall Street Journal,* 5 Mar.
"Kindling Spirit." 1992. Readers Digest. July 8.
Kinks. 1979. "Catch Me Now I'm Falling." From *Low Budget.* Arista Records.
Kirst, Michael W. 1991. "Improving Children's Services: Overcoming Barriers,
Creating New Opportunities." *Phi Delta Kappan* (Apr.): 615–18.
Klein, Tovah, et al. 1993. "No Place to Call Home: Supporting the Needs of
Homeless Children in Early Childhood Classroom." *Young Children* 48,
no. 6:22–31.

Knickman, J., and B. Weitzman. 1989. "Forecasting Models to Target Families at High Risk of Homelessness." Vol. 3. New York: New York University Health Research Program.

Knox, Richard. 1991. "Jobless Miss Out on Care." *Boston Globe,* 29 Sept., A-1.

Kobosa, S. 1982. "The Hardy Personality: Toward a Social Psychology of Stress and Health." In *Sociology of Health and Illness,* ed. G.S. Sanders and J. Suls. Hillsdale, N.J.: Erlbaum.

Kohlberg, K. and R. Kramer. 1969. "Continuities and Discontinuities in Childhood Moral Development." *Human Development* 12: 436–39.

Kohn, M., L. Skinczynski, and C. Schoenbach. 1987. "Social Stratification and the Transmission of Values in the Family: A Cross-National Assessment." *Sociological Forum* 1:57–69.

Koller, Marvin, and Oscar Ritchie. 1978. *Sociology of Childhood.* Englewood Cliffs, N.J.: Prentice Hall.

Kozol, Jonathan. 1988a. *Rachel and Her Children.* New York: Crown.

———. 1988b. "A Reporter at Large: The Homeless and their Children" *New Yorker,* 1 Feb.

———. 1989. "The New Untouchables." *Newsweek Special Issue,* 6 Jan.

———. 1992. *Savage Inequalities: Children in America's Schools.* New York: Harper Perennial.

Kronenfeld, D., M. Phillips, and V. Middleton-Jeter. 1980. "The Forgotten Ones: Treatment of Single Parent Multi-Problem Families in a Residential Setting." Office of Human Development Services, Washington, D.C. Grant No. 18-P-90705/03.

Kroner, Mark J. 1988. "Living Arrangement Options for Young People Preparing for Independent Living." *Child Welfare* 67, no. 6:547–61.

Kryder-Coe, Julee, Lester Salamon, and Janice Molnar, eds. 1991. *Homeless Children and Youth.* New Brunswick, N.J.: Transaction.

Kufeldt, Kathleen. 1991. "Social Policy and Runaways." *Journal of Health and Social Policy Special Issue: Homeless and Runaway Youth* 2, no. 4:37–49.

Kune, Norman. 1992. *Ready, Willing, and Disabled.* Excerpted in the *Newsletter of the Association for Persons with Severe Handicaps* 1,2,13, (Feb./Mar.)

Kurtz, P. David, Sara Jarvis, and Gail Kurtz. "Problems of Homeless Youths: Empirical Findings and Human Services Issues." 1991. *Social Work* 36, no. 4 (July): 309–14.

Kuttner, Robert. 1988. "Bad Housekeeping." *New Republic,* 25 (Apr.)

———. 1991. "Child Care Red Tape that Keeps Mothers from Work." *Boston Globe,* 14 June, A-1.

LaBlanc, S. 1988. "The Least Ones." *Earth Matters* 37, no. 4:3.

Lakshmanan, Indira. 1995. "Under Poverty's Burden: In Massachusetts, a Quarter of a Million Children Are Growing Up Poor, in Rural Towns as Well as Cities. *Boston Globe,* 6 June. A-1.

Lamanna, Mary Ann, and Agnes Riedmann. 1991. *Marriages and Families.* Belmont, Ca.: Wadsworth.

Lamb, H. Richard. 1984. The Homeless Mentally Ill. American Psychiatric Association. Washington, D.C.

Lang, Michael. 1989. *Homelessness Amid Affluence: Structure and Paradox in the American Political Economy.* Westport, Conn.: Greenwood.

Larson, Olaf F. 1978. "Values and Beliefs of Rural People." In *Rural U.S.A.: Persistence and Change,* ed. Thomas R. Ford. Ames: Iowa State University Press.

Lauriat, Alison S. 1986. "Sheltering Homeless Families: Beyond an Emergency Response." In *The Mental Health Needs of Homeless Persons,* ed. E.L. Bassuk. San Francisco: Jossey Bass.

Lazere, Edward, et al. 1989. "The Other Housing Crisis: Sheltering the Poor in Rural America." Washington, D.C.: Center on Budget and Policy Priorites and Housing Assistance Council.

Lee, Barrett, and Bruce Link. 1991. "Images of the Homeless: Public Views and Media Images." Washington, D.C.: Office of Housing Research.

Lee, Barrett, David Lewis, and Susan Jones. 1992. "Are the Homeless to Blame? A Test of Two Theories." *Sociological Quarterly* 33, no. 4:535–52.

Lefebvre, Norman R. nd. "Quiet Stories: Loss, Separation, and Trauma." Tyngsboro, Mass.: Clearview Center of New England, Multi-Specialty Psychological and Consultation Services.

Lemert, Edwin. 1972. *Human Deviance, Social Problems, and Social Control.* Englewood Cliffs, N.J.: Prentice Hall.

Leslie, Connie, and Pamela Abramson. 1989. "Can A Shelter Be A School?" *Newsweek,* 23 Jan., 51–52.

Levinson, Frances, et al. 1992. On Their Own—At What Cost? A Look at Families Who Leave Shelters. Citizen's Committee for the Children of New York. New York.

Lewin, Rober. 1992. *Complexity: Life at the edge of chaos.* New York: Macmillan.

Lewis, Michael, and Carolyn Saarni. 1985. *The Socialization of Emotions.* New York: Plenum Press.

Lexington-Fayette County Council. 1990. "By and for the Community. A Plan Addressing Homelessness in Lexington-Fayette, Kentucky.: Lexington: Lexington-Fayette County Council.

Liebow, Elliot. 1993. *Tell Them Who I Am.* New York: Free Press.

Lightfoot, Sara Lawrence. 1978. *Worlds Apart: Relationships between Families and Schools.* New York: Basic Books.

Limbaugh, Rush. 1993. "The Fraud of Homelessness Advocacy." In *The Way Things Ought to Be.* New York: Pocket Books.

Linehan, Michelle F. 1989. "Homeless Children: Educational Strategies for School Personnel." *Prise Reporter* 21, no. 2:1–2.

———. 1992. "Children Who Are Homeless: Educational Strategies for School Personnel." *Phi Delta Kappan* 61–66.

Link, Bruce, et al. 1993. *Lifetime and Five Year Prevalence of Homelessness in the United States.* New York: Columbia University.

Lipton, Frank, Albert Sabatini, and Steven Katz. 1983. "Down and Out in the City: The Homeless Mentally Ill." *Hospital and Community Psychiatry* 34, no. 9 (Sept.): 817–21.

Longfellow, Cynthia. 1979. "Divorce in Context: Its Impact on Children." In *Divorce and Separation*, ed. George Levinger and Oliver Moles. New York: Basic Books.

Lorch, Donatella. 1989. "Homeless Said to Do Poorly in School." *New York Times*, 12 Sept.

Luloff, Albert, Gus Zaso, and Yvonne Vissing. 1992. Report on Homelessness in New Hampshire to the New Hampshire Department of Education. Concord.

Lyson, Thomas, and William Falk, eds. 1994. *Forgotten Places: Uneven Development in Rural America*. Lawrence: Univ. Press of Kansas.

Maccoby, E.E. 1970. "The Taking of Adult Roles in Middle Childhood." In *Readings in Child Socialization*, ed. K. Danzinger. New York: Pergamon.

MacLeod, Jay. 1995. *Ain't No Making It*. Boulder: Westview Press.

Magura, Stephen, Beth Silverman Moses, and Mary Ann Jones. 1987. "Assessing Risk and Measuring Change." Washington, D.C.: Child Welfare League of America.

Malone, M.E. 1992. "DSS Explores Program to Keep Families Intact." *Boston Globe*, 6 Apr., 21.

Manis, Melvin. 1955. "Social Interaction and the Self Concept." *Journal of Abnormal and Social Psychology* 51:362–76.

Marcuse, Peter. 1988. "Neutralizing Homelessness." *Socialist Review* 18, no. 1:69–96.

Martinez-Brawley, E. 1990. *Perspectives on the Small Community: Humanistic Views for Practitioners*. Silver Springs, Md.: National Association of Social Workers Press.

Maslow, A. 1970. *Motivation and Personality*, 2nd ed. New York: Harper and Row.

Massachusetts Department of Education. 1990. *Children Without Homes: A Report By The Massachusetts Department Of Education*. Boston: Massachusetts Department of Education.

Matchan, Linda. 1991. "Foster Homes in Short Supply." *Boston Globe*, 24 Sept. A-1.

————. 1992. "DSS Finds It's Doing Less with Less: Social Workers Say Budget Cuts Mean Fewer Services Despite Outcry for More." *Boston Globe*, 15 Apr., A-1.

————. 1993. "Children Living on Their Own: Looking for Help Can Seem Hopeless." *Boston Globe*, 11 Feb., A-1.

Mathews, Jay. 1992. "Rethinking Homeless Myths." *Newsweek*, Apr. 6.

McCall, Kathleen P. 1990. *Educating Homeless Children and Youth: A Sample of Programs, Policies, and Procedures*. Cambridge, Mass.: Center for Law and Education.

McCallum, Debra Moehle, et al. 1991. "Investigation of School Aged Children and Their Families in Doubled Up Living Situations." Tuscaloosa: University of Alabama.

McCarthy, Bill, and John Hagan. 1992. "Surviving on the Street: The Experience of Homeless Youth." *Journal of Adolescent Research* 7, no. 4:412–30.

McChesney, Kay Young. 1988. "Policy Implications of the Low-Income Housing Ratio for Homeless Families." Paper presented at the Society for the Study of Social Problems, Atlanta, 23 Aug.

———. 1990a. "Growth of Homelessness: An Aggregate Rather Than an Individual Problem" In *Homelessness: A Prevention Oriented Approach,* ed. R. Jahiel. Baltimore: Johns Hopkins (in press).

———. 1990b. "Family Homelessness: A Systemic Problem." *Journal of Social Issues* 46, no. 4:191–206.

———. 1991. "Macroeconomic Issues in Poverty: Implications for Child and Youth Homelessness." In *Homeless Children and Youth,* ed. Julee Kryder-Coe, Lester Salamon, and Janice Molnar. New Brunswick, N.J.: Transaction.

———. 1992. "Paths to Family Homelessness." In *Homelessness: The National Perspective,* ed. M.J. Robertson and M. Greenblatt. New York: Plenum.

McCluskey, Sandra H. 1990. "Study Blames Zoning and Rent Control for Housing Problem." CATO Institute News Release, 6 Feb., 29–30.

McKamy, Elizabeth Herman. 1976. "Social Work with the Wealthy." *Social Casework* (Apr.): 254–58.

Mead, George Herbert. 1962. *Mind, Self, and Society.* Chicago: Univ. of Chicago Press.

Meade, Christopher. 1993. "A Long Day's Journey into Night: Tracking Applicants through the Entitlements Maze." New York: Legal Action Center for the Homeless.

Mech, Edmund V., and Elizabeth L. Leonard. 1988. "Volunteers as Resources in Preparing Foster Adolescents for Self-Sufficiency." *Child Welfare* 67, no. 6:595–608.

Mellman and Lazarus Research. 1988. "A Survey of Attitudes toward Hunger and Homelessness in America." Washington, D.C.: Mellman and Lazarus Research.

Melton, G.B. 1983. *Child Advocacy: Psychological Issues and Interventions.* New York: Plenum.

Melvin, Bruce, and Elna Smith. 1971. "Rural Youth." In *Rural Poor in the Great Depression,* ed. David Rothman. New York: Arno.

Merton, Robert K. 1957. *Social Theory and Social Structure.* Glencoe, Ill.: Free Press.

Messinger, Alex. nd. "Unsheltered Lives: An Interdisciplinary Resource and Activity Guide for Teaching about Homelessness in Grades K-12." Vermont Department of Education.

Mihaly, Lisa Klee. 1991. *Homeless Families: Failed Policies and Young Victims.* Washington D.C., Children's Defense Fund.

Milburn, Noretta. 1990. "Drug Abuse among Homeless People." In *Data and Issues,* vol. 2 of *Homelessness in the United States,* ed. Jamshid A. Momeni. New York: Greenwood.

Miles, Barbara. 1988. "The Housing an Community Development Act of 1987 and the Stewart B. McKinney Homeless Assistance Act: Summary and Analysis." *CRS Report for Congress.* 88–481 E. Washington D.C., Library of Congress. 5 July.

Miller, D., and E. Lin. 1988. "Sheltered Homeless Families." *Pediatrics* 81, no. 5:558–674.

Miller, Henry. 1991. *On The Fringe: The Dispossessed in America.* Lexington, Mass.: Lexington Books.

Molnar, Janice M., et al. 1990. "Constantly Copromised: The Impact of Homelessness on Children." *Journal of Social Issues* 46, no. 4:109–24. Plenum, New York.

Molnar, Janice, Annelie Hartman, and Tovah Klein. 1988. *Transitional Shelter for Homeless Families: Early Childhood Component.* Better Homes Foundation, Bank Street College of Education, 18 Aug.

Momeni, Jamshid A., ed. 1990a. *Data and Issues,* vol. 2 of *Homelessness in the United States.* New York: Greenwood.

———. 1990b. *State Surveys,* vol. 1 of *Homelessness in the United States.* New York: Greenwood.

Monsma, Jim. 1990. One Church, One Home—Six Models of Church Based Housing Initiatives. McAuley Institute, Silver Spring, Md.

Moroz, Kathleen J., and Elizabeth A. Segal. nd. Homeless Children: Intervention Strategies for School Social Workers.

Morrissette, Patrick J., and Sue McIntyre. 1989. "Homeless Young People in Residential Care." *Social Casework* 70, no. 10:603–10.

Morrow, Gertrude. 1987. *The Compassionate School: A Practical Guide to Educating Abused and Traumatized Children.* Englewood Cliffs, N.J.: Prentice Hall.

Mowbray, Carol. 1985. "Homelessness in America: Myths and Realities." *American Journal of Orthopsychiatry* 55 (Jan.): 4–8.

Mulroy, Elizabeth, and Terry Lane. 1993. "Housing Affordability, Stress, and Single Mothers: Pathways to Homlessness." *Journal of Sociology and Social Welfare* 3:29–34.

Mulvey, Kevin P. 1988. *Today's Alcoholic Homeless.* Northeastern University: Boston.

NASW. 1988. "Families Swelling Ranks of Homeless." *NASW News,* Mar., 5.

National Association of Community Health Centers. 1990. A National Directory of Homeless Health Care Projects. Washington, D.C.

National Association of State Coordinators for the Education of Homeless Children and Youth. 1993. "Opening the Doors: Removing Barriers and Creating Opportunities for America's Homeless Chlidren and Youth." Baton Rouge, La.

National Center for Children in Poverty. 1993. "Five Million Children: 1993 Update." New York: Columbia University School of Public Health.

National Coalition for the Homeless. 1986. "Mid America in Crisis: Homelessness in Des Moines." New York: National Coaltion for the Homeless.

———. 1987a. *Broken Lives: Denial of Education to Homeless Children.* Washington, D.C: National Coalition for the Homeless.

———. 1987b. "Rural Homelessness in America: Appalachia and the South." Washington, D.C.: National Coalition for the Homeless.

———. 1988a. "Homelessness: The Nature of the Crisis. A Synopsis." *Youth Policy,* May, 18–21.

———. 1988b. Necessary Relief: The Stewart B. McKinney Homeless Assistance Act. Washington, D.C.

———. 1989. *American Nightmare: A Decade of Homelessness in the United States.* Washington, D.C.

———. 1991a. "Addressing Homelessness: Status of Programs under the Stewart B. McKinney Homeless Assistance Act and Related Legislation."

———. 1991b. "Fatally Flawed: The Census Bureau's Count of Homeless People." Washington, D.C.: National Coalition for the Homeless.

———. 1991c. "A Look at Rural Homelessness." *Safety Network* 10, no. 8:1.

———. 1991d. "McKinney Funding in Peril." *Safety Network* 10 (July):1.

———. 1991e. "Study Finds 20,000 Homeless in Rural Ohio." *Safety Network* 4 (Apr.): 2.

———. 1992a. "Addiction on the Streets: Substance Abuse and Homelessness in America." *Safety Network* 11, (Mar.–Apr.): 1.

———. 1992b. "A Place Called Hopelessness: Shelter Demand in the 90's." National Coalition for the Homeless.

———. 1992c. "NCH Releases Report on Homelessness and Substance Abuse." *Safety Network* 11, no. 3 (Mar.–Apr.): 1.

National Commission for Employment Policy. 1990. "Helping the Homeless Be Choosers: The Role of the Job Training Partnership Act in Improving Job Prospects." Washington D.C.: National Commission for Employment Policy.

National Commission on Children. 1991. "Beyond Rhetoric: A New American Agenda for Children and Families." Washington D.C.: National Commission on Children.

———. 1993. "Just the Facts: A Summary of Recent Information on America's Children and Their Families." Washington, D.C.: National Commission on Children.

National Congress for Community Economic Development. 1991. "Changing the Odds: The Achievements of Community Based Development Corporations." Washington, D.C.: National Congress for Community Economic Development.

National Housing Law Project. 1993a. "The Criminalization of Homelessness." Chicago: National Clearinghouse for Legal Services.

———. 1993b. "Moving a National Agenda on Homelessness Policy." Washington, D.C.: National Housing Law Project.

National Law Center on Homelessness and Poverty. 1989. "American Nightmare: A Decade of Homelessness in the United States." Washington, D.C.: National Law Center on Homelessness and Poverty.

———. 1990a. "Homeless Children Denied Education, Report Charges." *In Just Times* 1, no. 2.

———. 1990b. "Shut Out: Denial of Education to Homeless Children." Washington, D.C.: National Law Center on Homelessness and Poverty.

———. 1993. "No Way Out: A Report Analyzing Options Available to Homeless and Poor Families." Washington, D.C.: National Law Center on Homelessness and Poverty.

National Low Income Housing Coalition. 1992. "The 1992 Advocate's Resource Book." Washington, D.C.: National Low Income Housing Coalition.

National Network of Runaway and Youth Services. 1985. "To Whom Do They Belong? A Profile of America's Runaway and Homeless Youth and the Programs that Help Them." Washington, D.C.: National Network of Runaway and Youth Services.

———. 1991. "To Whom Do They Belong? Runaway, Homelessness, and Other Youth in High-Risk Situations in the 1990s." Washington, D.C.: National Network of Runaway and Youth Services.

National Priorities Project and Citizens Budget Campaign. 1992. "Reinvest in New Hampshire." Concord: National Priorities Project and Citizens Budget Campaign.

Neuffer, Elizabeth. 1991. "Abused Child Faces More Abuse in the System." *Boston Globe,* 23 Sept. A-1.

New Hampshire Department of Education, Bureau of Compensatory Education. 1990. "One Day Count of Homeless Students." Concord: New Hampshire Department of Education.

New Hampshire, State of. 1991. "Shelters and Services for Persons Who Are Homeless." Annual Report. Concord: New Hampshire Emergency Shelter Commission.

New Hampshire Governor's Commission. 1991. "New Hampshire in the 21st Century." Final Report. Concord: My Responsibility.

New Hampshire Task Force on Homelessness. 1989. "Homelessness: The New Hampshire Response." Concord:New Hampshire Task Force on Homelessness.

Newman, Katherine. 1988. *Falling from Grace: The Experience of Downward Mobility in the American Middle Class.* New York: Vintage Books.

Nichiols, Sue. 1986. "We Unwittingly Conspire Against Our Children." *Lansing State Journal,* 18 Apr. D-1.

Nowicki, Steven, and Bonnie Strickland. 1973. "A Locus of Control Scale for Children." *Journal of Consulting and Clinical Psychology* 40, no. 1:148–54.

Nugent, Tory. 1990. "Setting a New Course: Expanding Collegiate Curricula to Incorporate the Study of Hunger and Homelessness." Boston: National Student Campaign against Hunger and Homelessness.

Nyhan, David. 1991. "State Sponsored Child Neglect." *Boston Globe,* 13 Aug. 13.

O'Connell, James, and Janet Groth. 1991. "The Manual of Common Communicable Diseases in Shelters." Boston: Boston Health Care for the Homeless Program.

O'Connor, Karen. 1989. *Homeless Children.* San Diego: Lucent Books.

Ohio Department of Mental Health. 1985. "Homelessness in Ohio: A Study of People In Need." Columbus: Ohio Departmentof Mental Health.

Outland, George E. 1939. *Boy Transiency in America.* Santa Barbara, Calif.: Santa Barbara State College Press.

Packard, Vance. 1983. *Our Endangered Children: Growing Up in a Changing World.* Boston: Little, Brown.

Palmer, John L., and Joseph A. Penchman, eds. 1978. *Welfare in Rural Areas: The North Caroline-Iowa Income Maintenance Experiment.* Washington, D.C.: Brookings Institution.

Parker, Ruth, et al. 1991. "A Survey of Health of Homeless Children in Philadelphia Shelters." *AJDC* 145 (May): 520–26.

Parsons, Talcott. 1964. *The Social System.* New York: Free Press.

Parsons, Talcott, and Robert Bales. 1955. *Family, Socialization, and Interaction Processes.* New York: Free Press.

Partnership for the Homeless. 1989. "Moving Foward: A National Agenda to Address Homelessness in 1990 and Beyond." New York: Partnership for the Homeless.

Patton, Larry T. 1987. *The Rural Homeless.* Report prepared for the Health Resources and Services Administration, Public Health Service, U.S. Department of Health and Human Services under Requisition No. 305761.

Paula, Larissa. 1991. "Unemployment Rocks State: From Boom to Bust." *Portsmouth (N.H.) Herald* 11 Aug., A-1.

Pavenstedt, E., ed. 1967. *The Drifters: Children of Disorganized Lower Class Families.* Boston: Little, Brown.

Pear, Robert. 1993. "Ranks of U.S. Poor Reach 35.7 Million, the Most Since '64." *New York Times,* 4 Sept.

Pennsylvania Resources and Information Center for Special Education. 1989. *Prise Reporter* 21, no. 2 (Dec.): 3.

Phillips, Michael, et al. 1988. "Homeless Families: Services Make a Difference." *Social Casework* 26 (Jan.): 417–22.

Pires, Sheila, and Judith Tolmach Silber. 1991. "On Their Own: Runaway and Homeless Youth Programs That Serve Them." Washington, D.C.: Georgetown University CASSP Technical Assistance Center.

Piven, Frances Fox, and Richard Cloward. 1971. *Regulating the Poor.* New York, Vintage.

———. 1982. *The New Class War: Reagan's Attack on the Welfare State and Its Consequences.* New York: Vintage.

Plotkin, Martha, and Ortwin Narr. 1993. "The Police Response to the Homeless: A Status Report." Washington, D.C.: Police Executive Research Forum.

Poarch, Camille. 1990. "I Did My Homework on the Dashboard of a Car: Homeless Children and School." *People's Voice,* fall.

Powell, Phyllis. 1994. Personal communication with the author. Concord, N.H., 16 May.

Power, N.S. 1965. *The Forgotten People: A Challenge to a Caring Community.* The Drift, Eversham Worcs, England: Arthur James Limited.

Powers, Jane L., John Eckenrode, and Barbara Jaklitsch. 1990. "Maltreatment among Runaway and Homeless Youth." *Child Abuse and Neglect* 14:87–98.

Proch, Kathleen, and Merlin Taber. 1978. "Helping the Homeless." *Public Welfare* (Spring): 5.

Rafferty, Yvonne. 1991. "Developmental and Educational Consequences of Homelessness on Children and Youth." In *Homeless Children and Youth,* ed. Julee Kryder-Coe, Lester Salamon, and Janice Molnar. New Brunswick, N.J.: Transaction.

Rafferty, Yvonne, and Marybeth Shinn. 1991. "The Impact of Homelessness on Children." *American Psychologist* 46 (11):1170–79.

Rafferty, Yvonne, and Norma Rollins. 1989. *Learning in Limbo: The Educational Deprivation of Homeless Children.* New York: Advocates for Children of New York.

Rainey, Kenneth D., and Karen G. Rainey. 1978. "Rural Government and Local Public Services." In *Rural U.S.A.: Persistence and Change,* ed. Thomas R. Ford. Ames: Iowa State University Press.

Redburn, F. Stevens, and Buss, Terry F. 1987. *Responding to America's Homeless: Public Policy Alternatives.* New York: Praeger.

Redlender, I. 1989. Testimony presented before the New York City Council Select Committee on the Homeless. 6 Jan.

Redmond, Sojia Parker, and Joan Brackman. 1990. "Homeless Children and Their Caretakers." In *Data and Issues,* vol. 2 of *Homelessness in the United States,* by Jamshid A. Momeni. New York: Greenwood.

Reid, Alexander. 1990. "Child Abuse Outpaces Rise in Personnel." *Boston Globe,* 11 Mar., 25.

Reiss, David. 1981. *The Family's Construction of Reality.* Cambridge, Mass.: Harvard Univ. Press.

Rescorla, Leslie, Ruth Parker, and Paul Stolley. 1991. "Ability, Achievement and Adjustment in Homeless Children." *American Journal of Orthopsychiatry* 61, no. 2 (Apr.): 210–20.

Ribadeneria, Diego. 1992a. "Boston City Hospital Reports Rise in Child Malnutrition." *Boston Globe,* 25 Sept., 1.

———. 1992b. "Children's Welfare Slips, Study Finds." *Boston Globe,* 22 Mar., 3.

Rico, Christine. 1989. "Guide to Church Alternative Investment." *Corporate Examiner* 17:1–8.

Rife, J., B. Toomey, and R. First. 1993. Homeless families in rural and nonurban communities. *Journal of Human Services in the Rural Environment* 12, no. 2:5–11.

Rife, J., R. First, J. Belcher, D. Wheeler, and J. Johnson. 1995. "Redefining the Health Care Needs of Persons Who Are Homeless and Mentally Ill." *Journal of Applied Social Sciences.* In press.

Rist, Ray. 1973. *The Urban School, a Factory for Failure.* Cambridge, Mass.: MIT Press.

Rivlin, Leanne. 1990. "Home and Homelessness in the Lives of Children." In *Homeless Children: The Watchers and the Waiters,* ed. Nancy A. Boxill. New York: Haworth.

Roberts, Sam. 1991. "Anger, Assumptions and the Rush to Limit Welfare." *New York Times,* 27 Sept. A-1.

Robertson, Marjorie, and Milton Greenblatt. 1992. *Homelessness: A National Perspective.* New York: Plenum.

Robin, Stan. 1981. *Perspectives on Rural Mental Health,* vol. 9 in *New Directions for Mental Health.* San Francisco: Jossey-Bass.

Rodges, Harrell. 1990. *Poor Women, Poor Families: The Economic Plight of America's Female Headed Households.* Armonk, N.Y.: M.E. Sharpe.

Roob, Nancy, and Ruth McCambrige. 1991. "Private Sector Funders: An Examination of Their Role in Homelessness Projects." Boston: Fund for the Homeless, Boston Foundation.

Ropers, Richard. 1988. *The Invisible Homeless: A New Urban Ecology.* New York: Human Sciences Press.

———. 1991. *Persistent Poverty: The American Dream Turned Nightmare.* New York: Plenum.

Rosenbaum, Sara, Christine Layton, and Joseph Liu. 1991. *The Health of America's Children.* Washington D.C.: Children's Defense Fund.

Rosenblatt, R.A., and I. Moscovice, I. 1978. "Establishing New Rural Family Practices: Some Lessons from a Federal Experience." *Journal of Family Practice* 7:755–63.

Rosenman, Mark, and Mary Lee Stein. 1990. "Homeless Children: A New Vulnerability." In *Homeless Children: The Watchers and the Waiters,* ed. Nancy A. Boxill. New York: Haworth.

Rosenthal, Robert, and Lenore Jacobson, 1968. *Pygmalion in the Classroom.* New York: Holt, Reinhart, and Winston.

Rossi, Peter. 1989. *Down and Out in America.* Chicago: University of Chicago Press.

———. 1994. "Troubling Families: Family Homelessness in America." *American Behavioral Scientist* 37, no. 3 (Jan.).

Rossi, Peter, et al. 1986. *The Condition of the Homeless in Chicago.* Social and Demographic Research Institute, University of Massachusetts at Amherst.

———. 1987. "The Urban Homeless: Estimating Composition and Size." *Science* 235 (Mar.): 1336–41.

Rossi, Peter, and James Wright. 1987. "The Determinants of Homelessness." *Health Affairs* (Spring): 19–32.

Roth, Dee, Gerald Bean, and Pamela Hyde. 1986. "Homelessness and Mental Health Policy: Developing an Appropriate Role for the 1980s." *Community Mental Health Journal* 22, no. 3 (fall): 203–14.

Rothman, David, ed. 1971. *Rural Poor in the Great Depression.* New York: Arno.

Rothman, Jack. 1991. *Runaway and Homeless Youth.* White Plains, N.Y.: Longman.

Rowe, Dorothy. 1982. *The Construction of Life and Death.* New York: Wiley and Sons.

Rural Congregation Creates Prevention Loan Fund." 1990. *homewords* 3, no. 3:4.

Rural Sociology Society, Task Force on Persistent Rural Poverty. 1993. *Persistent Poverty in Rural America.* Boulder: Westview.

Russell, Diana. 1986. *The Secret Trauma.* New York: Basic Books.

Ryan, Charlotte. 1991. *Prime Time Activism.* Boston: South End Press.

Ryan, Phyllis, Ira Goldstein, and David Bartlett, 1989. *Homelessness In Pennsylvania: How Can This Be?* Coalition on Homelessness in Pennsylvania and the Institute for Public Policy Studies of Temple University. January.

Ryan, William. 1976. *Blaming the Victim.* New York: Random House.

Saarni, Carolyn. 1985. "Indirect Processes in Affect Socialization." In *The Socialization of Emotions,* ed. Michael Lewis and Carolyn Saarni. New York: Plenum.

Sagan, Carl, and Ann Dryan. 1988. "Give Us Hope." *Parade Magazine,* 27 Nov., 4–9.

Scales, Peter C. 1991. "A Portrait of Young Adolescents in the 1990s: Implications for Promoting Healthy Growth and Development." New York: Carnegie Corporation of New York.

Schaller, W. Neill. 1978. "Public Policy and Rural Social Change." In *Rural U.S.A.: Persistence and Change,* ed. Thomas R. Ford. Ames: Iowa State Univ. Press.

Scheff, Thomas. 1984. *Being Mentally Ill: A Sociological Theory.* 2d ed. Hawthorne, N.Y.: Aldine de Gruyter.

Scheie, David et al. 1991. "Religious Institutions as Partners in Community Based Development." Minneapolis: Rainbow Research.

Schonwald, Virginia. 1990. "The Homeless: If Everything Goes Right . . . Their Fragile Plight." *New Hampshire Premiere,* July, 33–36.

Schorr, Alvin. 1966. *Poor Kids.* New York: Basic Books.

Schorr, Lisabeth B. 1988. *Within Our Reach: Breaking the Cycle of Disadvantage.* New York: Anchor.

Schroepfer, Dorothy. 1994. Personal communication with the author. Concord, N.H., 4 June.

Schutt, Russell, and Gerald Garrett. 1992. *Responding to the Homeless: Policy and Practice.* New York: Plenum.

Schwartz, David, et al. 1988. *A New Housing Policy for America: Recapturing the American Dream.* Washington, D.C.: Temple Univ. Press.

———. 1991. "Preventing Homelessness: A Study of State and Local Homeless Prevention Programs." Orange, N.J.: National Housing Institute and American Affordable Housing Institute.

Sege, Irene. 1991. "Poverty Rose, Incomes Fell in '90, Say U.S. Officials." *Boston Globe,* 27 Sept.

———. 1992. "More Pain, No Gain for the Poor." *Boston Globe,* 9 Apr., A-1.

Segre, Jessica. 1992. "The Last Thing We Need is Another Shelter." *New England Journal of Public Policy* 8, no. 1 (spring/summer): 129–54.

Sexton, Patricia Cayo. nd. "The Epidemic of Homelessness." Journal?: 137–40.

Seyle, Hans. 1956. *The Stress of Life.* New York: McGraw Hill.

Shabecoff, Alice. 1992. "Rebuilding Our Communities." Monrovia, Calif.: World Vision.

Shaffer, D., and C.L.M. Caton. 1984. *Runaway and Homeless Youth in New York City.* New York: Oxford Univ. Press.

Shames, S. 1991. *Outside the Dream: Child Poverty in America.* New York: Aperture.

Shapiro, Issac, and Robert Greenstein. 1991a. A Painless Recession? The Economic Downturn and Policy Responses. Center on Budget and Policy Priorities. Washington, D.C.

Shapario, Issac, and Robert Greenstein. 1991b. "Selective Prosperity: Increasing Income Disparities since 1977." Washington, D.C.: Center on Budget and Policy Priorities.

Shapiro, Issac, and Robert Greenstein. 1993. "Making Work Pay: The Unfinished Agenda." Washington, D.C.: Center on Budget and Policy Priorities.

Shedlin, Allan, Jr., Gordon J. Klopf, and Esther S. Zaret. nd. "The School As Locus Of Advocacy For All Children." New York: Elementary School Center.

Sherif, M. 1936. *The Psychology of Social Norms*. New York: Harper.

Sherman, Arloc. 1992. *Falling by the Wayside: Children in Rural America*. Washington, D.C.: Children's Defense Fund.

Shinn, Marybeth, and Beth Weitzman. 1990. "Research on Homelessness." *Journal of Social Issues* 46, no 4:1–12.

Shumway, David. 1992. "Rural Homelessness in the Upper Valley." *New England Journal of Public Policy* 8, no. 1:739–52

Sieman, Dorothy, and Diane Doherty. 1990. Creative Sources of Funding for Programs for Homeless Families. CASSP Tecnical Assistance Center, Georgetown University. Washington, D.C.

Sinclair, Ward. 1987. "Grief is Growing on Farm Land." *Washington Post*, 24 May, A3.

Smathers, Bill. 1989. "GAIN Sponsors Conference." *Project GAIN News* 1 (spring): 1.

Snow, David, and Leon Anderson. 1987. "Identity Work among the Homeless: The verbal Construction and Avowal of Personal Identities." *American Journal of Sociology* 92, no. 6 (May): 1336–71.

———. 1993. *Down on Their Luck*. Berkeley: Univ. of California Press.

Snow, David, and M. Gerald Bradford. 1994. "Broadening Perspectives on Homelessness." *American Behavioral Scientist* 37, no. 4.

Snow, David, Leon Anderson, and Paul Koegel. 1994. "Distorting Tendencies in Research on the Homeless." *American Behavioral Scientist* 37, no. 4:461–75.

Snyder, Mitch, and Mary Ellen Hombs. 1983. *Homelessness in America: The Forced March to Nowhere*. Washington D.C.: Community for Creative Nonviolence.

Solomon, Carmen D. 1988a. "Cash Welfare Funds and Homeless Families with Children." *Congressional Research Service*.

———. 1988b. "The Family Support Act of 1988: How It Changes the Aid to Families with Dependent Children (AFDC) and Child Support Enforcement Program." *Congressional Research Service*.

"Special News Report on People and Their Jobs in Offices, Fields, and Factories." 1993. *Wall Street Journal*, Mar. 9. A-1.

Spencer, Milton. 1986. *Contemporary Macroeconomics*. New York: Worth.

"Spotlight: Coordinating Services for Homeless Persons." 1990. *homewords* 3, no. 3:1.

Srole, Leo, et al. 1975. *Mental Health in the Metropolis*. New York: Harper Rochbooks.

Stark, L. 1987. "Blame the System, not Its Victims." In *Homelessness: Critical Issues for Policy and Practice*. Boston: Boston Foundation.

————."Rural Homelessness Still Hidden." *Earth Matters* 37, no. 4: 19–22.

Stasny, E., B. Toomey, and R. First. "Estimating the Rate of Rural Homelessness: a Study of Nonurhban Ohio." *Survey Methodology* 20, no. 1:121–38.

Stavsky, Lois, and I. E. Mozeson. 1990. *The Place I Call Home: Faces and Voices of Homeless Teens*. New York: Shapolsky.

Steele, Brandt. 1986. "Notes on the Lasting Effects of Early Child Abuse throughout the Life Cycle." *Child Abuse and Neglect* 10:283–91.

Steeley, Renita. 1991. "Open Letter to the *New York Times*." *Extra* 4, no. 8 (Nov./ Dec.): 3. Published by Fairness and Accuracy in Reporting, New York.

Stein, Charles. 1992. "More Young Children Join State Welfare Rolls." *Boston Globe*, 20 May, 1.

Steriti, Lisa. 1988. "A Needs Assessment of the Somerville Homeless Population." Boston: Northeastern University and University of Massachusetts.

Stern, Mark. 1984. "The Emergence of the Homeless as a Public Problem." *Social Service Review* (June): 291–301.

Stimpson, James. 1984. "Policy and Research on Homeless." Paper presented for panel on Shaping Nation's Health Agenda of the Homeless Mentally Ill." U.S., D.H.H.S. American Public Health Association, 12 Nov.

Stoto, Michael, et al. 1990. *Health People 2000*. Washington, D.C.: National Academy Press.

Stricki, Irene. 1994. "Unheard Voices: Participants Evaluate the JOBS Program." Washington, D.C.: Coaltion on Human Needs.

Stronge, James H., ed. 1992. "Educating Homeless Children and Adolescents: Evaluating Policy and Practice." Newbury Park, Calif.: Sage.

Struening, E., and D. Padgett. 1990. "Physical Health Status, Substance Use and Abuse, and Mental Disorders among Homeless Adults." *Journal of Social Issues* 46, no. 4:65–81.

Sullivan, Patricia A., and Shirley P. Damrosch. 1987. "Homeless Women and Children." In Russell Schutt and Gerald Garrett *The Homeless in Contemporary Society*. New York: Plenum.

Sullivan, Ronald. 1989. Welfare Benefit Upheld For Homeless Mothers. *New York Times Metropolitan*, 12 Sept.

Summer, Laura. 1991. "Limited Access Health Care for the Rural Poor." Washington, D.C.: Center on Budget and Policy Priorities.

Sutherland, Edward, and Harvey Locke. 1936. *Twenty Thousand Homeless Men*. Chicago: J.B. Lippincott.

Taeuber, Cynthia, and Paul Siegel. 1990. *Counting the Nation's Homeless Population in the 1990 Census*. Washington, D.C.: U.S. Bureau of the Census.

Tan, Evelyn. 1991. "One of Every 16 Families on Welfare." *USA Today*, 28 Feb.

Taylor, Charles. 1992. *Multiculturalism and the Politics of Recognition*. Princeton, N.J.: Princeton University Press.

Taylor, Martien. 1988. "Homelessness: The Nature of the Crisis." *Youth Policy*, May, 18–21.

————. 1989. "Making A Difference: A Resource Guide on Homelessness for Students." Washington, D.C.: National Coalition for the Homeless.

Terr, Lenore C. 1991. "Childhood Traumas: An Outline and Overview." *American Journal of Psychiatry* 148, no. 1:10–20.

Thomas, Jack. 1992. "Down and Out in Boston." *Boston Globe*, 12 Feb., 65.

Thomas, W.I. 1923. *The Unadjusted Girl*. Boston: Little, Brown.

Toomey, Beverly. 1992. "Final Report on Rural Homelessness in Ohio: A Five Year Replication Study." Columbus: Ohio State University.

Toomey, Beverly, and Richard First. 1991. *Rural Homelessness in Ohio*. Columbus: Ohio State University.

Toomey, Beverly, Ricyhard First, R. Greenee, and L. Cummins. 1993. "Counting the Rural Homeless: Political amd Methodological Dilemmas." *Social Work Research and Abstracts* 29, no. 4:23–27.

Trillin, Calvin. 1989. "Uncivil Liberties." *Nation*, 13 Feb.

Tucker, William. 1987. "Where Do the Homeless Come From?" *National Review*, 25 (Sept.): 35.

————. 1990a. *The Excluded Americans*. Washington, D.C.: Regnery Gateway.

————. 1990b. "The Source of America's Housing Problem: Look in Your Own Back Yard." *Policy Analysis*, Feb. 6.

Tye, Larry. 1990. "Seeking Shelter, the Street People Are Finding Scorn." *Boston Globe*, 27 Aug.

U.S. Bureau of the Census. 1989a. *Changes in American Family Life*. Current Population Reports Series, no. 163, Aug.

————. 1989b. *Statistical Abstract of the United States*, 109th ed. Washington, D.C.: USGPO.

————. 1986. "The Continued Growth of Hunger, Homeless, and Poverty in America." By Laura Waxman and Lilia Reyes. Washington, D.C.

————. 1987a. "The Continuing Growth of Hunger, Homelessness, and Poverty in America's Cities." Washington D.C.

————. 1987b. "A Status Report on Homeless Families in America's Cities: A 29 City Survey." Washington, D.C.

————. 1993. "Ending Homelessness in America's Cities: Implementing a National Plan of Action." Washington, D.C.

U.S. Congress. 1984. Joint Hearing before the Subcommittee on Housing and Urban Development of the Committee on Banking, Finance and Urban Affairs and the Subcommittee on Manpower and Housing of the Committee of Government Operations. *HUD Report on Homelessness*. 98th Cong., 2nd sess. 24 May.

U.S. Congress. 1987. Stewart B. McKinney Homeless Assistance Act. Public Law 100–77, codified at 42 USC SS 11 301–11472.

————. Select Committee on Children, Youth, and Families. 1990. *Children's Well Being: An International Comparison*. 25 July.

————. Select Committee on Children, Youth, and Families. 1989. *U.S. Children and Their Families: Current Conditions and Recent Trends*. 101st Congress, Sept. 101–356.

U.S. Department of Education. 1988. "Double Jeopardy: Homeless and Illiterate." *Clearinghouse on Adult Education* 17 (Oct.): 3–6.

———. *Report to Congress on Final Reports Submitted by States in Accordance with Section 724(b)(3) of the Stewart B. McKinney Homeless Assistance Act*. Washington, D.C.

———. 1992. *Serving Homeless Children: The Responsibilities of Educators*. Washington, D.C.

U.S. Department of Health and Human Services. 1989. "Conference Proceedings of the National Conference on Health Care for Homeless Mothers, Children, and Youth." 24–26 Jan., Washington, D.C.

U.S. General Accounting Office. 1985. *Children and Youths: About 68,000 Homeless and 186 in Shared Housing at Any Given Time*. # GAO/PEMD-89-14. Gaithersburg, Md.: U.S. General Accounting Office.

———. 1985. *Homelessness: A Complex Problem and the Federal Response*. Washington D.C.

U.S. House. 1989. Select Committee on Children, Youth, and Families. *U.S. Children and Their Families: Current Conditions and Recent Trends*. Sept.

———. Committee on Children, Youth, and Families. 1987. "The Crisis in Homelessness: Effects on Children and Families." Washington, D.C.:GPO.

———. Select Committee on Children, Youth, and Families. 1990. *Children's Well Being: An International Comparison*. 25 July.

———. Select Committee on Hunger. 1987. "Hunger among the Homeless: a Survey of 140 Shelters, Food Stamp Participants and the Homeless." Washington D.C.: GPO.

U.S. National Center for Health Statistics. 1990. "Advance Report of Final Divorce Statistics, 1987." Monthly vital statistics. Report 38, no. 12, supp. 1, 15 May 15.

VanderPloeg, J., and Andy Wiggins. 1989. "Homelessness: A Multidimensional Problem." *Children and Youth Services Reviews* 11, no. 1:45–56.

Vermont Department of Education. 19990. *Unsheltered Lives*. Montpelier: Compensatory Education Unit.

Vermont National Education Association. 1989. "Vermont-NEA Endorses March for Housing." *Today* 56, no. 3:1.

Vissing, Yvonne M. 1991. *Case Profiles of Homeless Children in New Hampshire*. Concord: New Hampshire State Department of Education, Bureau of Compensatory Education.

Vissing, Yvonne M. 1992. "Homeless Children Having Children." *New England Journal of Public Policy* 18, no. 1 (spring/summer): 393–406.

Vissing, Yvonne, Dorothy Schroepfer, and Fred Bloise. 1994. "Homeless Students, Heroic Sudents." *Phi Delta Kappa*, Mar., 535–39.

Vissing, Yvonne. 1994. *Serving Homeless Students: A Resource and Information Guide*. Concord: New Hampshire Department of Education, Homeless Education for Children and Youth.

Vissing, Yvonne, and Joseph Diament. 1996. "Are There Homeless Youth in my Community? Differences of Perception between Service Providers and High School Youth." *Journal of Social Distress and the Homeless* 4:287–99.

———. 1994. *Enumerating Homeless Teens in the Seacoast Area*. Portsmouth, N.H.: Greater Piscataqua Community Foundation.

Vissing, Y.M., J.C. Salloway, and D. Siress. 1994. "Organization of Alzheimer's Services for Rural Areas." *Educational Gerontology* 20, no. 3:303–18.

———. 1994. "Training for Expertise vs. Training for Trust: Issues in Educational Gerontology." *Educational Gerontology* 20, no. 8:797–808.

Vissing, Yvonne, Murray Straus, Richard Gelles, and John Harrop. 1991. "Verbal Aggression by Parents and Psycho-social Problems of Children". *Child Abuse and Neglect* 15:223–38.

Volz, Greg. 1993. "Making a Difference in the Attack on Homelessness—Legal Services at Work." *Economic Development and Law Center Report* 22, no. 2:3–9.

W.T. Grant Foundation. 1988. "The Forgotten Half: Pathways to Success for America's Youth and Young Families." Final Report on Youth and America's Future. New York: Commission on Work, Family, and Citizenship for the William T. Grant Foundation. Nov.

Wagenfeld, Morton O. 1982. "Psychopathology in Rural Areas—Issues and Evidence." In *Handbook of Community Mental Health*, ed. Peter Keller and Dennis Murray. Washington, D.C.: Human Services Press.

———. 1990. "Mental Health and Rural America: A Decade Review." *Journal of Rural Health* 4:507–22.

Wagenfeld, Morton O., and Nancy Buffem. 1983. "Rural Mental Health Management: Rewards, Stresses, and Strategies." *International Journal of Mental Health* 12, no. 1-2:89-107.

Wagner, David. 1993. *Checkerboard Square*. Boulder: Westview Press.

Walker, Adrian. 1992. "Spare Change for Sale." *Boston Globe*, 6 Apr., 21.

Wasem, Ruth Ellen. 1992. "Homelessness: Issues and Legislation in the 102d Congress." Congressional Research Service.

———. 1993. "Emergency Food and Shelter Program for Homeless People." Congressional Research Service.

Weber, Margret. 1988. *Religious Funds for Social Justice: The 1987–88 Directory*. Greater Minneapolis Council of Churches.

Weil, S. 1952. *The Need for Roots*. London: Routledge and Kegan Paul.

Weiss, Stephanie. 1988. "No Place Called Home." *NEA Today*, Sept., 10–11.

Weitzman, Beth, James Knickman, and Marybeth Shinn. 1990. "Pathways to Homelessness Among New York City Families." *Journal of Social Issues* 46, no. 4:125–40.

Werner, Emily. 1984. "Resilient Children." *Young Children*, Nov.

Werner, Emily, and R. Smity. 1982. *Vulnerable But Invincible: Study of Resilient Children*. New York: McGraw Hill.

Westchester Initiative for Homeless Children. 1993. "Slipping Through the Cracks." Mt Kisco, N.Y.: Plan for Social Excellence.

Whitbeck, Les B., and Ronald L. Simons. 1990. "Life on the Streets: The Victimization of Runaway and Homeless Adolescents." *Youth and Society* 22, no. 1:108–25.

White, Andrew. 1993. Community Organizing Special Issue: The Power to Be Heard. *City Limits* 5, no. 18:n7.

White, Richard. 1992. *Rude Awakenings.* San Francisco: Center for Self Governance.

Whitman, B., P. Accardo, M. Boyert, and R. Kendagor. 1988. "The Developmental Impact of Homelessness on Children." Unpublished manuscript. Knights of Columbus Developmental Center, Cardinal Glennon Children's Hospital, St. Louis, Mo.

Whitman, David. 1988. "Hope for the Homeless." *US News and World Report,* 29 Feb., 25–35.

———. 1989. "Shattering Myths about the Homeless." *US News and World Report,* 20 Mar., 27–28.

Whittemore, Hank. 1988. "We Can't Pay the Rent." *Parade Magazine,* 10 Jan., 4–6.

Wilkinson, Kenneth P. 1978. "Rural Community Change." In *Rural U.S.A.: Persistence and Change,* ed. Thomas R. Ford. Ames: Iowa State University Press.

Will, George. 1991. "Why Poverty is a Public Health Problem." *Boston Sunday Globe,* 23 June, A29.

Williams, Carol. 1991. "Child Welfare Services and Homelessness: Issues in Policy, Philosophy, and Programs." In *Homeless Children and Youth,* ed. Julee Kryder-Coe, Lester Salamon, and Janice Molnar. New Brunswick, N.J.: Transaction.

Williams, Lydia. 1991. *Mourning in America: Health Problems, Mortality, and Homelessness.* Washington, D.C.: National Coalition for the Homeless.

Winick, M. 1985. "Nutritional and Vitamin Deficiency States." In *Health Care of Homeless People,* ed. P. Brickner et al. New York: Springer.

Winkler, Karen. 1993. "Communitarianism Move Their Ideas Outside Academic Arena." *Chronicle of Higher Education* 39, no. 33 (21 Apr.): 7.

Wolf, Linda. 1991. "The Welfare System's Response to Homelessness." In *Homeless Children and Youth,* ed. Julee Kryder-Coe, Lester Salamon, and Janice Molnar. New Brunswick, N.J.: Transaction.

Wood, David. 1989. "Homeless Children: Their Evaluation and Treatment." In *California Children, California Families: over the Brink: Homeless families in Los Angeles,* ed. D. Wood, et al. Sacramento: State of California Assembly Office of Research.

Wright, James D. 1987. "The National Health Care for the Homeless Program." In *The Homeless in Contemporary Society,* ed. R.D. Bingham, R.E. Green, and S.B. White. Newbury Park, Calif.: Sage.

———. 1988. "The Mentally Ill Homeless: What Is Myth and What Is Fact." *Social Problems* 35, no. 2 (Apr.): 182–92.

———. 1988. "The Worthy and the Unworthy Homeless." *Society* 25, no. 5:64–69.

———. 1989. *Address Unknown: The Homeless in America.* Hawthorne N.Y.: Walter de Gruyter.

———. 1990. "Homelessness Is Not Healthy for Children and Other Living Things." In *Homeless Children: The Watchers and the Waiters,* ed. Nancy A. Boxill. New York: Haworth.

———. 1991. "Health and the Homeless Teenager: Evidence from the National Health Care for the Homeless Program." *Journal of Halth and Social Policy* 2, no. 4:15–35.

Wright, R. Dean. 1988. "The Problem of Homeless Children and Children of Homeless Families in Iowa: Final Report Presented to the Iowa Department of Education." Des Moines: Iowa Department of Education.

Wright, R. Dean, and Susan E. Wright. 1989. "Assessing the Educational Needs of Iowa's Homeless Youth." Des Moines, Iowa: Sociology Department, Drake University.

Wylie, Mary. 1987. "Re-Institutionalization in New York." *Networker* (Nov./Dec.): 39.

Wyman, Mary, and William Tranor. 1993. "The 1994 American Directory of Programs for Runaways, Homeless Youth, and Missing Children." Washington D.C.: American Youth Work Center.

Yates, Gary L., Julia Pennbridge, and Avon Swofford. 1991. "The Los Angeles system of care for Runaway/Homeless Youth." *Journal of Adolescent Research* 12, no. 7:555–60.

Yates, Gary, Julia Pennbridge, Avon Swofford, and Richard MacKenzie. 1991. "Los Angeles System of Care for Runaway and Homeless Youth." *Journal of Adolescent Health* 12, no. 7 (Nov.): 555–60.

Yeich, Susan. 1993. *The Politics of Ending Homelessness.* Lanham, Md.: Univ. Press of America.

Zelizer, Viviana. 1981. *Pricing the Priceless Child.* New York: Basic Books.

Zigler, Edward. 1982. "Controlling Child Abuse in America: An Effort Doomed to Failure." In *Socialization and Personality Development*, ed. Edward Zigler, Michael Lamb, and Irvin Child. New York: Oxford Univ. Press.

Zigler, E., S. Kagan, E. Klugman. 1983. *Children, Families and Government: Perspectives on American Social Policy.* New York: Cambridge Univ. Press.

Zigler, Edward, and Mary Lang. 1991. *Child Care Choices: Balancing the Needs of Children, Families, and Society.* New York: Free Press.

Zigler, Edward, Michael Lamb, and Irvin Child. 1982. *Socialization and Personality Development.* New York: Oxford Univ. Press.

Zigler, Edward, S.L. Kagan, and E. Klugman. 1983. *Children, Families and Government: Perspectives on American Social Policy.* New York: Cambridge Univ. Press.

Zimmerman, Carle, and Nathan Whetten. 1971. "Rural Families on Relief." In *Rural Poor in the Great Depression*, ed. David Rothman. New York: Arno.

Zwicka, K. 1990. Rural Homelessness: A Review of the Literature. Paper presented at Interagency Council of the Homeless, region 5 conference, Chicago. April.

Index